DATE DUE			

Women of the Andes

Women and
Culture Series

The Women and Culture Series is dedicated to books that illuminate the lives, roles, achievements, and status of women, past or present.

Fran Leeper Buss
La Partera: Story of a Midwife

Valerie Kossew Pichanick
Harriet Martineau: The Woman and Her Work, 1802–76

Sandra Baxter and Marjorie Lansing
Women and Politics: The Invisible Majority

Estelle B. Freedman
Their Sisters' Keepers: Women's Prison Reform in America, 1830–1930

Susan C. Bourque and Kay Barbara Warren
Women of the Andes: Patriarchy and Social Change in Two Peruvian Towns

SUSAN C. BOURQUE and KAY BARBARA WARREN are first place Hamilton Prize winners for 1979. The Alice and Edith Hamilton Prize is named for two outstanding women scholars: Alice Hamilton (educated at the University of Michigan Medical School), a pioneer in environmental medicine; and her sister Edith Hamilton, the renowned classicist. The Hamilton Prize competition is supported by the University of Michigan Horace H. Rackham School of Graduate Studies and by private donors.

Women of the Andes

*Patriarchy and Social Change
in Two Peruvian Towns*

Susan C. Bourque
and
Kay Barbara Warren

Ann Arbor
The University of Michigan Press

Copyright © by The University of Michigan 1981
All rights reserved
Published in the United States of America by
The University of Michigan Press and simultaneously
in Rexdale, Canada, by John Wiley & Sons Canada, Limited
Manufactured in the United States of America

Library of Congress Cataloging in Publication Data

Bourque, Susan Carolyn, 1943–
    Women of the Andes.

    (The Women and culture series)
    Bibliography: p.
    Includes index.
    1. Women—Peru—Case studies.   2. Women—Peru—
Chucchín.   3. Women—Peru—Mayobamba.   4. Chucchín
(Peru)—Social conditions.   5. Mayobamba (Peru)—
Social conditions.   I. Warren, Kay B., 1947–
II. Title.   III. Series: Women and culture series.
HQ1572.B68   1981   305.4'2'0985   81-811
ISBN 0-472-09330-4   AACR2
ISBN 0-472-06330-8 (pbk.)

To our parents

HELEN J. AND JOSEPH E. BOURQUE

ELVA R. AND BRUCE G. WARREN

and for

JUNE NASH

JILL CONWAY

PEGGY HENNESSEY, M.M.

AÍDA RAMIREZ BUSTAMANTE

Acknowledgments

This is a book we wanted to write. The people to whom it is dedicated—our parents, June Nash, Jill Conway, Peggy Hennessey, and Aída Ramirez Bustamante—have been our special sources of inspiration throughout the various stages of the project. Each, in her or his own particular way, has a commitment to cross-cultural understanding that has deeply influenced our lives and work.

Financial support for the research has been provided by the Andrew W. Mellon Foundation, the Social Science Research Council, and faculty grants from Smith College and Mount Holyoke College. We are especially grateful to the Andrew W. Mellon Foundation for its commitment to interdisciplinary, collaborative research.

One of the pleasures in undertaking this project has been the interaction with the lively and challenging intellectual circles in which we have worked. We have a special appreciation for the Peruvianists and Latin Americanists who have shared their insights with us during the period of our field work in Peru. The people of Chiuchin and Mayobamba have been central contributors; they have our special thanks for helping us to understand the meanings behind the actions we attempted to decipher. In addition, we would like to acknowledge the support and assistance of: Mario Vázquez, Julio Cotler, Enrique Mayer, Blanca Figueroa, Ximena Bunster, Elsa Chaney, Richard N. Adams, Scott Palmer, William Lofstrom, Wendy Stickel, Janet Ballantyne, Richard Laszewski, the Maryknoll sisters and fathers, and Padre Marzal.

Also among the Peruvians we would especially like to thank friends who have shared their homes and friendship with us: Julio and Elsa Uribe, Odilia, Silvio and Edmunda Huertas, Andrés Cueva, Hortencia, Jorge and Tati Castro, and Julia Polastri.

A number of people read all or parts of the manuscript, asking critical questions, offering helpful comments, and sharing the complexities of interdisciplinary, cross-cultural analysis. Our thanks to Carmen Diana Deere, Cynthia Enloe, Penny Gill, Dorothy Green, Billie Jean Isbell, Louise Lamphere, and Catharine Stimpson. At the University of Michigan we found special support for the project from Elizabeth Douvan, Louise Tilley, Dorothy McGuigan, Sherry Ortner, and Robin Jacoby.

Part of the initial research was carried out during a summer at the Cornell University Center for International Studies and a spring at the University of Texas (Austin) Institute of Latin American Studies. Our thanks to Tom E. Davis and our colleagues Douglas Ashford, Tom Kirsch, and Eldon Kenworthy at Cornell. Also in Ithaca we were grateful for the friendship of Laura Holmberg, Rosalind Kenworthy, and Elizabeth Yanof. At the University of Texas our thanks to William Glade and our colleagues Ann Graham, Ann and Henry Dietz, Jay and Suzanne Lehnertz, B. J. Fernea, and Richard Graham for making the stay so pleasant. Alida Metcalf was a most willing research assistant at several critical points and was especially helpful in the first rounds of the bibliographic research and editing in Texas and Northampton.

We count ourselves fortunate to live in the rich intellectual climate of the Five College consortium in western Massachusetts. Friends and colleagues at the other institutions whose support has been especially important to this research are: Susanna Barrows, John Cole, Len Glick, Ralph Falkingham, Sylvia Forman, and Howard Wiarda. The government department at Smith College has been a source of intelligent and willing colleagues who value and support interdisciplinary work. Teaching with Donna Divine helped test and develop some of our ideas, as well as maintain our sense of humor through the comfort of abiding friendship.

A most enriching circle of colleagues and friends has developed in our association with the Research Project on Women and Social Change, an interdisciplinary group of scholars located at Smith College and funded through a grant from the Andrew W. Mellon Foundation. This group has worked together over the past three years to better understand the process of change as it is manifest in the lives of women in a variety of cultural and historical settings. Exchange and interaction in this group has been a remarkable and exciting experience. Our special appreciation to: Martha Ackelsberg, Mark Aldrich, Donna and Thomas Divine, Evan Daniels, Sue Freeman, Philip

Green, Kathy P. Parsons, Thomas Pettigrew, Marilyn Schuster, Carolyn Sherif, Miriam Slater, Diedrick Snoek, Susan Van Dyne, and Iëda Wiarda. Joan Scott has been an important source of encouragement and insight for our endeavors.

Other friends who helped in many ways include: all the Bourque family, John Bollard, Barbara Frankel, Norman Kurtin, Lisa Leghorn, Margaret Lloyd, the late Jeanne McFarland, and Wendy Warren.

At the University of Michigan Press, Carol Mitchell has been a superb editor and a moving force behind the Women and Culture series. Our thanks also to Sally Donahue, Pat Kuc, Marty Ockenfels, and Susan McIntosh who all helped in the typing of numerous drafts. Mary Jo Powell, Jennifer Jackman, and Mary Moran provided vital editorial assistance and Stephen Petegorsky valuable photographic advice, in addition to making our prints.

Finally, our collaboration over the years—in the fieldwork, analysis, and writing of this book—has been a source of joy for both of us.

Contents

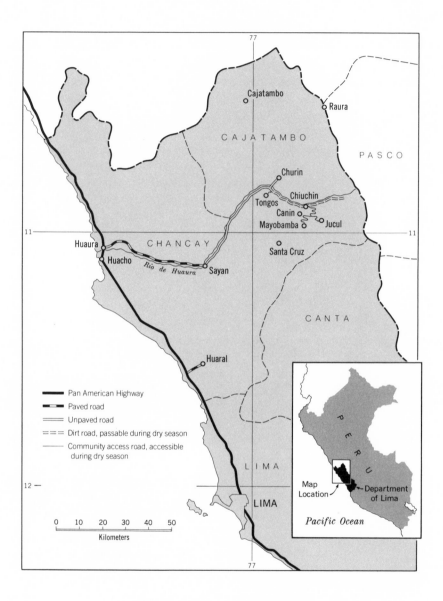

DEPARTMENT OF LIMA

PORTION MENTIONED IN THE TEXT

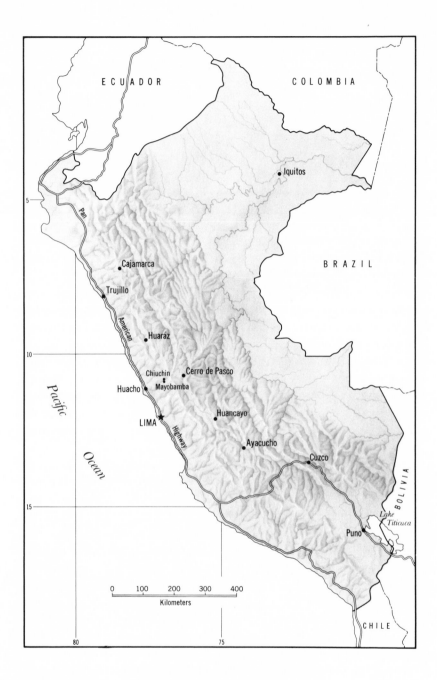

ECUADOR

COLOMBIA

• Iquitos

BRAZIL

5

Pan

• Cajamarca

Trujillo

American

10

• Huaráz

Chiuchin • Cerro de Pasco

Huacho • Mayobamba

Pacific

• Huancayo

LIMA ★ Highway

Ocean

• Ayacucho

• Cúzco

BOLIVIA

15

Lake
Titicaca

• Puno

| 0 | 100 | 200 | 300 | 400 |

Kilometers

CHILE

80   75

RELIEF MAP OF PERU
SHOWING CITIES MENTIONED IN THE TEXT

Introduction

During the past decade, cross-cultural studies of women's lives have sparked reevaluations of data, methods, findings, and theory in the social sciences. In this study of sexual hierarchies and social change in Peru we contribute new perspectives on and interpretations of women's social realities. On the one hand, we present an ethnographic account of the texture of Andean women's lives; on the other, we clarify the range of analytic models and theories formulated during the last ten years to conceptualize women's experience. Our examination of women's lives emphasizes the connections between theory building and ethnographic detail as we move beyond the politics of interpersonal relations to assess the impact of the broader social, political, and economic systems that structure and constrain everyday life.

The fieldwork for this study was carried out in a rugged area of the Andes, relatively isolated from national society until the twentieth century. The towns of Mayobamba and Chiuchin, located in the districts of Checras and Santa Leonor, lie on the western slopes of the Andes in the hinterlands between the departments of Lima and Cerro de Pasco. The settlements are small. Chiuchin is a trade center, located at 2,400 meters, of about 250 residents; Mayobamba, located above Chiuchin at 3,400 meters, is an agricultural community of about 450 residents. A precipitous road, carved into the mountainsides along the river basin in the 1940s, connects Chiuchin to the coast. Local residents completed a twisting, vertical extension of the road between Chiuchin and Mayobamba in 1968. This is a bilingual, Quechua-Spanish region where, according to the 1972 census, 62 percent of the population was literate in Spanish. Neither community has electricity or sewage, and potable water, while available since the 1960s in public faucets, is rarely found in people's homes.

Chiuchin expanded when agriculturalists from the higher towns moved to the settlement to exploit the distributive possibilities of the road. The road was the first link capable of carrying motorized vehicles between this region of the *sierra* (the rural highlands) and the coast. Chiuchin's entrepreneurs own and operate general stores, supplying dry goods, beer, coca leaves, alcohol, tin goods, shoes, and necessities brought in by truck and bus from the coastal towns some six hours away. The most enterprising townspeople have also converted their second floor or spare rooms into boardinghouse hotels to accommodate the students, from the neighboring peasant communities who study in Chiuchin, and the steady trickle of Peruvian tourists who come to use the hot spring baths located on the property of a *hacienda* (a large estate) that adjoins the town.

Chiuchin is composed of people actively interested in pursuing the opportunities that the extension of coastal contact offers. Despite its small size, it has the air of an important trade center, an interesting place to be where there is much action, especially in contrast to the highland towns. After spending even a week in one of the surrounding agricultural communities, one experiences in Chiuchin a heightened sense of activity: so much is available, there are strangers present, and the bus and trucks arrive every day. The town conveys this sense of activity without the benefit of a paved street, electricity, running water, or central plumbing.

Chiuchin is also the seat of several extensions of the central government's bureaucracy despite the fact that it is not the district capital—that honor is reserved for one of the highland agricultural communities. The national police force (*guardia civil*) and the agricultural extension agent have their local headquarters in the town. The secondary school operates there as well. In short, it is a town with extensive ties to both coastal urban society and to the rural Andean agricultural communities which surround it.

Mayobamba, in contrast, is a much more traditional agricultural community. Registered officially as an Indigenous Community (now termed a Campesino Community) on December 18, 1935, the total extension of the community is approximately 4,000 hectares which are located at altitudes ranging from 3,000 to 4,600 meters. About 1,000 hectares are under cultivation.[1] The system of land tenure involves both communal and private holdings. All nonirrigated pasture land south and west of the town has been retained in communal ownership and the town cultivates 4 hectares of alfalfa for the community's dairy herd. Also, communal lands for dry farming potatoes, the staple crop, are made available to all *comuneros*, or officially inscribed heads of household. *Comuneros* are assigned two fields in each of eight annually rotated areas. The community as an entity plants two large, central fields of potatoes each year as well. Despite the continuing importance of communally controlled land, private property has increased in economic importance and virtually all irrigated, high quality land is now in private hands. Water flow to the irrigated fields, however, is regulated by the community.[2]

In Mayobamba wealth is determined by the extent of irrigated land a family owns, which in turn determines the amount of cattle that can be raised. Both men and women inherit land, although there is a preference for males to inherit more extensive lots.[3]

Quechua and Spanish are spoken in Mayobamba; only a few monolingual Quechua speakers are found among the older women. Men are almost twice as likely as women to have had some education and more likely to have completed five years of school. Whereas 60 percent of the men have had five years of schooling, only 45 percent of the women have comparable school achievement.[4]

In both Mayobamba and Chiuchin reciprocal work exchanges as well as wage labor are used for agricultural work. Fictive kin relationships are constructed at important rites of passage and become the basis for labor exchanges for both men and women.[5] Barter with other highland communities, using overland trade routes and llama packs, is still practiced, though coastal trade is much more important.

Given these ethnographic characteristics, where can we locate Mayobamba and Chiuchin in comparison to other Andean communities? How representative of Peruvian rural settlements are these towns? Social scientists note correctly the variation to be found throughout the Andes. It is probably misleading to talk in terms of "typical towns" as if one could identify an average settlement in the historical, geographic, economic, and cultural complexity of the Andes. From our point of view, Chiuchin and Mayobamba illustrate the processes of change which, though uniquely manifested in each Peruvian town, share a generalized directionality with other rural communities. Chiuchin and Mayobamba are interesting precisely because they combine some traces of the past—labor exchanges, communal lands, subsistence agriculture—with the forces that will shape rural futures—growing class stratification, migration, and involvement in the coastal cash economy. The towns have mixed precapitalist and capitalist economies. While Quechua is still spoken by many, Spanish is increasingly the language of everyday discourse. The inhabitants of these towns see themselves as *serranos* (people of the highlands), not as ethnic Indians, and many are very closely tied to urban national society through kin who have migrated to coastal cities in search of work and higher education. The towns themselves are small and isolated enough to maintain some independence in their everyday affairs, and yet they are involved in the national economy and political system.[6]

This region of rural Andean society is heavily marked by sexual hierarchy, whether we are talking about small agrarian communities with strong collective traditions or commercial towns serving as supply links to the national economy. Sexual hierarchy is exemplified by women's differential access to important resources, such as land and irrigation water, the lower rates of literacy and acquisition of schooling, and their limited roles in local political structures.

We wanted to understand how *individual* women and men perceive and evaluate sexual divisions of work, community politics, and the currents of social change that are propelling rural people into expanding participation in coastal, urban, industrial society. At the same time, we wanted to examine the structures of power in the political and economic institutions that transcend individual lifetimes yet shape the experiences and life chances of each individual.

Our study attempts to show how women's subordination is institutionally structured, yet negotiated, disputed, and changed through the conscious actions of women and men. Our approach seeks the links between social ideologies, sexual divisions of labor, and differential access to central institutions. We explore how these linkages perpetuate sexual hierarchy for women and men in the Andes. The following central questions have focused our work:

1. How do women and men perceive sexual subordination? Do women act on their consciousness of sexual hierarchy? Do women's perceptions contribute to their oppression? Do women formulate strategies for change based on their understandings of subordination?

2. Is there greater equality between the sexes when sexual divisions of work are minimized?

3. Are class and ethnicity more important than sex in shaping women's and men's life experiences?

4. With growing urbanization, the expansion of commerce, schools, national legal systems—in short, with the forces of development and modernization—what has happened to women's status?

A word needs to be said also about the diversity of the experience of Andean women. One of our goals in this study is to provide the reader with an appreciation of the variety and range of experience to be found in the lives of the women in Mayobamba and Chiuchin, and by extension to suggest the variation to be appreciated in the experience of Andean women in general. Again, what we see as most interesting about the women of these communities is what they suggest about the patterns of change and the forces behind them which would apply broadly throughout the region.

We have known the women of Chiuchin and Mayobamba for the past fifteen years. Their lives and experience are of interest to us because we have shared their homes, hospitality, and friendship. Moreover, their lives pose intriguing intellectual problems which bear on the issues facing women in more industrialized communities as they seek to unravel the puzzle of sexual hierarchy. The experience of Andean women with social change may help us solve the central riddle of our own experience with modernization and industrialization: which kinds of changes enhance women's status and opportunities, and which restrict women's options? The women in our study experience change in their involvement in the cash economy, their integration in and dependence on urbanized coastal society, the penetration of national political institutions, and expanded educational and migration opportunities. Consequently, an examination of their lives reveals the impact of these changes, the links between these processes, and how such changes affect the relationships between men and women. This study explicitly addresses how social change can lead to greater parity between men and women and how change can also reinforce the preexisting subordinate status of women.

While we began field work in this area of Peru in 1965, we have specifically focused on women since 1974. Over the course of four years we spent a total of twelve months in the two communities. With participant observer techniques, we shared the daily rounds of

women: their sewing circles, trading expeditions, preparations for
fiestas, community rituals, births, deaths, and daily agricultural and
commercial tasks.

We chose an open-ended methodology throughout our study
which gave us access to people's values and perceptions. We did not
seek responses to predetermined attitude scales. We wanted the wom-
en and men of Chiuchin and Mayobamba to define for us the appropriate categories of experience. In practice this meant that we depended
on long, relatively unstructured conversations which took place
around the cooking hearths, on walks to the fields, or around dinner
tables. In addition, we joined public events from soccer matches to
public fiestas. Our fieldwork journals incorporated our observations,
our transcriptions of interviews and conversations, as well as our first
attempts to explore the patterns of our findings. In this book we
present a detailed and theoretical analysis of these patterns. In the
course of our fieldwork we talked to the vast majority of people in
Mayobamba and Chiuchin. We selected representative quotes from
those interviews to illustrate and document analytic points throughout the text.

Contact with these settlements over the past fifteen years gave us a
chance to observe long-term developments in both families and communities. We knew the towns and their political structures before the
military came to power in 1968. Thus, we have had the opportunity to
watch the course of the self-proclaimed Peruvian Revolution and to
trace its impact on the rural population: the hopes and fears it
aroused, as well as the limits and failures in the implementation of its
policies. We have watched the communities formulate, test, and re-
formulate strategies to garner benefits from national coastal and government institutions. This process reflects the politics of national integration and the complex interface between government policy and
citizen response, the challenges posed to political leaders, and the
risks involved for rural citizens. We have traced the migratory experiences of families as they establish networks of ties to Lima and other
coastal cities for jobs and education.

In looking at these general patterns of change we have been particularly anxious to understand the experiences of women and men to
see what impact sex has on their respective options in the rural areas
and in migration to the urbanized coast. The chapters which follow
are an attempt to present a systematic discussion of the interaction

between certain types of change and sexual subordination, between the local patterns of work, politics, and family life which structure subordination, and those elements of social change which perpetuate or alleviate sexual hierarchy.

Chapter 1 is an introduction to the complexity and variety of individual women's lives in rural Peru. We begin with biographical portraits of women who represent important contrasts in economic positions, marital arrangements, and labor force participation in order to understand what it means to be a woman in this society. This chapter focuses on three women's lives in the commercial settlement of Chiuchin and on four women's lives in the neighboring agricultural community of Mayobamba.

Chapters 2 and 3 step back from the particulars of the ethnographic case study and consider important issues of theory, methodology, and interpretation. These chapters evaluate the analytic approaches to women's subordination and social change. Chapter 2 presents a critique of bias in such disciplines as political science and anthropology and the impact of this bias on what we know of women's lives. Here we define and discuss the issues underlying the concepts of sexual subordination, parity, and power. Our goal is to phrase these key concepts so they become productive tools for multicultural theories of women's varying social and economic positions. Chapter 3 reviews four contemporary approaches to the cross-cultural study of women: the separate spheres, the sexual division of labor, the class analysis, and the social ideology perspectives. Our analysis probes these frameworks for unexamined assumptions, questions their comprehensiveness, and compares their potential for capturing the complexities of women's positions in class stratified societies in Latin America and North America. We conclude that a synthesis of the social value and class analysis approaches is possible and extremely useful. While some researchers stress the incompatibility of these models, we argue that one can successfully negotiate the analytic territory between them.

In the remaining chapters we demonstrate our analytic model in a finely grained comparative analysis of women's lives in Chiuchin and Mayobamba. In chapter 4 we begin with a closer look at women's life cycles, the cultural alternatives for marriage and household organization, and the politics of domestic life. We present the range of family situations and the consequences for women and men of each option, provide a discussion of women's attitudes toward fertility, and discuss the meaning of the changes that occur in family life and structure which are brought about by increased involvement with coastal society. We view the family as a crucial element in the study of social change because changes in the broader society are often reflected in the relationship between the sexes in family units. Moreover, as will become apparent in the pages which follow, the women of Mayobamba and Chiuchin view their families as critical relationships to which they are firmly committed. The choices they make and the strategies they adopt are made with reference to the central value of the family in their lives.

In chapters 5 and 6 we discuss rural economic structures and trace the impact of sexual divisions of labor and the agrarian class system on sexual hierarchies. In chapter 5 we discuss the consequences of women's participation in the economic life of the two communities. We ask if high levels of economic involvement and a minimal division of labor have led to parity between men and women. In chapter 6 we describe the class structure within each community and examine the differences between male and female experiences in the class system. This application of our analytic model demonstrates the interplay of sex and class in women's perceptions and organization of work.

In chapter 7 we consider women's political participation and how family structures, economic organization, and cultural values combine to constrain women's access to public office, public influence, and community policy. Finally, in chapter 8 we evaluate the differential impact of social change, specifically education and migration, on the options of the sexes in rural communities. Here we consider the impact of national government reforms and development policies on women in rural communities.

Throughout our analysis of the economy, the polity, the family and social change we specify the key elements of rural and national realities that perpetuate and transform women's subordination. The analysis moves beyond stereotyped notions of Andean women by focusing on the women of Chiuchin and Mayobamba, and portraying the complexity of their lives and interactions with the institutions that subordinate them to men. The analysis clearly shows that women are not hapless victims, immobilized in the face of the forces of an economy and a political system marshalled against them. Rather our material suggests that women mobilize a variety of resources to help them cope with their limited and restricted influence. The task, then, is to understand how the mechanics of subordination operate and what strategies offer the best route for promoting sexual equality.

Notes

1. Figures on land use are drawn from Morris (1964).
2. For a more traditional ethnographic treatment of Mayobamba, see Morris et al. (1968).
3. The pattern in Mayobamba seems to follow that noted for a number of Andean communities in Lambert's (1977, p. 15) summary: "Virilocal residence is preferred and sons take priority in the division of inheritance, particularly when land is scarce. The favoritism shown toward male offspring reflects a cultural ideal rather than economic requirements, since the division of labor by sex is not rigid and a day's work by a woman is, in fact, reckoned as the equivalent of the same amount of work by a man. The inequality of the sexes in matters of inheritance was probably greater in the last century than it is now. . . ." See also Flores-Ochoa (1979, p. 96) for inheritance patterns among herders.
4. Adapted from Morris et al. (1968, pp. 275, 288).
5. The use of kinsmen and fictive kin in reciprocal relationships has been found in varying degrees throughout the Andes. See Lambert (1977) and Alberti and Mayer (1974). As both Mayer (1974) and Isbell (1978) note, these ties and obligations may be maintained despite the influence of the coastal cash economy. In Mayobamba and Chiuchin, reciprocal obligations and wage labor coexist.
6. If one thinks in terms of a spectrum of rural community types ranging from those which are culturally autonomous, monolingual Quechua speaking, maintaining Quechua traditions, and erecting barriers to Peruvian state expansion at one end, to communities whose economies and cultures have been thoroughly integrated into and shaped by the expansion of coastal mestizo society at the other, Mayobamba and Chiuchin would be placed toward the latter end of the spectrum. See Deere and León de Leal (n.d.) for an important study of economic variation in agrarian communities.

I

Mother's Day:
Ritual Ironies and Realities

By the eleventh of May it is spring in Chiuchin. The surrounding mountains are still green from the rainy season. In another six weeks the predominant colors will be brown and red, but early in May the highlands are green. On the eleventh of May in 1975, Chiuchin was full of more than the normal level of early morning activity as the local population geared up for the celebration of *El Día de la Madre*, Mother's Day. While it is a totally imported holiday organized primarily by mestizo school teachers who come from the coast, Mother's Day in its translation to the high Andes takes on the stamp of local personalities and customs.

The women of Chiuchin were busy at home. But women from the higher hill towns with children in the secondary school had already come down the mountain on foot and had gathered in the central plaza. A Mayobamba mother with two boys in the high school arrived early, announcing that she had been ordered to come to the ceremony or her sons would be thrown out of the school.

To celebrate the day, a group of Chiuchin men, dressed in their best suits, began the serious business of drinking. They congregated in one of the two local restaurants and by 10 A.M. were exchanging rounds of beer and cane alcohol, both brought from the coast. All the men wore a wild carnation from the surrounding hills, red for those with living mothers and white for the rest.

For dress occasions, the men of Chiuchin have adopted somber blue suits and white shirts, contemporarily styled, yet with a distinctive *sierra* touch in the cut of the coat and the fit of the shirt collar. Women's clothing for the occasion was traditional and thus colorful: orange and pink blouses and full, flowing ankle-length skirts of equally bright colors. The skirts rest on top of several layers of em-

10

broidered felt underskirts (*pulleras*) that give the skirts a billowy quality. Women had freshly washed and braided their dark hair, gleaming
in the sunlight from under their stiff, white, broad-brimmed hats.
This was, after all, Mother's Day and very few women in Chiuchin or
in any of the surrounding areas were not mothers.

Events were scheduled for 10 A.M. in the central square that is actually part of the road that runs through the town. For the Mother's Day
activities, the school teachers had enlisted the support of the local
police to supervise the school boys in sweeping the square, arranging
chairs for the guests at the ceremony, and drawing the lines for the
afternoon football games.

By noon all the preparations had been completed. The enclave of
now rather tipsy fathers from the school's parents committee found
their way from the storefront tavern on the corner to the chairs for
the official participants. The school children, all freshly scrubbed and
dressed in the national uniform of grey and white with red ponchos
for the girls, stood in a formation of slightly squiggly lines, surrounding a color guard. There were four or five benches for the audience
set between the boys' and girls' formations, but most of the mothers
preferred to distribute themselves around the curb outlining the
square. There, they managed their preschool children or talked
among themselves, and in general showed no willingness to move
toward the predetermined spot for the audience. By now all the
women had arrived; two merchant women, Pilar and Hilaria, puffed
to their places at the last second, carrying with them an air of industry
and important activity temporarily interrupted.

The program began with the Peruvian national anthem, and pro-
ceeded through a series of songs, poems, monologues, and skits. Of
the sixty school children assembled, about ten contributed to the performance, with the offspring of the leading merchants playing predominant roles.

The skits were suited to the Mother's Day theme: the ungrateful
son who kills his mother for the love of a wanton woman; a son who
steals for his mother, is caught, and forgiven when it is learned that he
has done the deed for his mother; a daughter who criticizes her
mother's scarred hands until her grandmother tells her they were
scarred when the mother saved the daughter from a fire. The audience showed polite, parental appreciation of the skits.

Throughout all of the presentations there was an undercurrent of activity. Half a dozen of the men found their way back to the two closest taverns to continue drinking, members of the audience chatted with those seated next to them, and the school teachers bustled back and forth whispering about a calamity with the punch they were preparing for the reception following the program. To the distress of the school teachers, someone had contributed a spoiled egg, which threatened to ruin the taste of the thirty good ones in the punch.

As the program drew to a close, the teachers asked the president of the Parents Association, celebrating since early morning, to say a few words. The president was delighted to accept the invitation and launched into a series of self-congratulatory remarks on his contributions to local education. He hit his stride when he turned to his main theme: the puzzling issue of why it is that men, despite the fact that they are men, are obligated to respect and pay homage to women, and especially to their mothers. He had little success in unraveling the mysteries of this contradiction. The audience, tired and restless and sensing that he was foundering, tried to silence him with applause. Eventually he tired of his subject and sat down. One of the female school teachers ended the ceremonies with an invitation to the mothers to try the revitalized punch.

The Mother's Day celebration is an apt starting point for our discussion of the lives of Andean women. The vast majority of Andean women are mothers, and motherhood is an important aspect of their lives. The Mother's Day celebration in Chiuchin brings the community together to demonstrate some of the public expectations regarding women and motherhood as well as some of the continuing tensions in the lives of these Andean women and men.

We will trace the sources of women's subordination in the Andean towns of Mayobamba and Chiuchin, by exploring their interaction with men and other women in the local economy, in politics, in the family, and in the currents of change affecting life in rural Peru. In the following pages we ask how women and men view participation in community life and their interactions with one another. To understand women's status it seems most useful to focus on the structures and processes within community life, the patterns of interactions among women and men which create, reinforce, and, at times, alleviate subordination. Neither subordination nor women's reactions to it are simple phenomenon, and while it is possible to catalogue manifestations—such as lower rates of educational achievement, wage compensation, monolingualism, and limited access to valued resources—our purpose is also to understand how Andean women and men perceive and explain sexual hierarchy in their lives.

The lives of these women demonstrate the ways in which cross-cutting commitments and loyalties to family networks—which include parents, spouses, siblings, and children—are critical to the survival of the family unit. Women's strategies which emphasize family survival, combined with cultural norms restricting women's opportunities, may limit women's choices and perpetuate their subordinate status.[1]

To introduce the shape and complexity of Andean women's lives, let us turn to a series of short descriptions of Chiuchin and Mayo-bamba women. These biographical sketches provide a sense of the variation one finds in women's choices about marriage, husbands, and families; their work involvements; their self-perceptions and evaluations of other women; and their present options and hopes. These descriptions portray women of different ages, levels of education, social statuses, and aspirations. They represent a cross-section of the women who make their homes in this area of the Andes and the varying interpretations they bring to their own experience. The sketches also identify the interplay of factors that shape women's lives, the economic opportunities available to them, the cultural constraints upon sex roles, and the domestic arrangements in which they live, including both marriage choices and kin networks. The sketches demonstrate how these factors intersect in actual lives of individuals, giving rise to a range of female experience.[2]

Women's Lives in the Commercial Center of Chiuchin

In Chiuchin, women are involved in almost all aspects of the town's expanding economy. An individual woman's economic participation is organized and constrained by two factors: the kind of household in which she lives and her access to capital with which to start a business. The following three sketches exemplify variations in household composition and economic positions for the residents of Chiuchin. Pilar, as we will call her, lives in an extended family with her mother-in-law, husband, and children. Over the years, she and her husband have built up one of the town's most successful dry goods stores and sent their children to the coast for professional training. In contrast, Hilaria stands at the center of a domestic kinship network that traces relations through women. Members of this network operate a series of interdependent businesses, including a restaurant and bakery. Finally, Genoveva lives alone without a man or children and maintains weak ties with her highland and coastal relatives. She is a day laborer working for several businesses in town. Understanding the opportunities and restrictions that these domestic and economic situations pose is critical.

Pilar: Marriage and the Creation of a Successful Business Partnership
At the Mother's Day celebration, Pilar did not last through the president's remarks. She has no patience with his drinking and his abuse of his hardworking wife. Pilar left in the middle of the speech, explaining that she had better things to do. Pilar is the wife of a wealthy Chiuchin merchant. At fifty, with three years of primary education, she is a woman well tuned to the *sierra* rhythm, living in a traditional marriage to a highly energetic and entrepreneurial husband. The family has experienced dramatic vertical mobility through the success of their business and the educational achievements of their three older sons, all now located on the coast.

Pilar comes from an agricultural community in the mountains located eight hours by foot from Chiuchin. She moved to Chiuchin when she married Esteban twenty-five years ago. She is serious and soft-spoken with the high-pitched voice common to women in the *sierra*. She is a very hardworking, private person who shows affection by engaging a friend in a short conversation or sending word that a merchant has brought vegetables to town. Despite her reticent manner, she can be tough and self-reliant, running the business without assistance when her husband travels to the coast. Esteban, her husband, came to Chiuchin from a nearby peasant community located in the altitudes above the commercial center. Esteban is still an official member of his natal community and retains land there. In 1945, however, he established a small store in Chiuchin, which twenty-eight years later had become a major business in the region. Over the years, he has retained the respect of the local citizenry. Esteban is an attractive, solidly built man with an outgoing, enthusiastic nature. His leadership qualities and drive have singled him out as a man of ideas and action, and he has been elected to district office.

Esteban met Pilar when she was still young in her home community. Esteban had visited her community to see his sister. According to

Pilar, the sister advised Esteban to marry her from the outset because of Pilar's reputation as a good worker, a woman capable of doing everything, including working in the fields. Their courtship began in Huacho, a provincial town on the coast, where Pilar had gone to live with an older brother. (Huacho, six hours by bus from Chiuchin, is a central link in the network system that gives rural highland dwellers periodic exposure and access to urban society and national Peruvian life.)

As Pilar tells the story, Esteban began their three-year courtship by trying to establish a friendship with her older brother. The brother began to wonder why Esteban hung around so much. Eventually, Esteban traveled to Pilar's community to ask Pilar's father for permission to marry her. The father sent word to Pilar to return home and, when she arrived, asked her if she knew anything about Esteban's plans to marry her. Thinking back on the event, she recalls that she was timid and confused and did not know what to say, so she denied any knowledge of Esteban's intentions. Her father responded by saying that perhaps this was her luck or destiny (*suerte*) and she in turn agreed that perhaps it was. All three—Esteban, Pilar, and her father—journeyed to Chiuchin where the couple was married. At the time, Esteban was twenty-seven and Pilar was twenty-five.

Pilar has four children, three boys and a girl. The three boys live in Lima. The oldest has graduated from high school and is now a teacher in the capital. The second boy is in law school, and the third is in his first year of architecture. The youngest, and only girl, is seven and a star pupil in the Chiuchin elementary school. Educational achievement has been highly valued in Pilar and Esteban's family, and the roots of this appreciation are deep. Esteban's eighty-year-old mother, who lives with them in Chiuchin, while now deaf, is literate. She was taught by her own mother, who had been a teacher in one of the highland communities. All three of Esteban and Pilar's sons have been sent to the coast for high school and all three have excelled. The two in Lima universities board with families who are not relatives. Esteban visits them regularly when he travels to resupply the store's stock. Pilar sends them food, their favorite dishes, and awaits their visits back to Chiuchin. She considers the atmosphere of their Lima boardinghouse to be cold and impersonal. Her efforts to befriend the woman who runs the boardinghouse were met with rejection. The Lima woman failed to reciprocate Pilar's greetings and would not accept the gifts of food she had brought from the *sierra*. At the same time that Pilar sees the advanced training of her children on the coast as a necessity to ensure their well-being, her preference remains for life in the *sierra*.

Esteban and Pilar have a simple home and shop located on the main street just off the square. The building is a single story, of cement construction with a corrugated metal roof. The store occupies one half of the first floor; separated from the store by a curtain is the living room/bedroom. Behind the bedroom there is a kitchen with a four-burner kerosene stove and small table. An addition to the back of the home includes four bedrooms rented to Peruvian tourists. In 1975, Esteban was in the process of remaking one of the back bedrooms into a bathroom with running water and a flush toilet. The addition of the bathroom and plans to provide electricity from a small generator represent dramatic improvements to their property, for none of the other boardinghouses in town offer such facilities.

Unlike their neighbors and chief competitors, Pilar does not offer meals to their clientele. Esteban asked her if she would add this enterprise and Pilar rejected the idea. She argues that meals are a huge bother because of the limited and unpredictable supply of food in Chiuchin. Moreover, she finds tourists very demanding. She reasons that she could not take on this added obligation without further help.

Given the volume and rate of activity at their store, it is almost impossible to imagine Pilar taking on more responsibilities. She already plays an active role in the store's management, spending long hours behind the wooden counter supplying people's needs. The store offers a broad range of merchandise brought from the coast: rice, noodles and bread; locally produced potatoes; highly priced fruit; an occasional vegetable not produced in the high altitudes; tinned foods for special occasions; matches, kerosene, batteries, rubber shoes and other products of the urbanized coastal society to which the people of the *sierra* have grown accustomed.

Both Pilar and Esteban trade off their days in agricultural work and in their other activities so that one of them can always attend the store. Esteban is frequently building and hires other men to help him. On these occasions Pilar must prepare meals for the entire work party. Pilar for her part goes off to bake bread or to care for her animals. Esteban does all of the buying for the store, and this takes him to the coast for several days at a time. During these periods, Pilar takes on all the responsibilities.

Pilar has no family help beyond her young daughter and must hire additional workers to complete her tasks. She hires Genoveva, another Chiuchin woman, to help her with the boardinghouse laundry, a laborious, time-consuming task of washing, drying, and ironing sheets, all by hand.

In addition to the store, the rooming house, and her fields, Pilar raises a variety of small animals. She religiously saves scraps for her pigs. She would not dream of eating their meat but raises them to sell to people living on the coast. Through experience she has found that she must spend her earnings immediately on what she intends to buy, or else Esteban will use the money to buy more stock for the store. Pilar used the income from the sale of the last pig to purchase blankets for the boardinghouse.

Pilar does not have a group of close female friends. Nor does she have a group of relatives close at hand. She is not a member of the family friendship groups composed of women who spend their afternoon sewing or crocheting together at their stores. She could not participate, for this would require closing the shop and could result in loss of potential business. Without a close group of relatives she has a limited amount of consistent company. She does crochet and knit, but both activities are secondary to the store and the frequent interruptions it brings.

Pilar assesses Esteban highly. She respects his accomplishments and his public stature but notes that his worst period of drinking was when he held district office. In this position he could not avoid drinking because there were too many public obligations and occasions when there was no alternative. Pilar felt that she had no recourse in these situations, no way to stop his drinking once it had begun. In certain circumstances she has been able to elicit a promise from Esteban before an event, such as a wedding, that he will limit his drinking and he has kept his word. If, however, she encounters him in the midst of drinking with a group of friends and endeavors to get him away, the other men remark to Esteban, "Why are you so henpecked that you allow yourself to be ordered about by a woman?" Pilar is infuriated by other men who draw him into bouts of drinking and she tries to get the shop closed at night to avoid this occurring. Whenever there is a public meeting she fears that it will end in a drinking bout at the store. On more than one occasion after a dance or a fiesta she has gone out to search the streets, found Esteban sprawled over a rain barrel, and brought him home to sleep it off for a day.

Pilar is not a sentimental woman, but she is generous, giving, and warm in the reserved fashion of the *sierra*. She judges herself well treated by the world, with three healthy sons making their way in the larger society in professions that should insure her future well-being. She feels fortunate to have had a daughter, someone to take her place, to help her with her work, and to take special care of her when she feels tired or ill. Her husband is prosperous, industrious, and well-respected. She recognizes their status in Chiuchin and marks it with a somewhat narrow social circle. She likes the life of the *sierra*—working in the fields, caring for her animals—and she is adept at managing the store. She has no desire to make her life on the coast, which she has found cold and uncaring in her contacts there.

Hilaria: Kinship Networks and Interdependent Businesses
The Mother's Day celebration included a brief marching exercise by all the school children. As they straggled by in rough age and height order, several children too young to be in school scrambled to join the parade. Running along at the end of the group came Tico, Hilaria's youngest son, struggling with all his energy to keep up with the bigger boys. Hilaria and her mother collapsed in laughter watching this spectacle. The scene of these two women together in some degree of delight over Hilaria's offspring is not unusual, for they are at the center of an important series of networks and enterprises based on family bonds. Hilaria is one of the most highly educated women in the town and the least involved in agriculture. Born and raised in Chiuchin, she has no ties to the *campesino* communities. Her family was one of the original Chiuchin families and continues to own some of the prized and limited land on the valley bottom. Hilaria is a woman who desired more education and was frustrated by the attitudes of her father. Her own relations with men are complex. She, like other women who run their own businesses, is involved in a network of friendship, family, and kin ties that relate to a series of diversified economic activities.

Hilaria is a very short woman, rounded in pregnancy, but strong shouldered and active. She is especially proud of her long, black hair that falls over her shoulders to her waist when she combs it out from her usual braids. The darkness of her hair matches the black dresses, sweaters, and pants that she, along with the rest of her family, has worn as a sign of mourning since her father's death. Hilaria enjoys the company of others, is assertive about her own opinions, and proud of her competence and tough-mindedness as a merchant.

At thirty-three Hilaria has two children and a third on the way. She finally married the father of the second boy when he threatened to carry off his son if she would not agree to marry. Her mother was not in favor of her daughter's marriage, causing some tension between them. As her mother recalls the discussion: "I told her not to get married, what could she possibly want from it? She has two children. She saw how her father treated me; she knows how men are. Finally I told her if she was going to get married to go out to the corral and do it there. I told her not to expect any banquet from me, and I told him the same thing."

Hilaria retorts: "Mother, you'll be the source of my destruction, my perdition. You didn't want me to marry Juan (the father of the first child) and now you object to Felipe." Hilaria's romance with Juan was fully expected by most people to end in marriage. Juan had a reputation as a romancer, but he also had a great deal of land and cattle and came from a wealthy family in a highland community. He was recognized as one of the most eligible men in the district. Hilaria, for her part, was viewed as a highly competent, intelligent woman. She had petitioned her father to allow her to continue school beyond the primary grades. When this failed, she studied for three years on the coast to be a seamstress. She also attended a course for peasant women at a coastal development center sponsored by the Catholic Church. From the course she received some general instruction in leadership, community development techniques, and cooperatives. Hilaria seems to consider her relationship with Juan past history and notes that Juan's increasing drunkenness is a sign that it would have been a hopeless match. In contrast, marriage to Felipe has proven to be rather untaxing. He is a truck driver on routes in a neighboring region. He comes to Chiuchin every week and visits Hilaria's shop on the square for a day. She travels down to his coastal town once or twice a year as a kind of holiday. Consequently, Hilaria's life has not changed much with her marriage. She continues to make her home in Chiuchin, which she feels is a beautiful place, one she would never leave permanently

for the coast. She runs her business, a restaurant, and takes in occasional Peruvian tourists in the upper rooms. She sleeps with her two
children and her mother in a little room behind the shop. The restaurant serves as the chief distribution point for bread from her brother's
bakery.

Her brother, the baker, is the youngest of her mother's three children, six years younger than Hilaria. He has a boyish, ebullient quality about him, an openness and freshness toward the world. His latest
enthusiasm has been to buy a gasoline motor to drive a mechanized
kneading machine for his bakery. Without the kneading machine his
task as a baker was grueling. With the machine it is still a time-
consuming, largely manual operation; but his production has increased substantially. Bread is less frequently served in this part of the
sierra than potatoes and is viewed as something of a luxury since it is
not made at home and must be purchased. The bakery business
supplies the commercial establishments throughout the districts of
Santa Leonor and Checras. Baking is only the most recent of the
brother's professions and is related to his recent marriage, the birth of
his son, and his father's death.

As the only boy, the brother was sent on to high school on the coast.
Hilaria was far more academically motivated, but her father turned
down her pleas for more education. Instead the brother went to
school somewhat against his own inclination and returned to
Chiuchin before completing the course of study. He did learn enough
math and composition to qualify for a job with a trucking company
working in a mining town. He took care of the payroll and other
administrative details, including organizing the boarding arrangements for the truckers. During the process of hiring a cook for the
workers' kitchen, he met his wife. He hired her for the position of
cook and began to court her.

His wife, Melinda, was born in a highland community. She went to
primary school in the *sierra* and then went to Lima to work as a
domestic. She studied for a year while she was in Lima and worked in
what she describes as a nice home in a wealthy section of Lima. When
all of her brothers and sisters left the *sierra* community, she felt obligated to return home to care for her parents; she was also tired of
work as a domestic.

After about four months of courting, Hilaria's brother brought
Melinda home to meet his mother, announcing that this was her new

daughter-in-law. When Hilaria's mother recalls the event, she remembers telling them that they could not continue living together, that they had to get married: "What would happen if he got bored with her? I saw his intentions, he has so much of his father in him, I know what happened to my daughter, and I know all the problems that follow. I wanted to avoid all that."

They did marry and the young couple now have a baby son they both adore. The grandmother complains that the baby is spoiled, but no one else seems disturbed.

Economically, Hilaria and her kin have mobilized a network of closely related individuals who often eat together, share domestic tasks, and promote each other's businesses. The two adult generations of this family have strung together a series of enterprises that combine to give them and their offspring a comfortable life. Hilaria, her mother, and brother share access to capital in the form of valley-bottom agricultural land, the restaurant, and the bakery. None of these enterprises is very large, but together they have become quite successful. While each adult specializes in one business, the family freely exchanges labor to assist each other.

Hilaria tends the restaurant. She does all the purchasing, some cooking, and spends most of her time somewhere in or about the restaurant where she can attend to customers. She presides over an informal sewing and crocheting group that gathers in the restaurant during the slow afternoons. Hilaria also manages the boarding rooms above the shop. Her sister-in-law, Melinda, helps in all of this work, shares the child care and washing, and does much of the food preparation. The grandmother works in her fields, hiring male workers when she needs assistance. Hilaria's brother runs the bakery with a young assistant. When all the women are occupied he will take a turn with his son.

Genoveva: A Day Laborer without Husband or Children

Genoveva did not attend the Mother's Day celebration. Not a mother and not attached to a man, she represents a third form of living situation and economic position in Chiuchin. Genoveva is a large woman with thick grey hair, small eyes, and smooth skin. She is now fifty years old and is beginning to worry about the future because she has never married or had any children. As she puts it, "A woman who is single must worry about old age, losing her physical strength, and not being able to work." Genoveva figures that she is strong enough to work for another twenty years but worries that after a certain point there will be no one to take care of her. "For this reason," she concludes, "women should marry."

For the time being Genoveva supports herself as a laborer. She cooks in the dark, smoky kitchen of a local restaurant and washes sheets for families that take in boarders. From time to time, she helps other women who must meet deadlines for crocheted bedspreads ordered by coastal families. On the one hand, women in the town look out for her and make sure that she makes enough money to get by. On the other hand, women feel that she has made poor choices and is suffering the consequences.

Genoveva prefers to live in Chiuchin because she is able to earn a living there, whereas in the higher agricultural towns, such as her home town, wage labor for women is virtually nonexistent. Nor could she be an independent agriculturalist in a highland town because some of the work is considered too heavy for women. She would have to find money to hire men to irrigate the fields and to do service to the community on her behalf. Some years she is able to plant small amounts of corn in her home community, an activity that brings her the satisfaction of working in the fields. As reminders of her agrarian past, Genoveva is often accompanied by her dog and a pet chicken that she dotes on and carries in a cloth when she thinks that its feet are tired.

Genoveva has always worked and valued her independence, although she has not always understood the high cost of not having children. She left school after three years, not because she had lost interest but, she explains, because her father died and she had to work to help support the family. She supported her younger brother through high school and helped him migrate to the coast where he became a successful businessman. In retrospect she feels she martyred herself in her efforts to advance her brother's career. Later, Genoveva followed him to the coast and became a servant in a middle-class Peruvian home.

Although she worked as a servant for five years in Lima, Genoveva never adjusted to coastal life. She missed the face-to-face relations of rural communities. She was disturbed by the anonymity of coastal society. She recalls that in Lima she would stand at the gates of her employer's house and watch strangers pass by, wondering if they were perhaps distant relatives. On top of these feelings of isolation, she resented the regimented routine that servants were subjected to, as well as the pecking order established among the women working in the house. In the *sierra* after her father's death she was independent, working hard, but deciding for herself which tasks needed attention and when she would eat and rest. In Lima she found herself working under someone's command and forced to obey another's orders. Finally she was fired.

When Genoveva returned to her home town, she wanted to continue supporting her family and maintaining a measure of independence. She believes that these values precluded marriage, commenting, "I didn't want to be under the authority of a husband, to do his will. A woman who marries has to do all the work in the home and then children come. She must follow her husband's plans. If I had married, my husband might never have let me work. Perhaps he would have helped my family a little, but he would not have given them everything they needed." Genoveva also points out that the choice to remain single when she returned to the *sierra* was not totally hers because men are not interested in an older woman. Rather they prefer to marry younger girls of eighteen to twenty.

For Genoveva, the future is clouded primarily because she has no living children, not because she has remained unmarried. As other townspeople argue, work has little meaning unless one has children. In turn, children will support their parents in old age. Highland aunts now help Genoveva, sending her agricultural surpluses in exchange for assistance in the corn and potato harvests. Her brother, who still lives on the coast, also helps her financially. Genoveva wonders what will happen after the death of her older relatives. Her brother's children have little sense of their responsibility to their aunt. They have grown up on the coast and know nothing of life in the *sierra*.

Women's Lives in the Agricultural Community of Mayobamba

Mayobamba, a settlement of 450 people, is located at 3,400 meters (11,000 feet) above sea level on mountainous slopes overlooking Chiuchin. Mayobamba is a town of peasant agriculturalists who grow potatoes, raise dairy cattle and sheep, and produce broad beans and cheese for regional and national markets. Unlike Chiuchin, Mayobamba is officially recognized as a "peasant community" (earlier termed an "indigenous community") by the national government. This status as a recognized community protects communal lands from sale, calls for the formal political organization of the community, and serves as the basis for a continuing tradition of such communal works as road building and maintenance of the irrigation canals. The political organization of the community centers on the formal role of family heads, called *comuneros*. The body of *comuneros* elects community officials, allocates access to communal lands and organizes communal work projects. Generally, *comuneros* in Mayobamba are adult men who act as the representatives of nuclear or extended families.

Despite the fact that Mayobamba is organized as a community, it had no Mother's Day celebration. Lacking Chiuchin's complement of coastal school teachers, the community let the day pass unmarked. In some respects the lack of such a celebration demonstrated the more limited penetration of coastal values into the highland community as well as the more restricted public role of women in Mayobamba.

In addition to the communal aspects of Mayobamba's social and economic organization, townspeople are individually active in the production of cash crops, agricultural surplus, and animal products for regional and national markets. The wealth and productive capacity of a family in cash crops or animal husbandry is directly related to the amount of private land they own. Land is acquired through inheritance or purchase, and there is substantial variation in the amount of land owned by individuals in Mayobamba. A wealthy man will own eight to twelve irrigated fields; a poor man will own none and consequently be forced to either rent fields from an absent family or sharecrop with a wealthier man.

Women's lives in Mayobamba contrast with those of their counterparts in Chiuchin because of the very different productive bases in agricultural and commercial settlements. In Mayobamba, an individual woman's economic participation is structured by two primary factors: the kind of marital relationship she has (whether she is formally married, lives in a consensual union, or is a single mother) and the access she has to private land through inheritance or marriage.

The following three sketches demonstrate the impact of variations in the marital relations and wealth of women in this agricultural settlement. Carmen and Mercedes are cousins who live with their husbands in satisfying marriages. They are peasant agriculturalists with small herds of dairy cattle and very restricted private land. Both are well adapted to life in the *sierra,* although they have made very different economic choices and have placed different values on economic mobility. Mariana, as a single mother with two children, must depend on her father, a day laborer, for access to communal land for subsistence. She is a woman with little security and few options because she has not married and because of the poverty of her family. Finally, Concepción is a woman from a relatively wealthy family who managed to continue school through the first two years of university. Her life reflects the variety of reasons *sierra* women migrate to the coast and the opportunities and restrictions they find in urban, coastal life.

Carmen and Mercedes: Contrasting Patterns of
Satisfaction with Sierra Life

Carmen had walked down to Chiuchin the afternoon of the Mother's Day celebration. She spoke with friends about the activities in Chiuchin and commented on her disappointment that there had not been any public display in Mayobamba. Carmen and her husband, Marcos, have been married for thirty years and both agree that they are well suited to one another. They live in a small compound, surrounded by a shoulder-high stone fence and guarded by a ferocious rooster who has the run of both the courtyard and house. The compound consists of three small stone structures, two one-room buildings for storage and a third for living. Outside the main house is a covered dining area with a wooden table, a bench, a few chairs, and a dried mud stove with several different cooking levels sculptured over the central fire chamber. The room looks very much like the interior of all cooking and eating units in Mayobamba. Carmen made the stove herself. Like all the women of Mayobamba and Chiuchin, she does the cooking in her home: "Marcos could cook if he wanted to, but he pretends not to know how. When he cooks, he complains that he can't find anything, so that I am forced to do it."

Carmen is a robust, cheerful, and gregarious woman. She loves jokes and teasing, particularly gently teasing Marcos. She has never lived for any extended period of time on the coast and never went beyond the first years of primary school. She takes life in the *sierra* very much on its own terms and seems satisfied with its slow but demanding pace and the reciprocal demands of the extended kin structure in which she and Marcos make their social world.

Carmen and Marcos were married when Marcos came from a

neighboring highland community to seek a wife in Mayobamba. After finding that water and land were more abundant than in his home community and marrying the daughter of one of the town's more prosperous *comuneros,* Marcos decided to stay and make his home in Mayobamba. The decision to relocate to his wife's community has had some drawbacks for Marcos. He has never felt fully accepted as a *comunero* in Mayobamba. Although he has held some minor offices in the town, he has never been elected to the presidency. Moreover, during community meetings when he has presented differing opinions, he has felt that his views fail to carry the proper weight because he is not originally from Mayobamba. Additionally, Marcos has not directly benefitted from the wealth of his wife's family. Both of Carmen's parents are still alive and have not distributed their private landholdings to their children. Consequently, Marcos and Carmen have made do with relatively little over the years. The marriage has never been materially prosperous, but neither party seems particularly disappointed by lack of wealth.

Carmen and Marcos have demonstrated very little interest in social mobility in Mayobamba. Marcos did not inherit land in his home community. In Mayobamba, the community fields he was assigned by virtue of his marriage and permanent settlement are located at a substantial distance from the town. He has made very few improvements on the plots. The family keeps guinea pigs, a few chickens, sheep, and several cows they received from Carmen's parents. Marcos has some specialized skills as a carpenter that bring in a little additional income to supplement subsistence agriculture.

Carmen and Marcos never lived in a consensual union. Because of her family's insistence, they were married almost immediately following their courtship. As Carmen explains it, her parents felt marriage would provide her with some degree of protection, that with a formal marriage a woman has some negotiating power: "Marriage is more secure, with marriage a woman won't be left. If you have a piece of paper that says you were married and your husband leaves, then you can use it to complain and get justice. If you aren't married, you have no way to get help from the father of your children."

Carmen believes in the complementary character of male-female tasks and argues that it would be very difficult for a woman to survive without a man in Mayobamba. In agriculture, she believes that men and women share work by performing different but coordinated tasks. In her view, men are better suited for heavy work in the fields, while women take an active part in agricultural activities that do not require as much strength. Despite the complementarity of agricultural tasks, in Carmen's view men should (as they actually do) direct these activities. She also extends this division of labor and structuring of authority from agriculture into the home to the control of property and income. Sharing work and income, for her, implies a hierarchy of control of husbands over wives. Men, in her experience, control most of the family income and make the major financial decisions for the family.

Marcos and Carmen have lived life very much within the constraints of Mayobamba. Their one son completed high school, moved to the coast where he has a job, and returns to the community only for fiestas. He has no intention of permanently returning to agricultural work. Both daughters live on the coast, are married, and have produced grandchildren. Neither Carmen nor Marcos had particularly ambitious plans for their children, and they seem completely satisfied with their children's choices. Neither of them would encourage their children to return and settle in Mayobamba, though they enjoy visits and seeing the grandchildren.

Carmen and Marcos spend a great deal of their time with an extended kin network that includes Carmen's parents, a brother and sister, and a cousin and her husband. They frequently eat evening meals with Carmen's cousin Mercedes and her husband, Cesar. The two couples are very close and the cousins enjoy spending time together. Both women have good marriages to hardworking men, and both share positive feelings about life in the *sierra*. Mercedes is about fifteen years younger than her cousin. She is about the same stature with the same good health and gregarious personality. But in contrast to her cousin, Mercedes gives the impression of ceaseless activity and liveliness.

For all that they have in a common commitment to *sierra* life, the attitudes toward economic experimentation and mobility of Mercedes and Cesar are very different from those of Carmen and Marcos. Mercedes and Cesar have made a concerted effort to expand their agricultural activities and to combine agriculture with commercial enterprises.

As a young man Cesar migrated first to a mining center and later to the coast in attempts to find work. His family had very little land and his two older brothers had preceded him to the mines as an alternative to the dwindling productivity of *sierra* agriculture. His older brothers located a job for him in the mines, but Cesar found the job incredibly difficult. Further attempts to find satisfactory work in Lima also proved unsuccessful. He finally returned to Mayobamba and decided to try his hand at agriculture. His work on the coast had allowed him to amass a little capital and considerable commercial experience. He married Mercedes and together the two have constructed a series of agricultural enterprises that have allowed them to expand their landholdings and livestock investments.

When the access road that links Mayobamba to the main road at the bottom of the valley was completed in 1968, Mercedes and Cesar began offering room and board to the bus drivers and the occasional traveling merchants. Mayobamba is not large enough to support a full-time restaurant or hotel, and this activity is very much secondary to their primary activities as agriculturalists. This enterprise, however, is an example of the ways in which Cesar and Mercedes have responded to new opportunities to improve their economic situation.

Like Cesar, Mercedes began life at the lower end of the economic scale in Mayobamba. She was one of three illegitimate daughters of a Mayobamba woman. Her mother is still alive and has, as a widow and head of household, *comunera* status. Her father, now dead, was from a neighboring community. The father never recognized Mercedes as his daughter and she has never received any inheritance from him, nor has she as yet received any from her mother. When Mercedes first began to live with Cesar they had a consensual union. They lived as *convivientes* during their early years together and through the birth of two children. There seems to have been a turning point in their lives about ten years ago, just as they started their new business of providing board and room for visitors to Mayobamba. As Mercedes recalls the circumstances, she insisted on a legal marriage at that point. Having suffered in her own life the ill effects of illegitimacy on inheritance, she wanted to insure that her children would not have the same disability. As Mercedes recounts the experience, she told Cesar that she was unwilling to make all the efforts at expanding their income without some guarantee that her children would be sure to enjoy the fruits of those extra efforts. Cesar consented and the couple was married by the district secretary.

Cesar and Mercedes have attempted to expand their sources of income through hard work and astute responses to new economic opportunities. They began by taking care of a large herd of cows belonging to another *comunero* for a year. Their pay was half the offspring of the herd during the year. With this beginning, Cesar and Mercedes have built up their own small herd that is restricted in number by the size of their landholdings on which fodder is grown. When the herd becomes too large or they need money for a new business venture, they sell a cow to coastal merchants.

Another economic strategy has been to increase and diversify their agricultural production by acquiring irrigated land. Cesar has inherited a few small plots and they have purchased others. The irrigated land is used to produce broad beans and fodder for cattle. The beans are a cash crop that bring a good price on the Lima markets. The cattle also represent a response to the national market and a form of investment. Cesar's coastal experience has come into good use in his ability to organize and, to some extent, control the marketing of his products. He is in charge of this aspect of their lives.

The growing dairy herd and the beans are a source of pride for both Cesar and Mercedes. Both express pleasure, without self-consciousness, at the beauty of the bean blossoms and the handsomeness of their animals. The proceeds from their endeavors support their three sons in school on the coast, another form of investment. Cesar and Mercedes decided against the Chiuchin school, feeling that the educational opportunities of Lima were worth the increased expense. They are using a kinsman's home to board the boys.

Mercedes and Cesar are probably the only Mayobamba couple ever to have taken what might be loosely described as a holiday together. Following the very advantageous sale of their bean harvest in Lima, the couple decided to travel to Huancayo, in the central *sierra,* by train. This spectacular journey on the engineering marvel constructed by Henry Meiggs in the 1870s took them through countless tunnels and switchbacks and over the highest train pass in the Americas. They adored the trip and describe their adventures in the second-class car with a precision that reveals their delight in the experience.

Cesar and Mercedes are perceived as very enterprising members of the community. Their efforts to improve their economic situation are viewed as appropriate behavior for people who start adult life with relatively little. Mercedes has few complaints about her present situation, which seems full of possibilities, or with her marriage to Cesar. He attempts to control his drinking and he works very hard. The couple share a set of aspirations for their own lives and for those of their children. Mercedes assumes that Cesar has affairs with other women when he is away on business; but she refuses to ask him about this, dismissing it as predictable male behavior of little consequence. Her official marriage seems to guarantee her enough loyalty and her children enough security.

Mariana: The Single Mother

Mariana is a nineteen-year-old girl who seems out of place in a town where, due to heavy coastal migration, there are relatively few people her age. In a wealthier family, she might have been sent to Chiuchin to finish her primary education or perhaps to the coast to work with an aunt or uncle. But Mariana's family had little interest in educating daughters and no extra money or contacts for sending their daughter to the coast. Her parents cultivate potatoes on communal lands given to each household head in return for service to the community. The potato harvest ensures the family's subsistence. In Mayobamba, money for a higher standard of living, for dry goods, school supplies, and trips to the coast must come from the cultivation of cash crops, from raising dairy cattle, or from day labor in other people's fields. Mariana's family owns no private land on which to grow cash crops and fodder for cattle. Her father works as a laborer, earning 60 *soles* ($1.50) a day, taking other people's dairy cattle to pasture and clearing and preparing their fields to be planted in broad beans and alfalfa. Mariana and her mother take care of the family's five sheep, assist in the cultivation of potatoes, and earn a few dollars each year working in the bean harvest. Neither woman has found other sources of day labor because women are not generally hired for assistance in the fields (with the exception of the bean harvest).

Mariana seems more isolated than alone. She spends time with her mother, a quiet older woman who takes pleasure in caring for the grandchildren. Together, mother and daughter oversee the house, which is sparsely furnished even by Mayobamba standards. The kitchen is a low dark room with a few cooking pots and little in the way of reserves of firewood, cheese, or bread. The room does not serve as a social center for evening visits as it would in the houses of Carmen and Mercedes. Rather, Mariana's family is more self-contained, partly out of choice and partly because they do not have close kin in the town.

Mariana is skillful and industrious without an outlet for her abilities. She walks through town spinning wool on a wooden bobbin or takes the low trail out of town to pasture animals. She talks of crocheting but never finds the money to buy thread. In addition, Mariana is a highly verbal woman, a storyteller without an audience, who, if given a chance, effectively portrays local personalities and their conflicts.

At one point, Mariana had an opportunity to escape Mayobamba and settle on the coast. Her brother, a mechanic, invited her to visit him in Huacho, a coastal town. Mariana never had a chance to shed her *sierra* awkwardness in the city: she became pregnant two months after her arrival and returned to her mother in Mayobamba to give birth to her first child.

Mariana's life is shaped by poverty and by the fact that she is a single mother (*madre soltera*) with two daughters aged three years and six months. She is bitter about her experiences with men, whom she terms "the mean ones, the lizards, who tell girls lies and deceive them." She is not the only woman to complain that some men seduce women, promising marriage, but later abandoning lovers. Mariana is also bitter toward women whom she perceives as competitors for the affection of eligible men. Yet she empathizes with women who have been left by their lovers with children to raise.

Finding someone to share a permanent relationship that will end in marriage is felt to be next to impossible for the *madre soltera*. Single mothers are viewed by other women as the victims of short affairs, in which the couple never lived together and there was no feeling of long-term responsibility. After having a child and failing to establish a more continuous relationship with its father, the single woman may seek other lovers. Some argue that single mothers take subsequent lovers out of resentment and with a desire to belittle the initial lover. Others stress that men are unlikely to marry the woman because they, too, want to evade increased responsibility.

As a single mother, Mariana has none of the benefits of the *conviviente* or the marriage relationships. She is formally a member of her father's household and gains access to communal land and potatoes through her father. She remains under his authority until he dies. At that point, if she is still unmarried, she or her mother will be given the status of the head of household. This solution will not resolve Mariana's problems, for she will still be without private land, and, thus, the means to gain cash income. She will still be without the labor of a man in the fields. In such circumstances it is probable that she will become a secondary wife, exchanging sexual favors for a man's labor. There are several women in Mayobamba in this situation. These patterns of poverty may be perpetuated through Mariana's children. They may be forced to hire themselves out as laborers if they do not inherit land. Alternatively, they might migrate to the coast or the mines to seek better opportunities outside the agricultural communities. In this situation, the value of male children is obvious. They may be able to replace the missing husband's labor in the family until they move on to establish a separate household or migrate.

Concepción: The Option of Migration from the Sierra
Concepción, who migrated to the coast fifteen years before, was in Lima on Mother's Day. She returned from an exhausting morning at her market stall. Business had been unusually busy with customers clamoring to buy Concepción's chickens for a special midday meal. She looked forward to the afternoon with her family in their partially completed home in a dusty working-class development east of the city. She regretted that only half her children would be with her. Concepción is an example of a Mayobamba woman who successfully migrated in search of education. Her adult life, while primarily spent in Lima, gives ample illustration of the adaptability of *sierra*-based kin networks in helping families meet their needs, whether those be to pursue professional aspirations, meet the daily necessities for work, or survive in the face of disaster.

Concepción was born into one of the wealthier Mayobamba families. Her father holds substantial private land and cattle. Her mother, an indomitable *sierra* woman, raised five surviving children, two boys and three girls. Concepción's life has been characterized by her strong desire to study. Her first move to the coast was in pursuit of high school education. Concepción's family had planned to send her younger brother to the coast to continue his studies. An elder sister, already working on the coast, offered him a place to live. At this point, Concepción began to lobby for more schooling as well. It took a lot of protesting, but eventually she convinced her father to let her go. Her mother agreed, and the older sister offered to keep both children. Life on the coast required some changes. As Concepción recalls:

> When I first got to the coast I felt different from everyone else. I
> wanted to adapt quickly to the new way of life. I changed the way I
> dressed so that it wouldn't be so obvious that I was from the *sierra*. The
> most difficult adjustment was that coastal men call out compliments to
> the girls, "you're pretty, you're nice, I like you" as the girls walk by. I
> was fourteen at the time and this frightened me. This was not the
> custom in the *sierra*. At first I was afraid the boys would follow me. In
> time I learned not to pay any attention to this, that it was simply a
> custom of coastal men.

Concepción did very well in the Huacho school and was anxious to
continue studying after high school. She thought about nursing
or teaching and planned to go to Lima and enroll in a specialized
course of study. She managed to accompany her brother to Lima
and they lived together for a while. The brother, however, was unable
to make a success of it on the coast and decided to return to the *sierra*.
Concepción stayed on, sharing a room with some cousins. She found
employment in a department store where she could work during the
day and study at the preparatory academy in the evening to get
ready for her university entrance exams. She analyzed the entrance
procedure as a highly political affair requiring sponsorship. Concepción sought just this kind of sponsorship by contacting a Mayobambino who had moved to Lima and had ties with political parties.
She failed the entrance exams for the university twice and finally
managed to pass the third time.

Once in the university, she studied for two years, met a young man
from Huaral whom she married, and then became pregnant. When
the first boy was born, Concepción dropped out of the university and
found work. This time she found a job through a cousin, selling
poultry at a fixed stand in one of the large markets in Lima. The job
caused arguments between Concepción and her new mother-in-law.
The mother-in-law felt that married women should not work. As
Concepción explains it, "She was from the old school which felt that
women had to be the slaves of men, there to serve them and nothing
else." Despite her mother-in-law's objections, Concepción continued
to work. As she explains it, she felt she had to as long as her husband
had a limited income. Moreover, she had every intention of returning
to the university. But the babies came rapidly. The first boy was followed by a second and then two daughters. After the birth of the

fourth child, Concepción's young husband died very suddenly; he got sick, went to the hospital with chest pains, and died two days later.

Concepción's ties with her *sierra* family had never been broken. Throughout her time on the coast, visits were frequent and were viewed as mutually beneficial. With the loss of her husband, however, the linkages became more intensive as the family rallied around to assist her. The two young daughters went to live with their paternal grandparents in Huaral. Concepción explains that she sent them to ease the pain of her in-laws in the loss of their only son. Concepción's father decided to move to Lima from Mayobamba to accompany his daughter, and, from time to time, the youngest unmarried sister comes to stay and assist with the children.

The extended family decided to buy a plot of land in a development adjoining squatter settlements on the outskirts of Lima and hired a carpenter to help with the basic construction of a house. First, brick walls were constructed, forming a large living room and a garden open to the sun, a patio for cooking and washing, and two bedrooms. The interior will be completed little by little as the family saves the money. At the front of the house, there is room for a small shop to sell poultry, beer, or whatever else Concepción decides she will offer. Her hope is that eventually she can have a shop in her home and thus avoid the long trek across Lima to her present market stall.

Concepción has maintained her stall in the market, leaving her two young boys with her father during the day. Work in the market has become increasingly difficult because the transportation system of Lima is severely overburdened, forcing Concepción to spend long hours in waiting for transportation and then still more time in difficult traffic. Thus for Concepción, while her stall has provided a steady income, it has very real limitations and drawbacks.

While Concepción has made adjustments to life in Lima, her ties with her *sierra* family have been reinforced by the impersonality of urban life: "In Lima in the squatter settlements (*pueblos jóvenes*), it's pretty difficult to make friends. People are quite reserved. It's not like Mayobamba where you have known people since they were little." Many *sierra* women (as well as men) never make the adjustment to life on the coast. For women from agricultural communities, adjustment to urban life requires accommodation to very different economic roles as urban female consumers and workers. For instance, Concepción's mother cannot visit her daughter for long in Lima without becoming nervous about the amount of money people spend in their daily lives. During these visits her mother complains: "My daughter, I have to go back home to Mayobamba. Look at how much money you are spending. It hurts me to see you spending so much."

The concerns expressed by Concepción's mother reflect both the noncash basis of daily life in Mayobamba, where monetary expenditures may be infrequent, and the central role of a woman as administrator of household consumption in many *sierra* families. Concepción's mother, like most Andean women, oversees the storage of the family's harvests and decides what is needed for daily consumption. Consequently, her mother becomes very anxious when she sees her daughter's dependence on cash, knowing her own limited ability to earn money. On the coast, *sierra* women explicitly note the loss of control in those areas of life where they have had some control in their home communities. Complaints about the heavy dependence on cash, about being restricted to one-room homes in squatter settlements, or about the lack of farm animals relate to differences in lifestyles and women's roles in the *sierra* and urban economies. Some *sierra* women reject migration for reasons that are directly related to this sense of loss of control.

Yet other women have very different perceptions of the significance of migration for women's lives, speaking of improvements in their options on the coast. Concepción expresses the positive dimension of migration in her observations about the differences between marriages on the coast and in the *sierra:*

> There's a great deal of difference in marriage patterns between the coast and the *sierra.* Men who migrate usually adapt to the coastal pattern. On the coast, both spouses express opinions about life in their home. Men begin to leave behind the authoritarian practices of Mayobamba, where women are not allowed to offer opinions. In Lima, the man is still dominant, but less so because of the change in the social atmosphere. Also on the coast, women's work is less demanding and women can improve themselves through education. Women have jobs and they still do the work in the home. Women don't have to go to the fields; they don't have to do all the spinning and make all the clothes. The work in the *sierra* is physically much more difficult and takes much more time to accomplish.

Concepción's own hopes for her family's future on the coast firmly rest on her first son. She sees him as extraordinarily bright, worthy of many sacrifices, and her ultimate salvation. She follows an explicit policy of attempting to secure every opportunity for him, judging that he is her best single investment.

Critical Variables that Shape Women's Lives

Women's lives in the Andes are striking for their diversity. In the foregoing sketches a series of central variables emerge as shaping the diversity of women's life experiences: (a) the differing economic bases of rural settlements, (b) the varying strengths of kinship networks and high rates of geographical mobility, (c) the economic stratification within towns, and (d) the range of marital and domestic relationships available to women. These factors operate in conjunction with each other; they constrain individual women's options in such areas as political and economic participation, alternatives for structuring relationships with men, and choices for organizing family life.

It is very difficult, and probably inaccurate, to point to a specific variable as determining a woman's life. For example, Mariana's narrowed options in Mayobamba cannot be attributed solely to her impoverished financial circumstances. Rather, one would have to understand the full range of factors that reinforce economic stratification in an agricultural community. The patterning of class positions, marital relationships, and the varying strength of kinship networks all contribute to economic differences and narrowed options. In Mariana's case, one would have to analyze the impact of both economic and noneconomic factors on her options in comparison to other women's options in rural communities. Moreover, our list of factors does not exhaust all possibilities. Women's lives are also influenced by the particulars of their biographies, by their personalities, and by larger patterns of historical change on national and international levels. However, local economic, social structural, and cultural variables form the general background against which individual biographies and national historical change play themselves out.

The economic base of the settlements in which these Andean women live varies significantly and plays a critical role in the activities of all inhabitants. The agricultural community of Mayobamba and the commercial town of Chiuchin are involved in the same national economic system and market economy. These settlements differ, however, in their economic bases, dependence on cash economies, and the labor force participation they provide for their inhabitants.

In Mayobamba, the local economy focuses on agricultural production and animal husbandry. Women in Mayobamba work on family land as agriculturalists, raise the family's cows, sheep and other livestock, and take on heavy household duties. Official heads of household (*comuneros*) have access to communal land with which to produce subsistence potato crops. For women like Carmen, Mercedes, and Mariana, access to communal lands must be gained through husbands and fathers. Agriculture in Mayobamba also involves cash crop production on private lands. Women's limited access to cash with which to pay laborers or acquire land seriously restricts their ability to farm independently.

In contrast, in Chiuchin, the local economy is specialized in commerce, and local merchants gain their livelihood as intermediaries between coastal and highland economies. Pilar, Hilaria, and Genoveva are all heavily involved in rural cash economies and in kinds of work that are simply unavailable on a full-time basis for women in agricultural communities. Thus, Chiuchin's productive base creates a new set of economic opportunities for women. At the same time, Chiuchin is not a formal community and does not maintain communal lands. As a result, women are not guaranteed even mediated access to land on which to cultivate subsistence crops. Thus, for instance, poverty has very different meanings for the women of the two towns.

The economic contrasts between the settlements are somewhat softened in practice by people's attempts to maximize their options and participate in different types of production. Mayobamba peasants orient their production of livestock and broad beans to the national economy. They produce surpluses in order to trade with the coastal market and to purchase goods not available in the community. Chiuchin merchants attempt to maintain *comunero* status and kin ties in highland agricultural communities so that they will have access to such staples as potatoes. Furthermore, coastal migrants maintain kinship ties to their home communities. Along these networks, labor and goods are exchanged between urban and rural settlements without entering the cash economy.

A second central variable shaping rural lives are the networks of close relatives used by both men and women to promote local economic endeavors or to gain access to products and labor produced outside their home settlements. In theory, all individuals are born into a set of kinship relations that can be mobilized for mutual assistance. In practice, the kind of marital relationship a woman has with the father of her children influences the scope of kinship networks for herself and for her children. Formal marriages widen the potential family network, as do godparent relationships that are established at major transitions in the life cycle of the individual. Those who serve as a child's sponsor at baptism, first hair cuttings, and marriage maintain special fictive kin relationships with the family. These ties also may be mobilized for labor exchanges in agricultural work.

Networks are mobilized to cut across almost all social and economic divisions. They are facilitated by high rates of geographical mobility in the *sierra*. Inhabitants of *sierra* towns are forced to leave home communities when the local economy cannot support increasing population growth. Individuals who move to mining centers, commercial towns, or to urban centers on the coast establish new outposts for their family's networks. Migrants may settle permanently outside their home communities or they may save money from employment to use as capital for investments on their return to their home communities.

Migration is a particularly complex process and one that demonstrates the differential impact of social change on women and men. Most female migrants are marginally employed in service occupations as domestic servants or in businesses as vendors or as merchants with fixed stalls in the market. While they aspire to statuses of professionals with fixed salaries, most settle for wage labor or the variable income of small-scale vendors. For example, Genoveva and Concepción, who were originally from agricultural communities, migrated to the coast through kin networks which helped them settle and find employment in Lima. These women represent different responses to broadened economic opportunities in cities. Genoveva never adjusted to the impersonality of urban life, the authoritarian character of employers, and the submissiveness demanded of women in urban domestic service. On the other hand, Concepción had aspirations to economic mobility through education but found that marriage and children precluded the attainment of professional credentials. She now combines the jobs of raising her children and working in the market as a vendor. These women's experience as migrants exposed them to new relations to the cash economy, loss of traditional female roles as administrators of agricultural storage and consumption, and more flexible styles of male-female interaction.

A third key factor that shapes the lives of rural inhabitants is the economic stratification of families within particular rural settlements. In Mayobamba, broad differences in the amounts of private land and livestock that families own serve as the basis for local stratification. Landless families cannot invest in substantial herds of cattle and must work for others to gain access to cash with which to acquire products not produced in the town. Laborers are paid by the day so that there are real limits on their incomes. In contrast, families with land can invest in the production of cash crops and livestock as well as in part-time economic enterprises and in the education of their children.

In Chiuchin, local stratification is based on differences in individual access to capital with which to begin a store, boarding house, or restaurant. A merchant's income is derived from successfully meeting local demands at a reasonable price. Merchants are able to expand their incomes by staying open long hours and by using their knowledge of the local populations and their contacts on the coast. Those without capital must work as wage laborers. Men work in construction, whereas women work in lower paying jobs generated by tourism, such as cooking and washing sheets for local hotels. Laborers would be hard pressed to expand their incomes, which are already based on a full day's work.

For women, variations in their family's economic standing translate into significant differences in the ability to support education for daughters who are often given second priority to sons. Schooling past the fifth year is only offered in Chiuchin; advanced training is only available on the coast. Poor families cannot support children in schools away from home for long periods of time. In Mayobamba, the different educational levels of Concepción and Mariana relate in part to the different economic standings of their families. Being illiterate and only partially fluent in Spanish, the language of commerce and coastal life, has had a broad impact on Mariana's life.

A fourth central factor influencing rural women's lives is the range of marital relationships, varying from formal legal marriages to consensual unions and single motherhood. The kind of marital union a woman is involved in influences her economic position, the composition of her household, the shape of kin networks she can mobilize for assistance, and her children's inheritance.

In Mayobamba, Mercedes is a good example of a woman who acted assertively on her understanding of the link between economic stratification and different kinds of marital relationships. By her insistence on a formal marriage, she and her children will benefit from the upward mobility and growing investments of her business activities with Cesar. If she had remained in a consensual union (in a *conviviente* relationship) with Cesar, she might have been left with little or nothing in the event of a separation; in addition, her children would not have inherited from their father's estate.

In Chiuchin, however, access to capital for subsistence is not channeled so exclusively through men as it is in Mayobamba. In the commercial settlement women expand their business opportunities either by formal marriage or by creating domestic networks. These domestic organizations often incorporate relatives traced through mothers, daughters, and sisters, who pool resources and labor. As a result, single mothers and female *convivientes* are not blocked from economic mobility in Chiuchin if they can mobilize kinship networks for business or if they have inherited capital. In the commercial settlement, Pilar and Hilaria represent alternative routes for financial success, while Genoveva, who does not have a husband, an active network, or an inherited source of capital, is the least secure economically.

Before we further explore economics and politics, kin and domestic relationships, and social change in these towns, let us consider in more theoretical terms the alternative ways of conceptualizing the relations between men and women, defining dominance and subordination, and explaining the origin and perpetuation of differences in power between the sexes.

Notes

1. We are not arguing here that sexual hierarchy is maintained because it is "functional" (cf. Langness 1979; Pollock 1972).

2. We have self-consciously disguised the identities of individual women to protect their privacy. Nevertheless, we have decided to maintain the coherence and richness of actual lives rather than synthesizing "typical" individuals or "ideal types." The information for these sketches comes largely from women's autobiographical conversations with us, supplemented with our observations of their daily lives and interactions with others in their home communities.

II

Analyzing Women's Subordination: Issues, Distortions, and Definitions

Contemporary feminist movements, like their predecessors, struggle to understand the relationship between the subordination of women and the economic conditions of their lives. We share that goal in this study of women in the Andes. Moreover, we believe that the study of other societies as well as our own is an especially productive way to approach the issue of sexual subordination. Certainly by coming to an understanding of women's and men's lives in a range of cultures we are reminded that our own value systems, expectations regarding masculine and feminine behavior, and sexual divisions of labor are not universal, unchangeable, or especially long-lived historically. Multicultural studies allow us to pose and investigate such central questions as: Are women universally subordinate and devalued? Under what circumstances do societies promote sexual egalitarianism? Do sexual divisions of work inevitably result in differences in power and authority between the sexes? What implications do childbearing and nursing have for women's position within and outside the family?

Sources of Bias in the Study of the Sexes

As a result of renewed interest in women, researchers have begun to reexamine social scientific theories and analytical frameworks for distortions in existing portrayals of women's activities. Initially in this reexamination, many scholars were startled to discover the extent to which studies of history, politics, economics, religion, and social change have failed to incorporate women as sources of information and failed to portray women as actors in public affairs. The corrective response proposed by some was to fill in the existing gaps in our

knowledge by simply finding the missing data on women. Other researchers have found the character of bias to be more far-reaching.
They have concluded that questions, interpretive frameworks, and
research findings have been distorted by researchers' stereotyped assumptions concerning women's motivations, creativity, capacity to organize groups, concern with politics, and economic contributions.

Social scientists in such disciplines as political science, psychology,
and anthropology have undertaken critiques of accepted frameworks
and interpretations. As the critical literature from these disciplines
demonstrates, none of these fields has been free from distortions. In
fact, the problems of distortion and strategies for rectifying bias have
proven to be strikingly similar from discipline to discipline.[1] For
example, Bourque and Grossholtz (1974, p. 225) criticize political
science in the following terms: "In the choice of data to be analyzed
and in the interpretation of those data, the discipline insists upon a
narrow and exclusive definition of politics which limits political activity to a set of roles which are, in this society and many others,
stereotyped as male." The use of limited or biased frameworks restricts the degree of consideration given to women's involvements.
Moreover, researchers who are guided by such frameworks may force
their data into preordained categories which obscure the complexity
of actual patterns of participation and mask sources of inequality.

In a critique of psychology, Sherif points out the tenacity of sexist
bias in her discipline as well. In her analysis, she raises a fundamental
question about the structure of the field and argues that the ways in
which issues are raised and research questions defined accounts for
the discipline's continuing difficulties in treating women's experience. Sherif argues that: "Certain of its dominant beliefs about the
proper ways to pursue knowledge have made psychological research
peculiarly prone to bias in its conception, execution, and interpretation" (1979). In identifying the most hopeful routes for eliminating or
ameliorating such bias, Sherif notes the following potentially helpful
avenues:

1. The first is toward broadening psychologists' perspectives on the
pervasive influences of cultural institutions, of ways of living and working, and of social values upon the individual in any research situation. . . . Comparative research within the same country, cross-cultural
research, and an eye to history are the first essentials in enlarging this
vision of human beings, male and female. . . .

2. Second, there is great need for psychology to extend its cross-disciplinary borrowing beyond the biological disciplines. . . . It needs to learn from the social disciplines and humanities . . . about significant and enduring problems in human relationships. [1979]

Sherif argues that broadening the frameworks through which sex differences are viewed will help eliminate bias from psychological studies of the sexes. Her suggestions are appropriate for all of the social sciences.

Similarly, we would argue that one corrective for the limitations of existing social research may be found in cross-cultural and interdisciplinary studies which are self-conscious about the impact of social values on research. The present work embodies such an approach and is an effort to combine the insights and concerns of political science and anthropology.

Anthropologists who concentrate on the cross-cultural study of behavior have also joined the ranks of those who see important benefits to be gained in critiquing their disciplines. We pursue this disciplinary critique in detail because anthropological findings are often used to generalize about human origins, to question assumptions about human nature, and to reconstruct early human evolution. These issues are particularly important for the study of the sexes because they influence our ideas about the origin of sexual divisions of labor and family roles. In addition, we will examine anthropological methodologies as they bear on the study of contemporary societies.

Anthropological debates about early sexual divisions of labor and women's subordination draw on data from various fields: studies of nonhuman primates; archaeological investigations of the physical remains of our early ancestors and their settlements; ethnohistorical studies of other societies by travelers, missionaries, and colonial officials at early points of Western contact; and contemporary investigations of hunting and gathering, horticultural, pastoral, and peasant societies. Data from these sources are used in reconstructing the early stages of human evolution, often by projecting present patterns back into the distant past. In some cases, as with primate and archaeological studies, the goal is to reconstruct very early human evolution hundreds of thousands and even millions of years ago. In other cases, as with ethnohistorical studies, the goal is to reenvision cultural patterns before contact with the West introduced great changes through conquest, colonization, and the decimation of indigenous populations through disease.

Each kind of evidence for the origins of sexual divisions of labor, however, presents social scientists with profound ambiguities in interpretation. The uncritical use of data from each source has contributed to distortions in the reconstruction of women's activities in early societies. In the case of primate studies used to project back to early protohuman social organization, the range of patterns of behavior and social organization is wide. By selectively choosing among studies of such primates as chimpanzees, baboons, orangutans, and mountain gorillas, one can come up with evidence for amazingly different theories for the early evolution of sexual divisions of labor and family formations. Which primate should be used as a model for early human development is still a problematic issue. From recent critiques of evolutionary reconstructions we are also learning that our image of early human society as primarily dependent on men's hunting for subsistence and technological development is erroneous. In fact, foraging was probably very significant in early cultural development.[2]

Ethnohistorical accounts written by explorers and colonists are another source of data for the reconstruction of early patterns of sexual divisions of labor. These accounts are especially interesting because early explorers and missionaries sometimes showed anthropological curiosity about the beliefs and behaviors of other societies. While the resulting diaries and histories give us some indication of cultural diversity before long-term colonization transformed indigenous societies, these accounts must be read with great care. Early writers often imposed their own judgments and interpretations on the societies they encountered. In some cases, chroniclers created hierarchical images of another society's social organization and religion when, in fact, duality existed between female and male principles. In other cases they found sexual parity and female independence an anarchical oddity to be condemned. Leacock and Nash (1977) conclude that ethnohistorical accounts can be decoded for bias and that they are important sources of documentation for cultural patterns that developed independently of Western society.

Finally, the use of data from present-day societies to project toward the past is difficult because in many cases societies have been in direct or indirect contact with neighboring groups, settlers, traders, and colonial officials for hundreds of years. Generally, cultural contact has had substantial impact on these societies, displacing populations to less productive zones, establishing new patterns of leadership, promoting isolated nuclear families, and introducing market economies where other forms of exchange were common.[3] The interpretation of present-day sex roles and antagonisms, for example, is clouded by the fact that the behaviors in question may be indigenous or they may be the indirect consequences of larger patterns of change caused by reduced group mobility and rising intergroup hostilities.

The study of the origins of sexual hierarchy will be a challenge for anthropology because the data are very ambiguous and inconclusive at this point. Which primates most closely represent our antecedents, how one interprets accounts of early European chroniclers, and which aspects of present foraging and agricultural societies represent past forms of social organization are important methodological questions for the field.

In this study, the issue of origins is secondary to our central concern with the social, cultural, economic, and historical factors which perpetuate and transform sexual hierarchies in the modern period. However, as Nash (1976) and many others have pointed out, the concern with the contemporary issue of women's position does not free us from the obligation of locating sources of distortion and reappraising biased or incomplete interpretations.[4] Since the present study is based on prolonged fieldwork in another society, we believe it is especially important to discuss the ways in which data collection in contemporary social science often contributes to distorted information on women.

The participant observer fieldwork technique, for which anthropology is famed, is often an unwitting source of bias, especially for studies of societies where men predominate in social organizations outside the household. Generally in order to gather cultural data for analysis, anthropologists spend a year or two in a community living through the annual round of activities and important events and interviewing members of the settlement. Researchers often find that key informants, who are active members of the community, provide useful interpretations of ongoing events. These informants often select the anthopologist, rather than the other way around. They are likely to have had contact with more urbanized settlements and national organizations in the broader society; they are more often formally educated, literate, and used to dealing with strangers. They have the gift of not only narrating events, but also of talking on the metalevel about the nature of cultural events, groups, and values. Key informants provide critical, often extremely insightful material on their community and its relationship to the larger political and economic system. They may also provide anthropologists with moral support and friendship in the sometimes isolating and difficult experience of doing fieldwork.[5] Significantly for the character of the data that field-workers bring home, men and women are not equivalently likely to be selected as key informants (or to select to work with the anthropologists for that matter). To the extent that the field project is conducted in a society where rates of education and contact with national society are higher for men, chief informants will tend to be males unless females are especially sought out. Women may not be given the methodological chance to speak out for themselves on a deeper level of rapport.

Anthropological researchers analyze the data they collect from community interviews, observations, and detailed discussion with key informants. In the process of moving from many discrete conversations, discussions, interviews and events toward a coherent, analytical understanding of social life, the researcher may unconsciously introduce a second form of distortion: an overly institutionalized view of social reality. A closer examination of this tendency will show that it has important implications for anthropological portrayals of the sexes. Whatever the subject of their investigation, anthropologists are likely to focus on "a community" (be it a town, plantation, neighborhood, or a particular organization) which becomes the unit of study and the level at which the field-workers generalize their findings. Researchers work toward the clearest, least ambiguous notion of the community's basic structures and its relation to the broader society. They often concentrate interviewing and analysis on the formal institutions of the community: perhaps an economic cooperative, a local church, land-owning groups, or community political organizations. Such groups are viewed as the mainsprings of society because they are thought to integrate individuals into a broader set of relationships and to serve as models for community social organization and value systems. Roles in these formal, public organizations are given greater importance than they might deserve. The end result of these tendencies in research is often a highly institutionalized and, perhaps, an overly masculinized view of society, especially when men dominate

leadership roles in community groups. Anthropologists may by implication negatively define women as nonparticipants, although in fact
they are active members of alternative organizations. Women's roles
and work in so-called informal groups may be misinterpreted and
trivialized because formal institutions are taken as the measure of
employment and leadership. The formal-informal and public-private
distinctions are artifacts of the field investigator's classifications rather
than accurate reflections of social reality in many cases.

As Reiter concludes, the problem is one of a "double-bias," that is,
our biased assumptions and expectations combined with the male-
centric biases of many informants in the societies we study (1975a).[6]
Biases need not be conscious. They may be perpetuated quite effectively in studies not dealing explicitly with sex roles. Furthermore,
biases do not honor the boundaries of different theoretical perspectives (or political viewpoints, for that matter), as Nash has shown in a
critique of studies of social change (1976). As she points out, the social
sciences have accepted stereotyped notions of women's participation
in social change, have failed to analyze the differential impact of
industrialization on men and women, and have attributed women's
responses to change (especially when they are conservative) to
feminine nature rather than questioning the factors which shape their
attitudes and values.[7] Enlarging our knowledge of women and moving away from earlier distortions does not free us from controversy,
but it does allow us to take part in debates that will have a long-term,
demystifying effect on the comparative social sciences.

Defining the Terms for Cross-Cultural Comparisons

The term *sexual subordination* has been a difficult one for scholars in
comparative fields to define although there have been many interesting attempts to characterize it. The concept has generated a vocabulary of synonyms and antonyms which are worth examining in some
detail. In social scientific literature, sexual subordination is often
reduced to an examination of women's positions or statuses as subordinates. A subordinate status is one that is deemed to be inferior,
devalued, second-class, dependent, dominated, exploited. In this vocabulary, sexual subordination contrasts with relations of sexual parity in
which women's status is independent, autonomous, and given equivalent value to men's status. One would be mistaken, however, if one

contrasted these two sets of terms and defined subordination as simply a ranking of individual statuses or social positions.

Subordination is not simply a status or a social state, rather it is the product of social processes and structural relations between men and women. Thus, we emphasize that sexual subordination involves broad structural limitations that stress the identity of femaleness over more variable individual qualities and other social identities (such as age, occupation, class, ethnicity, and family).[8] While subordination need not be collectively perceived or understood by its victims, it is categorically imposed by larger social processes.

Subordination involves those social processes which shape the structural relationship of dominant to subordinate. Subordination may also be understood as a relative and thus changing condition. As a result, it is possible for analysts to talk about a society in which women are becoming more (or alternatively less) subordinate. It is also possible to speak comparatively of the women in one society (or community) being more or less subordinate than women in another society by comparing the broader systems of sexual hierarchy and/or parity.

Sexual subordination may be contrasted with *sexual parity;* that is, an egalitarian relation between the sexes. Unfortunately (for motives that are transparent), a mythic image of women ruling and dominating men is often projected as the singular alternative to male dominated societies. The assumption is that, where males do not rule, society is inevitably organized in a matriarchal inversion of conventional patriarchal power relations between the sexes. Clearly this unnecessarily hierarchical interpretation is a misreading of what parity between the sexes logically entails. We suggest that parity involves relations of equivalence, though not necessarily sameness or identity (in the mathematical sense), between the sexes.[9]

There are at least two alternative models of parity, neither of which requires replacing one form of sexual hierarchy with another. On the one hand, sexual parity would be fostered in an egalitarian society with a minimal sexual division of labor. The person (rather than a male or female) would be treated as the basic social unit in the widest range of social contexts. Sex roles, to the extent that they were marked at all, would be highly flexible and individually variable. In such a society, competence, not sex, would determine how decisions are made, resources allocated, and activities undertaken.[10]

An alternative model of parity would give men and women equivalent, counterbalancing, and potentially conflicting roles in institutionalized decision making, the allocation of resources, and the articulation of social values. The sexes might be economically specialized yet highly interdependent. For example, men might be hunters and women agriculturalists with both sexes enjoying the political powers to regulate access to resources and define social issues. Men and women would have distinct institutional and material bases for their powers.[11] Sex roles would be marked, but not unequivocally ranked, in such a society.

Actually the second model is by far the more controversial since some comparativists see counterbalancing powers where other researchers see separate and unequal sources of control which mask sexual hierarchy for the participants. Whether or not a given society fulfills the criteria for the second model generates heated debate among cross-cultural analysts. One group of observers contends that a society is ordered (that is, it originated and reproduces mutual relations) according to the principle of counterbalancing powers. They cite such evidence as marriage patterns, land transfer practices, inheritance, rituals, symbolism, and decision making to demonstrate the ordering principle of counterbalancing powers. In contrast, a second group of observers analyzing the same society (hopefully at the same historical point) will argue that female subordination and sexual hierarchy exist nonetheless, masked perhaps, but still the operative principle controlling the creation and distribution of values and critical resources. What is at issue here is not just different data and different methodologies, but more crucially different conceptualizations of subordination and hierarchy.[12]

Gough, for example, says we should look at control—at who controls women's sexuality, labor, and their range of involvements in society. She argues that men's control over women's resources (including women's very definition of themselves) varies broadly by levels of technoeconomy so that hunting and gathering societies are more egalitarian than state-organized societies:

> In general in hunting societies, however, women are less subordinated in certain crucial respects than they are in most, if not all, of the archaic states, or even in some capitalist nations. These respects include men's ability to deny women sexuality or to force it upon them; to command or exploit their labor to control their produce; to control or rob them of

their children; to confine them physically and prevent their movement; to use them as objects in male transactions; to cramp their creativeness; or to withhold from them large areas of society's knowledge and cultural attainments. [1975, pp. 69–70]

Gough talks about a relative *lack* of sexual subordination when there are high levels of interdependence and reciprocity between men and women. For example, she speaks of those hunting and gathering societies in which "there is rank difference, role difference, and some difference respecting degrees of authority between the sexes, but there is reciprocity rather than domination or exploitation" (1975, p. 70).

Draper discusses other aspects of foraging societies that promote sexual egalitarianism including:

... women's subsistence contribution and the control women retain over the food they have gathered; ... a similar degree of mobility for both sexes; the lack of rigidity in sex-typing of many adult activities, including domestic chores and aspects of child socialization; the cultural sanction against physical expression of aggression; the small group size; and the nature of the settlement pattern. [1975, p. 78]

These anthropologists would agree that parity is fostered in the case of foraging societies, such as the !Kung of the Kalahari or the Mbuti of the Congo, when the sexual division of labor is minimized and flexible, and when both sexes are active in reciprocal exchanges of the products of their work. The communal nature of hunting and gathering societies (which do not have differentiated leadership roles, marked contrasts in social status, or differences in the accumulation of material wealth and property) reinforces sexual parity. As we will detail later, evidence indicating greater male and female parity in prestate and preclass societies has led some anthropologists to focus on the emergence of the state as a crucial transition in the formation of sexual hierarchies.

Many anthropologists, like Gough and Draper, emphasize the control of the *material* aspects of social life—that is, cultural adaptations to the environment, economic systems, technologies, and sexual divisions of work—as key to hierarchical or egalitarian relations between the sexes. Ortner emphasizes *ideology*, the specific value and symbol systems which rationalize and justify any asymmetrical pattern of material control. From this perspective women's inferior status in society is evidenced by:

> (1) elements of cultural ideology and informants' statements that explicitly devalue women, according them, their roles, their tasks, their products, and their social milieu less prestige than accorded men and the male correlates; (2) symbolic devices, such as the attribution of defilement, which may be interpreted as *implicitly* making a statement of inferior valuation; and (3) social-structural arrangements that exclude women from participation in or contact with some realm in which the highest powers of the society are felt to reside. [Ortner 1974, p. 69]

Note that Ortner does not rely solely on ideological factors though her perspective underscores their importance. Like the more materialist analyses, Ortner also mentions patterns of differential access as a contributor to women's status. Our view is that women's subordination has both material and ideological dimensions.

Conceptualizing Power and Influence

That women are sexually subordinate in a given society should not be interpreted as implying that women by definition have yielded control over all aspects of their lives to male-centric institutions. In fact, women extend control, influence, and authority to negotiable and disputed areas of daily life in all societies. By analyzing women's strategies to act on society, one can pose and answer such central questions as: What factors contribute to or restrict women's extension of control and authority? What lessons do women learn from conflicts over decision making in negotiable situations? Do women gain insight into their subordinate condition through indirect manipulations of institutions from which they are excluded on the basis of sex?

Women's influence in public affairs is significant even in societies in which they are denied formal roles as participants in key organizations. For example, in sexually hierarchical societies women act as mediators between kin groups in marriage alliances; they influence men's political careers through praise or criticism; and they occupy positions as sorcerers, saints, and midwives. Along these lines, Nelson has analyzed the politics of women's mediating roles and has concluded that women exercise power in the patrilineal, patrilocal, and patriarchical societies of the Middle East because of:

... the crucial role women play as structural links between kinship groups in societies where family and kinship are the fundamental institutions of everyday life. . . . The implications for power are obvious in that by these networks of relationships, the woman is in a position to channel or withhold information to the male members of the kindred. And in this position the woman influences decision making about alliances, actually sets up marriage relations, and informs male members of the household what is going on in other homes. But of course the "home" in question is not that of a tiny nuclear family, but of a wider family group. And this family group is one upon which many of the affairs of the society—social, economic, political—turn. [Nelson 1974, p. 559]

There is no doubt that women in these pastoral and sedentary societies are influential and that they have successfully elaborated strategies that focus on kinship for gaining influence.[13] Yet we would argue with Nelson's conclusions that women *exercise power* through these interstitial roles in patriarchical societies. The problem is definitional and has important consequences for the analysis of women's position cross-culturally. Nelson holds that power is "the reciprocity of influence" and so she is able to observe that "women's segregation is also male exclusion" in the Middle East. The model is one of men and women who autonomously operate out of specialized niches to manipulate each other in small ways to perpetuate a mutually satisfying status quo. Such phenomenological interpretations reduce sexual subordination to the politics of interpersonal relationships, and as a result they fail to make an important analytical distinction between power and influence.

The academic controversy over the meaningful distinction between power and influence has critical ramifications for our understanding of the subordination and control with which Andean women and their counterparts in other societies actually live. It is deceptive to limit the definition of power *either* to visible decisions and who has the resources to affect them *or* to the effect of predecisions concerning what is on or off a community's agenda.[14] The ability to determine which issues become relevant for political discussion and decision making may be more important than any specific decision that gets made. Of course, this perspective gives an elusive quality to power which may become difficult to measure and to identify when it is actually being exercised.

Our own study of power relations between the sexes in Andean communities grows out of an increasingly acute sense that to understand explicit and implicit power in any community we must go behind the public decision-making procedures and examine the values and routinized relations that precede and undergird those visible power relations. It is there—both before the meeting and after the meeting—that the subordination of women and their efforts to overcome that asymmetry are most often created and reproduced. At the same time, we believe that the more traditional attention to decisions and the formal distribution of economic and political power also reveal important dimensions of the relationships between men and women in Andean society.

Undoubtedly power is relative, has various sources and expressions, and operates on political and psychological levels. One can speak of the power to define and enforce definitions of the rules of the game in a society or community. One can also speak of power as control over the access to crucial material and nonmaterial resources, however they may be defined. Those who are powerful may not necessarily be definers of central values or regulators of access but they must stand to benefit in some structurally favored way from the existing social order and its perpetuation.

Influence, also a relative term, represents the development of strategies by a group (or by individuals) to limit the exercise of power on itself and on others. Cross-culturally, men's power is institutionally based; that is, it is embedded in and derived from important political, economic, and religious organizations. To the extent that women are structurally excluded from key institutions, they must depend, more exclusively than men, on strategies of influence. Influence may involve very direct, public actions that are unambiguous attempts to deny another's definitions of reality. Or strategies may work toward an anonymous authorship of a change in plans through behind-the-scenes jockeying.[15] Women's influence involves culturally formalized strategies which are generally recognized as legitimate by both sexes.

From this discussion of terms, then, it should be clear that power is not only publicly or formally exercised and that influence is not always privately and informally achieved.[16] The chief contrast between power and influence, which we stress in this context, is that they emanate from structurally different positions in the institutionally perpetuated social order. Where women are subordinate, they stand in a structurally disadvantaged position both to the political processes that define the issues subject to decision making and to the institutions that allocate resources in the community. Women's control, which ranges from substantial to minimal, is exercised through strategies of influence that attempt to limit or redirect the powers of those who are structurally superordinate.

To explain in broader, cross-cultural terms how women's and men's relative positions are shaped and perpetuated, we must now build on our discussion of subordination, parity, power, and influence. In the next chapter we examine four models of society that have been constructed to reveal the interconnections of factors producing and reproducing women's structural position.

Notes

1. The critical literature on sexism in social scientific problem formulation, data collection, analysis, and interpretation has received much attention in the 1970s. Those interested in pursuing disciplinary critiques should consult Bourque and Grossholtz (1974), Reiter (1975a), Boals (1975), Jaquette (1976), Millman and Kanter (1976), Lamphere (1977), Carroll (1979), and Sherman and Beck (1979). The journal *Signs* regularly publishes updated disciplinary criticism.

2. For more on foraging and early human evolution, see Slocum (1975), Liebowitz (1975), Gough (1975), Tanner and Zihlman (1976), and Zihlman (1978).

3. See Bodley (1976), Murphy and Murphy (1974), and Draper (1975) for further examples of the impact of cultural contact on sex roles.

4. The growing cross-cultural literature which challenges stereotyped assumptions about women's attitudes toward social change includes Jopling (1975), Murphy and Murphy (1974), Rubbo (1975), Chaney (1974), and Elmendorf (1976).

5. Levy's (1973) interviews of anthropologists document the social and psychological dynamics of fieldwork for the researcher.

6. See also Slocum (1975) and Faithorn (1976) for analyses of bias in anthropological research.

7. While we have cast this problem in terms of the dimensions of anthropological fieldwork, it has parallels in many other disciplines. Bourque and Grossholtz (1974) identify the bias in elite studies undertaken in the United States which systematically ignore women. Jaquette makes a similar point in her critique of the disciplines in the introduction to *Women in Politics* (1974). A very sophisticated consideration of the theoretical dimensions of the problem is found in Elshtain's work on the public and private domains, which traces the use of these modes of analysis in the history of Western political

thought (1974, 1979). See also McCormack's essay in Millman and Kanter (1976), and the review essay by Carroll (1979). Cloward and Piven (1979) describe a similar phenomenon in their analysis of female deviance.

8. This approach contrasts sharply with recent phenomenological trends which focus on the individual as a unique cluster of interacting social identities such as sex, age, kin group, regionality, and class (see, for example LaFontaine's introduction, 1978).

9. Dumont (1970) discusses the Western confusion of "equal" and "equivalent" in a way that has shed light on our understandings of parity.

10. Actually some foraging societies composed of small, highly mobile bands approach the egalitarianism of this model. The Mbuti Pygmies of northern Zaire are one example of this form of parity (Turnbull 1961).

11. The Iroquois and the Huron, before Western expansion, were examples of this second form of sexual parity (J. Brown 1975; Wallace 1970; Sacks 1976; Leacock 1977).

12. For good examples of some of the conceptual issues, see Chiñas (1973), Harris (1978), and Schlegel (1977), as well as our discussion of the "separate spheres" model in chapter 3.

13. Two dimensions of this influence merit special attention. First, as Sharma (1979) points out for India, in sex segregated societies the cultural patterning of authority within women's society may reinforce structural subordination and undercut collective mobilization as women. Second, as Goldschmidt and Kunkel (1971) have found for peasant societies, kinship and household structures may be influenced by the character of *external* forces emanating from the state such as governmental policy, contractual access to land, and economic opportunities outside the rural sector.

14. Bachrach and Baratz distinguish between power and influences as follows:

> Thus, power and influence are alike in that each has both rational and relational attributes. But they are different in that the exercise of power depends upon potential sanctions, while the exercise of influence does not. [1970, p. 30]

Our distinction between the two concepts points out and emphasizes the structural and institutionalized source of the ability to sanction. For the initial debates over conceptualizing power see Dahl (1961) and Bachrach and Baratz (1962).

15. Netting (1969), J. Collier (1974), and Lamphere (1974) discuss direct strategies, while C. Nelson (1974) and Harding (1975) stress the importance of private modes of influencing public affairs. Gomm (1979) and Constantinides (1979) have insightfully analyzed a third category of strategies involving the ritual expression and redefinition of women's influence so that the system of sexual hierarchy remains intact.

16. One can imagine cases in which strategies of influence would have a broad and persuasive impact on both men's and women's behavior. For instance, Netting (1969) notes that among the Kofyar of the Jos Plateau in Northern Nigeria, women may publicly ignore or challenge husbands' at-

tempts to regulate their behavior. Structurally Kofyar men are favored by a patrilineal social organization which regulates land resources and arranges marriage alliances. In addition, residence rules direct women to live with the husband's family after marriage. Yet married women control who visits the homesite, take public lovers, freely leave their husbands, and decide whether to invest their labors cultivating women's crops, engaging in trade, or working on their husband's fields. Netting says that men, who are noted for being independent and stubborn on their own account, have limited recourse when a woman decides to go her own way. Women's individualized influence is especially strong among the Kofyar because women have access to their own agricultural harvests, produce crafts for sale, and engage in trade. Also women's strategies for influence play on the general scarcity of marriageable women in this polygamous society. The Kofyar are an example of a society in which women are highly valued and have efficacious strategies for limiting the implications of men's structural superiority. Sangree (1979), however, describes the structural and psychological tensions of this marriage system for the women in another Jos Plateau group, the Irigwe.

III

Analyzing Women's Subordination: Alternative Frameworks

Patriarchy, as we are using the term in this book, refers to the social organization of the family, the community, and the state in such a way that male power is reinforced and perpetuated. There are a number of explanations for this social form. In this chapter we explore some of the principle analyses of patriarchy, the mechanisms, structures and processes which guarantee its reproduction and lead to women's subordination. The focus of our examination is not on the origins or first causes of sexual hierarchy or patriarchy. Rather, we are concerned with explanations of (a) the contemporary perpetuation of sexual divisions of labor and female subordination and (b) the factors contributing to changes in female subordination through expanding, contracting, or redefining sexual hierarchies.

In this analysis we are concerned with the impact of three broad sets of variables on women's position in Andean society:

1. The technological and economic organization of rural agricultural production and trade in the context of local material conditions and the national economy.
2. The social organization of rural institutions including the family, local community, and agrarian class structures.
3. The social ideologies, world views, and belief systems that guide rural populations' perceptions, values, and activities on local and national levels.

Our concern is with the impact of public, organizational, collective aspects of social reality on the definitions and flexibility of sex roles, sexual divisions of labor, and men's and women's relative positions in society.

From the outset, however, we should make clear that by emphasizing the social and institutional aspects of daily life we are by definition excluding certain forms of explanation. For instance, we will not evoke biosocial explanations—such as instincts, psychological drives, or demographic imperatives—for sexual divisions of labor and women's roles.[1] Nor do we find ourselves entirely comfortable with social psychological explanations of sexual differences and hierarchies.[2] Obviously there are biological and psychological constraints on social realities, and some social scientists are attempting provocative arguments for connections between the psychological and institutional aspects of everyday life as they contribute to the reproduction of sex roles.[3] In order to pursue such links, however, one must have independent analyses of the institutional context of sex roles.

Our analysis uses a different methodology and vocabulary than the biological and psychological interpretations. Such differences are symptomatic of larger analytic and theoretical differences and contrasting phrasings of core questions.[4] It is our experience that agrarian societies invest great energy in directing the experiences and behaviors of individuals so that men and women live *different* lives. We ask: How do social systems perpetuate contrasting lives for men and women? What are the broader consequences of sexual differentiation? We answer such questions by examining the institutional organizations, patterns of interaction, and the meanings of social encounters for the populations of rural communities.

In the last fifteen years, social scientists, especially anthropologists and political scientists, have done a great deal of productive theorizing about women's subordination. In reviewing the cross-cultural literature, we have found that major explanations can be grouped into four perspectives: the separate spheres; sexual division of labor; class analysis; and social ideology. Each of these approaches emphasizes particular dimensions of male-female relationships and isolates certain principal factors as prime shapers of life experiences, patterns of labor force participation, and authority in the family and community.

Some researchers assert that these perspectives are mutually exclusive and competing explanations. In contrast, we emphasize the ways that different approaches can be understood as conceptually building on each other to form more comprehensive explanations of sexual hierarchy. Our method questions the flaws of explanations that are incomplete in themselves, yet notes the contributions such frameworks make to more encompassing explanations. In the process of being recombined into new frameworks, the insights of earlier perspectives take on new significance. We attempt to balance a critical review of theory with a concern for the concrete applications of these perspectives to the analysis of women's and men's lives. When possible we have chosen analytical applications of these approaches to issues dealing with Latin American women. This venture benefits from the rich social scientific literature on Latin American women as studied by Latin American and North American scholars.[5] Finally, throughout our review we have looked at the ways these perspectives have been used to study women in the United States.

The goal of this theoretical review is to question the major contemporary explanations of sexual hierarchy before we turn to an in-depth analysis of the social realities of Peruvian women. We will begin with the separate spheres perspective because it denies that women are, in fact, subordinate and parallels many of our society's folk theories of women's position in the United States.

The Separate Spheres Approach: Woman as Queen of Her Castle

The separate spheres perspective argues that even in so-called hierarchical societies women enjoy parity with men through their control of a separate, domestic sphere of activity. This view emphasizes the complementary character of women's work in maintaining the household and children with men's work in the public world of business and politics. The equivalence of men and women, according to this view, arises from marriage and the creation of a household through which the sexes structure specialized, complementary, and interdependent roles. In the domestic sphere, women gain power and respect as wives and mothers precisely because they are different from men and do not share male values, sources of authority, and personality characteristics.

This approach emphasizes the broad range of activities that women organize and administer in the home. Women are specialists in decision making with regard to the care and early training of children as well as the maintenance of the home. Women's claim to a separate sphere is legitimated by attributing to them specialized, specifically female powers and qualities: spiritual strength, moral superiority, nurturance, and emotional sensitivity. These qualities legitimize women's primary authority as mothers within the home and their central focus and power within the family. It follows, then, that there is no reason why women would want to give up their sphere to compete with men in the public world.

This perspective generally denies that subordination is an adequate description of women's position by suggesting that women's control over the private sphere compensates for limitations placed on their participation elsewhere. Implicit in some versions of this approach is the belief that women would be reluctant to extend their participation into men's sphere for fear that it might trigger male encroachment into women's affairs, or that it might undermine women's claims to moral superiority and thus their ability to use moral suasion.

Both North American and Latin American scholars have used the notion of separate spheres to argue that men and women have equivalent power. One version of this argument concludes that equivalence finds expression in the political symbolism of women's ability to counterbalance male virility (*machismo*) in public with female moral superiority (*marianismo*) in the home. For instance, Jaquette in her analysis of the sociological significance of female archetypes in Peruvian literature argues that women "have a stake" in Latin American concepts of masculine sexual aggressiveness (*machismo*).

> The Latin American woman correctly perceives role differentiation as the key to her power and influence. Even the notions of the "separateness" and "mystery" of women, which are viewed in the North American context as male propaganda chiefly used to discriminate against women, are seen in the Latin American context as images to be enhanced, not destroyed. [1973a, p. 20]

According to this interpretation, women gain power as wives and mothers through moral superiority over husbands and sons who are committed to a sexual double standard. Women come to signify the strength and stability of the family and society. Jaquette believes that the monogamy and sexual self-denial practiced by wives give them "leverage" and "traditional influence" over their husbands. Mistresses are also said to exert control over those errant husbands who are dependent on them sexually (1973a, pp. 23, 26). Thus, according to this analysis, wife, mistress, and husband are interdependent for their cultural identities and powers within distinct spheres.

Stevens (1973) further characterizes the woman as wife in Latin America in a description of the feminine cult of *marianismo*. Wives should exhibit self-sacrifice, humility, sadness, and patience. Ideally, such women receive compensation for self-denial and other-directedness in that they are said not to have to worry about being abandoned as a result of their husbands' infidelities, nor do they suffer from conflicts resulting from forced choices between mother-wife and career roles (Stevens 1973, pp. 98–99). Both authors conclude that Latin American women are unlikely to push for change in the images of the sexes or for wider participation in public life precisely because they enjoy power in a separate sphere.

These analyses are particularly vulnerable to criticism because they are based on images rather than actual examinations of the politics of family life. Neither author gives us a well-defined sense of the powers women exert or the sphere that women control. Since no evidence is given that women have a material base for the "power" they exercise in the family, one is left wondering if standing as a symbol of the moral order actually gives women much concrete power or influence. Also, the separate sphere analysis fails to deal with class issues implicit in the wife-mistress contrast.[6] Jaquette's and Stevens's analyses are largely directed toward urban society and segments of the middle and upper-middle classes in which wives do not work outside the home. Another version of the separate spheres perspective has been developed for rural peasant populations, once again arguing that women already enjoy parity with men in Latin American society.

Núñez del Prado Béjar (1975a, 1975b) makes a more complex case for the separate spheres approach by discussing distinct material bases for men's and women's authority in a Peruvian community of Indian agriculturalists. Her analysis links different material sources of authority to values which reinforce separate spheres and distinct social reference groups for men and women. For southern Peru, she argues that male-female relationships follow wider cultural patterns of Quechua society in which political and economic powers are carefully distinguished and separated. In this society, men are given authority over their wives and children as political representatives of the family in local government and politics. Women, however, have a distinct source of economic control that comes from their roles as the administrators of the family harvest. Wives measure out appropriate amounts of grains for family consumption, regulating supplies so that the family will have sufficient stores to last until the next harvest. Women also trade surpluses in local markets, barter for products their family does not produce, and control the family's religious expenditures. Men say that husbands are poor administrators of the domestic economy. They also are kept from intervening in household storage by cultural prohibitions and religious sanctions. As Núñez del Prado Béjar sees it, men and women engage in different kinds of work, involving cooperation with members of the same sex and contrasting criteria for successful performance. The sexes become interdependent and an equilibrium of power is established primarily through marriage and family relationships. Núñez del Prado Béjar shows how different spheres for men and women are created by patterns of economic and social relations in southern Peru. While one may differ with her analytical conclusions, the strength of this analysis lies in the specification of the social context in which sex roles are being examined.

For Latin America, we would suggest that there are significant limitations to the explanatory power of the separate spheres approach, especially when it is not coupled with other forms of explanation. The problem is that this perspective is not comprehensive enough to represent the complexities of Latin American reality. In questioning the appropriateness of the separate spheres perspective, we must ask if *separate* spheres of control actually exist for women and men. It is important to know if the household is best conceptualized as being distinct from the public world of work and male control of government. Also, we must ask if women actually have autonomous decision-making powers in the home. Answers to such questions must grapple with the limitations of women's control of the broader community and state.

Women in their sphere generally do not control the laws which govern marriage, divorce, legitimacy, inheritance, and education. Rather their control of crucial aspects of family and home can be undermined by public policy emanating from the domain of political affairs and regulated by community government and national law. In addition, women's authority in the home may be undercut by the intervention of fathers and husbands in domestic affairs. If husbands or fathers make high-level decisions, retain the right to override household decisions at any level, or serve as the catalyst for the reorientation of domestic activities to the presence of a male, then women cannot be said to have gained parity with men through control of a separate sphere. In short, the separate spheres approach errs in its narrow focus on the family. Women are portrayed as specialized in, rather than restricted to, a particular sphere with special authority and control. In contrast, we suggest that the household and family are closely integrated into the broader social fabric of the community. To the extent that male dominance is characteristic of the larger community, it will also be replicated in the household.[7]

An important contribution to the literature on the North American version of this argument that avoids the pitfalls we have signalled in other works is found in Cott's *Bonds of Womanhood* (1977). Cott argues that for the United States the idea of a woman's sphere was a nineteenth-century creation for middle-class women. The notion of a woman's sphere served a particular function with respect to the religious, secular, and political ideologies of the day. With regard to the origins of this concept, Cott writes:

> The shift of production and exchange away from the household, and a general tightening of functional "spheres" (specialization) in the economy and society at large, made it [the woman's sphere] seem "separate." [p. 199]

Yet Cott goes on to point out the interrelationship between a woman's sphere and society through the special role assigned to women as the moral guardians of society.

In viewing this sphere as intimately tied to religious and secular ideology, and thus not separate at all, Cott avoids the most common inconsistency of the general model. As an ideology, Cott argues that the notion of a woman's sphere played an important and positive role by providing women with:

> ... a social power based on their special female qualities rather than on general human rights. For women who previously held no particular avenue of power on their own—no unique sense of integrity and dignity—this represented an advance.... The ideology of woman's sphere formed a necessary stage in the process of shattering the hierarchy of sex and, more directly in softening the hierarchical relationship of marriage. [p. 200]

However, Cott goes on to warn that there were severe limitations in this notion as the basis for social ideology.

> But woman's sphere had the defects of its virtues. In opening certain avenues to women because of their sex, it barricaded all others. [p. 201]

Cott sees the notion of a separate woman's sphere as part of the historical development away from a more patriarchal family order in the United States. Moreover, she sees it as a temporary way station which gave rise to its own challenge in the form of the nineteenth-century feminist movement. Historically, then, a separate sphere did not provide an adequate solution to the condition of women's subordination.[8]

The separate spheres model is also a limited framework for analyzing women's contemporary position in the United States although this approach closely resembles conventional middle-class wisdom about the family. Again, the problem is the assumption that what goes on in the home is unaffected by what happens in the rest of the world, the nonhome. According to middle-class social ideology, the home is the sphere that women maintain for the husband's benefit as a refuge from the demands of working life, as the locus for the collection of property either in the form of children or tangible objects, and as a means for displaying and enjoying material success. Zaretsky argues that "the family, and the subordination of women within it, was necessary to preserve a refuge of spiritual and emotional life against the dehumanization of capitalist society" (1976, p. 115). But whose refuge, and is the home really a refuge or simply a new arena for materialistic accumulation and competition? To view the household as a separate domain seems an idealization of what is more appropriately described as an extension of the public world.

The argument for a separate sphere, even if it is restricted to the privileged upper-middle class, is usually based on two misconceptions. First, it is assumed that the sphere is separate, rather than intimately tied to the values of the larger society, including values of male dominance. While social values may emphasize that women's most meaningful place is in the home, it does not follow that wives are to be dominant within the home. In some cases women's limited authority in the domestic sphere is masked by their role as the primary consumer for the family. To the extent that women internalize the consumer role, they may substitute control over choices regarding subtle distinctions between commercial products for the serious erosion of their authority and influence in the home. The consumer-oriented economy, of course, depends on the illusion that differences and changes in products are significant.[9]

Second, one must question the assumption of a more person-oriented quality of life in the home. The concept of the home as the center of unalienated labor ignores the nature of full-time housework. So, too, evidence that the family is affected by political, economic, and social phenomena and that its structure is manipulated by political leaders for their own ends appears to shake any notion of the household as a separate sphere.[10]

In critiquing the separate spheres model we are pointing to the need for a framework which deals more adequately with women's work commitments both within and outside the home. The second approach to women's status attempts a more comprehensive analysis of the relation between women's work and their cultural status.

The Sexual Division of Labor Approach: You Are What You Work

The sexual division of labor perspective argues that the constraints on female involvement in the economy, resulting from sexual divisions of occupations and work tasks, shape women's position in sexually hierarchical societies. Some advocates of this approach see women's child care responsibilities as having a major restrictive influence on female economic participation; others emphasize women's general contributions to subsistence as fundamentally important in shaping women's social status and other domestic duties. All analysts from these viewpoints argue that women's primary responsibility for children is a cultural specialization, not just a physiological or psychological constraint. The sexual division of labor analysts begin with a framework that underscores women's major contributions to the subsistence activities—such as foraging, fishing, animal husbandry, and agriculture—in the economies of their respective societies. Women contribute 43.88 percent of the food consumed in all societies. The range of their contribution is from 32.24 percent to 50.73 percent (Aronoff and Crano 1975). These figures make it very clear that men do not monopolize the role of family provider, nor are women confined to household duties.

That there are marked specializations in work activities by sex throughout the world has been clearly demonstrated by anthropological analyses of large cross-cultural samples. In a worldwide survey of societies, Murdock and Provost (1973) find that certain tasks are exclusively masculine including lumbering, trapping, stoneworking, and mining. Other activities such as butchering, land clearing, soil preparation, herding large animals, and house building are men's work in *most* societies, though there are notable exceptions. Tasks which are women's work in *most* societies include fuel gathering, dairy production, spinning, laundering, water fetching, and cooking. Finally, a substantial range of labors are *not* systematically specialized by sex including crop planting, harvesting, milking, burden carrying, the care of small animals, loom weaving, clothing manufacture, and pottery making (Murdock and Provost 1973, pp. 207–10).

Anthropologists have tried to explain these broad statistical patterns in the sexual division of labor. J. Brown (1970) focuses her explanations on those factors which shape women's specializations. She concludes that

> societies are able to draw on womanpower *because their subsistence activities are compatible with simultaneous child watching.* Such activities have the following characteristics: they do not require rapt concentration and are relatively dull and repetitive; they are easily interruptible and easily resumed once interrupted; they do not place the child in potential danger; and they do not require the participant to range very far from home. [1970, pp. 1075–76; emphasis ours][11]

Subsequent statistical analyses of large samples of societies have sustained the outline of this argument while sidestepping the description of women's activities as especially dull and repetitive and pointing out that child care activities such as infant feeding are more culturally variable than one might think. Where the demands on women for subsistence production are high, cross-cultural analysis shows that infants are much more likely to be fed indigenously developed baby food as an early supplement to breast-feeding. Also, infants will be given earlier supplementary feeding in societies in which women are heavily involved in agriculture than in societies in which women work at home in craft production. The demands of breast-feeding and child care fall on women's shoulders. But at least some of these responsibilities can be shifted from any particular mother to other women by supplementary feeding combined with various cooperative and reciprocal child watching arrangements (Nerlove 1974; Burton, Brudner, and White 1977).

New studies build on Brown's analysis while questioning the rigidity and exclusivity of sexual divisions of labor. Burton, Brudner, and White (1977) suggest that the reason a particular sex performs a task may depend on how far away from home the work is done rather than on any special demands of the work or qualities of the sexes.[12] These anthropologists find a strong tendency for clear sexual divisions of specific tasks combined with an overall sexual sharing of responsibility for an entire production sequence (Burton, Brudner, and White 1977, p. 246). Generally men are more involved than women in raw material production at great distances from home settlements. However, the earlier women normally enter a production sequence, the wider their range of work activities since they are more likely to participate in all subsequent tasks in the production sequence. For example, in societies in which women clear land for agriculture, they are also very likely to be active in subsequent activities such as soil preparation, planting, crop tending, harvesting, and food preparation (Burton, Brudner, and White 1977).

The statistically based generalizations developed by sexual division of labor analysts give us a sense of broad patterns and possible functional explanations for sexual specialization on a worldwide basis. Rarely, however, do these anthropologists move from statistical descriptions to fuller accounts of women's position or to exploring the issue of subordination. These researchers are primarily concerned with comparative patterns of task involvement as studied independently of the political organizations, the value systems, and the ecological adaptations of particular societies. One limitation of this approach is the narrow scope of the questions addressed. Generally these analysts do not move beyond the description and functional analysis of behavior to investigate and explain the ways in which cultural systems give meaning to the organization of people's activities.

To find out if early female involvement in a production sequence tends to translate cross-culturally into broader patterns of sexual parity, we must look to a second, more materialist branch of the sexual division of labor approach. This alternative approach, which is especially well articulated in the work of Friedl, is less concerned with the prediction of behavior and more involved in the analysis of the ways specific societies socially organize access to important resources.

Social scientists such as Friedl do not give equivalent weight to all sexually specialized tasks but rather focus on sexual divisions of labor as they relate to specialized access to resources, economic exchanges, and political control.

> ... we define male dominance as a situation in which men have highly preferential access, although not always exclusive rights, to those activities which society accords the greatest value, and the exercise of which permits a measure of control over others. [Friedl 1975, p. 7]

Instead of comparing male and female tasks in different societies, this "access and exchange" approach concentrates on those activities that give one sex greater control over social and material resources than the other. Clearly, the routes of access to social and material resources must be studied in the context of particular societies. Land, for example, is a very different resource for nomadic foragers, who range over wide territories, subsisting on gathered plants and small game, than for horticulturalists, who may secure the right to farm particular parcels by membership in a lineage group. Through the examination of patterns of access to resources, this approach avoids treating tasks as if they existed in a vacuum and, by including data on the social context, implications, and cultural evaluations of men's and women's work, provides a fuller understanding of the sexual division of labor.

This approach holds that the form of production is a crucial determining variable of women's position because technoeconomies influence the range of occupations available in any given society. For example, hunting and gathering societies offer relatively little occupational specialization for either men or women; horticultural societies require some occupational specializations on a part-time basis; and agricultural societies have full-time craft, trading, religious, and governmental specializations complicated by the emerging significance of class differences. Methodologically, then, the sexual division of labor analysts find it important to categorize societies by their techno-economies (i.e., as foragers, horticulturalists, agriculturalists with plow technologies, industrial societies) before comparatively analyzing factors that account for women's status.

Friedl generalizes about the implication of economic participation for women's status in foraging and horticultural societies in the following terms:

Among hunters and gatherers and horticulturalists the relative power of women is increased if women *both* contribute to subsistence *and also* have opportunities for extradomestic distribution and exchange of valued goods and services. In situations in which women either do not contribute to the food supply at all, or, while working hard and long at subsistence tasks, are not themselves, in their own right, responsible for extradomestic distribution, their own personal autonomy and control over others is likely to be most limited.... Where men's chance for giving away goods and services are not markedly better than women's, there are fewer differences between the sexes in power and autonomy. [1975, p. 135]

The access and exchange approach to women's position is a very successful method of analyzing women's position in foraging and horticultural groups. The limitations of this framework become apparent as we move on to study peasant and urbanized societies in which agriculturalists are not autonomous populations but are subject to state politics and economics which regulate local affairs, establish the market value of agricultural surpluses available for trade, and foster the development of class differences and rural-urban dependencies.

The insights, as well as the limitations, of the sexual division of labor perspective become even clearer when it is applied to the United States. Friedl sees her access and exchange model as being useful for understanding married women's quest for parity in our own society.

But what of the working wife? If our analysis of foragers and horticulturalists is applicable, such a woman, if her income is used primarily for consumption within the household, may gain some degree of parity in domestic affairs, but this is limited to the confines of the family and does nothing for her prestige and power outside it. Unless her occupation is at a managerial or professional level high enough to enable her to distribute goods and services to persons outside the home, or her income is great enough to be maneuvered or manipulated or exchanged in business, political, or community contexts, her public power and autonomy are not significantly changed by the mere fact of her outside employment (in this, incidentally, she does not differ from her husband). The women's movement which stresses equality of opportunity for women in managerial and administrative positions is profoundly right from the standpoint of equalizing the public power of the sexes. [1975, p. 136]

This analysis, in concentrating on women's restricted economic involvement as the key to understanding structural subordination, is more comprehensive than a separate spheres analysis of women's position in class-stratified society. Friedl argues that the road to female equality will be paved by expanded female participation in strategic, high status areas of the labor force. The underlying assumption here is that the work presently done by females does not give them access to important resources and patterns of exchange. Other analysts drawing from a similar perspective would add that the work done presently by females in the United States is not valued and consequently those who are active in the female sectors of the labor force are the unwitting recipients of the negative connotations associated with low status work.

These analyses assume that there is nothing inherently negative in society's evaluation of "female" that would persist beyond the specific tasks a woman performs. Ideally, then, to change the work women do would be to transform attitudes toward women. As women increasingly share men's economic roles, especially those that are powerful, women will acquire a similar degree of economic independence and personal autonomy. Friedl's version of this argument adds that such changes will potentially transform women's roles in the family. According to her view, cultural values regarding family size, child spacing, and child care vary in conformance to women's customary work requirements in all societies.

The principle limitation of this access and exchange model is that it does not deal adequately with class and racial stratifications which are major, cross-cutting structural constraints on access to resources in state societies. In Friedl's model these issues remain implicit in the remedy for sexism—greater power and autonomy in high status, managerial work. What is needed is a more comprehensive model which builds on the sexual division of access and exchange and reveals women's varying access to resources and forms of labor force participation within a given society. The next framework makes economic class the center of gravity for the explanation of women's status in complex societies.

The Class Analysis Perspective:
The Development of Multiple Inequalities

The class analysis perspective explains women's subordination in contemporary societies as an outcome of the historical transformation of prestate societies to class-stratified, state-organized societies. This approach provides frameworks for examining the early transition from tribal to state societies as well as the modern impact of advanced capitalist economic systems on women's positions in newly industrializing and urbanizing countries.[13] This has been developed into the most comprehensive approach to date for the analysis of women's status, incorporating elements of both the sexual division of labor and separate spheres approaches into a broader historical argument.

At the heart of the class analysis is a generalized model of the process of state formation and its impact on women. Engels's *The Origin of the Family, Private Property, and the State* remains a paradigmatic statement of this process, though the ethnographic particulars of his 1891 argument have been revised with the twentieth-century expansion of anthropological knowledge.[14] Both Engels's early statement and modern revisions argue that women's subordination and dependency changed qualitatively with the development and expansion of state-organized societies.

This approach observes that *pre*state societies, such as tribal horticulturalists, were organized primarily on the basis of kinship groups (often lineages and clans) which maintained corporate control over access to resources and the organization of political, economic, and jural affairs. Prestate societies were not necessarily egalitarian, though some showed remarkable parity between the sexes, nor were differences in wealth and property unknown.[15] Yet the inequalities of economic class, involving differential relations to subsistence and production, failed to crystallize in these societies. The structure of prestate societies contrasted profoundly with the later development of the state.

> In pre-state societies, economy, polity, and religion are all familized; in state society, these spheres emerge as separate and public while the family becomes privatized. (Reiter 1975*b*, p. 278)

The emergence of state societies redefined and limited the political aspects of kinship relations and the economic centrality of households. Distinct economic classes with different relations to economic production developed. The new elites of the class system increased their control over resources, surpluses, and labor, supplanting the corporate control of kinship groups. Finally the state came to reflect the interests of the economic elites and, ultimately, to assume such

central functions as political administration, law making and en-
forcement, defense, taxation, and public works.

To summarize a very complicated set of changes central to this
perspective, the rise of the state brought a decline in the importance
of communal kinship organizations, a new significance to the ownership of private property, the reorganization of society into a class
system, a sharper separation of domestic production from social
production and production for exchange, and monogamous marriage. Class analysts differ in their assessments of which of these factors had the formative impact on women's position in state societies.[16]
All agree, however, that these political and economic transformations
brought new virulence to women's dependence and subordination as
domestic work became increasingly isolated and stripped of recognized value in broader social production and women's exploitation
took on a class as well as a sexual dimension.

In the process of state formation, households lost their centralized
position in politics and economics, but kept the demanding role of
producing, socializing, and maintaining new generations. This reorganization of household functions had different implications for men
and women, as Reiter observes:

> The crucial function of kin units in the maintenance of centralized state
> societies, and especially industrial capitalist ones, is hidden by its
> ideological submersion into privacy. In the process, the status of
> women—the holders of kinship functions and powers, a group increas-
> ingly defined by its participation in the reproduction and production of
> families—is reduced. [1975, p. 282]

The development of state societies resulted in highly differentiated
spheres and a sexual separation of forms of production for men and
women. According to the class analysis, women's status in state
societies was shaped by the increased isolation of private domestic
labor, their marginated position in public production, their general
role as a reserve labor force, and their varying class positions.

The expansion of Western political and economic dominions has
meant that all societies—be they foraging, horticultural, peasant, or
indigenous states—have felt the impact of class-stratified, market-
oriented forces. The class analysis perspective examines the impact of
Western expansion on colonial and contemporary society through a
materialist analysis of the development of the stages of capitalist

modes of production.[17] Western expansion, which established class-stratified societies with economies tied to the development of world capitalism, has most forcefully changed women's lives.

> ... behind the endless variety in the culture histories that have been unfolding over the past half millenium of colonialism and imperialism, certain processes are central. The undermining of women's autonomy and the privatization of their social and economic roles have consistently been linked with the break up of the egalitarian and collective social forms that are anathema to capitalist exploitation. [Leacock 1977, p. 15]

The class analysis approach focuses on European colonialism, the development of modern nation-states and the imperialist exploitation of third world societies as aspects of a general process that has tended to isolate women politically in atomized households and to exploit women by forcing them to work a double day, at home and in the wage labor market.

These economic processes have also weakened women's collective opportunities for independent mutual assistance, reciprocal exchanges, and joint work, all of which were vital to social production in prestate societies. As Leacock (1977) notes, women's sodalities, work groups, and economic networks operated in pragmatic and productive ways in tribal societies, contributing to women's autonomy and to the general social welfare of both men and women. In contrast, with colonialism women began to lose opportunities for panhousehold organizations. Networks linking women in class stratified societies no longer necessarily represented the common interests of their participants. For example, Burkett concludes that in Peru economic class, not sex, was the most important dimension of power and common experience for women during the colonial period.

> While we theorize endlessly about the oppression of women, we all too frequently forget that the position of the one [the elite women] is maintained only through the exploitation of the other [the lower-class, working women] and such a relationship leaves little concrete room for sisterhood. ... No matter how great the sanction and how meager the rewards, nonelite females were trapped in the public sector by their class status. The qualitative difference of need [for work] versus whim, survival versus desire was a fundamental dividing point by class. It was the divergence of experience between those [women] who had choice, however limited, and those who did not. [1977, p. 19, 23]

In societies that have been touched by Western colonialism, class is the preeminent definer of social relations, political interests, and economic choices and rewards. Female experiences, from this point of view, are more accurately understood as the products of class positions rather than any commonalities of sexual identity or subordination. The class analysis approach does not deny sexual subordination. Rather, this approach subsumes the study of women's position within a broader concern with class stratification and exploitation.

Of course the impact of Western economic expansion was felt not just during the colonial period. Rather, advanced capitalism in the twentieth century has had a renewed impact on class formation and sexual divisions of labor. In research focusing on rural Latin America, class analysts have examined changing patterns of labor force participation as agrarian production has shifted from nineteenth-century *haciendas* to modern commercial enterprises. The shift away from traditional *haciendas* has resulted from the reorientation of rural production to meet the demands of new urban and international markets. The consequent drive to modernize agriculture has introduced new skilled occupations, reduced the demand for unskilled laborers, enlarged the pool of semiproletarians, and increased the migration of workers in search of ways to supplement subsistence farming.[18]

Deere (1977a) presents a very subtle analysis of the expansion of modern capitalism and its impact on the exploitation of workers, the sexual division of labor, and women's local political authority in a northern region of Peru. Early in the twentieth century, large *haciendas* in this region still provided badly needed access to agricultural lands and pastures for resident laborers, sharecroppers, and renters, none of whom were able to accumulate sufficient land for independent farming. In exchange for access to land, whole families worked for the *hacienda,* tending the fields, caring for the herds of cattle, and taking care of domestic duties in the owner's household.

Haciendas were exploitative of both sexes, but special burdens fell to women. Contractual agreements between a family unit and the *hacienda* owners specified men's duties in the fields. Women, in contrast, were required to be continually available for house service, herding and milking, harvest processing, and cooking for labor gangs. No maximum obligation was established for women; they were infrequently compensated for work and then only at one-half the male rate. Deere concludes that *hacienda* owners manipulated the sexual division of labor and the devaluation of women's work to increase the rate of exploitation of peasant families (1977*a*, p. 57).

By the mid-twentieth century, the rural economy of this northern region of Peru was transformed by the opening of roads to urban centers and by the local establishment of a new milk processing plant, the subsidiary of a multinational corporation. Faced with market forces that increased land values and rewarded more mechanized dairy farming over traditional crop production, the *haciendas* sold marginal lands, reduced the unskilled agricultural labor force, and concentrated on improving herds and pastures.

Deere's analysis underscores the differential impact of modernization on workers by class and by sex. Proletarian laborers—who now work for wages, not primarily for access to land as on the former *haciendas*—are legally guaranteed minimum wages, protected by labor contracts, and covered by the Peruvian social security system. On modern dairy farms, women specifically benefit from cash earnings, a clearer definition of work requirements, and a recognized length for women's workday. Clearly, permanent workers sharing a similar class position in modernized enterprises have reaped rewards from economic development. Over time, special demands on women workers have diminished and greater economic parity between the sexes has resulted. Deere notes that economic parity, however, has not brought increased political recognition for women in local affairs (1977*a*, p. 58–65).

Permanent wage labor in commercial dairies, however, is an option open to only a rather small, privileged segment of the rural labor force. In fact, most peasants have not received direct benefits from capitalist expansion because of the reduced demand for laborers in capital intensive businesses. Many former *hacienda* workers must gain subsistence by farming small plots of land, engaging in minor commerce, and migrating in search of seasonal employment. Men, who are given wider options for cash earnings in the broader economy, search for temporary work outside home communities. The women of these families now specialize in subsistence agriculture. Deere argues that women agriculturalists have gained greater control over their labor in the process, though their workday remains very long and their primary goal is still subsistence. She proposes that women's increased participation in subsistence production, while men are absent as seasonal laborers, is accompanied by a higher female status in the family and wider female participation in community government (Deere 1977a, p. 63–67).

Modern capitalism and economic development have had an uneven impact on agrarian social classes and on women and men. Deere's study shows the importance of detailed case studies which avoid over-generalizations about the positive or subordinating effects of capitalism and technological modernization for women of different class positions. Deere seeks the explanation for women's changing and varying statuses in the requirements of a capitalist mode of production.

> Women's greater or lesser autonomy in social production, or in the reproduction of the labor force, is merely a reflection of the requirements for reproduction of the dominant mode of production. [1977a, p. 68]

The new requirements of modern capitalist production shape women's and men's labor force participation, household roles, and local political involvements. Sex and class present themselves as contradictions of varying intensities at different historical points in the process of changing modes of production (Deere 1977a).

Our analysis of rural Peru draws inspiration and core questions from the class analysis perspective. Yet we have chosen to leave two areas of questioning more problematic and subject to further analysis. First, we are concerned with the role of social and cultural values, attitudes, perceptions, and beliefs in reinforcing and transforming sexual hierarchy. Second, we want to pursue a conceptualization that examines those dimensions of sexual subordination which cross-cut class divisions in rural society. Our goal is to readdress the issues Burkett and Deere raise with a new framework which looks past observable patterns of behavior and toward the meaning of social interaction for the participants of different classes and sexes. In order to pursue this line of questioning, we must turn to the fourth, and final, framework for understanding women's lives.

The Social Ideology Approach: Reexaminations of Patriarchy

The social ideology approach holds that female subordination is not compensated for by women's role in the family, will not be ameli-

orated by women's acquisition of economic positions traditionally defined as masculine, and will not necessarily disappear in social exper-
iments working toward alternatives to class-based capitalist society.[19]
This approach seeks to understand sexual hierarchy as a product of
culturally created social ideologies and the material conditions of
women's and men's lives. According to the social ideology approach,
sexual divisions of work are not just behavioral specializations to be
exhaustively explained in functional and historical terms. Patterns of
labor force specialization also have an ideological dimension in that
they are perpetuated and legitimized by social ideologies of exclusion,
segregation, and avoidance. Only through analyses of the social world
views of participants in the labor force can we move from behavior to
meaning, value, and ideology. Social ideology models give new importance to sex role stereotypes, images, and values as aspects of
world views that are used to motivate and justify sexual hierarchy.
The social ideology framework moves past the analysis of discrete
stereotypes and toward an examination of the role that social
ideologies play in perpetuating female subordination. This framework sees social ideology as a set of cultural beliefs that shape people's
perceptions of such key dimensions of their social universe as gender,
class, and race.[20]

The conceptual work of relating sexual ideologies to the material
conditions of people's lives has preoccupied a range of social scientists. Social ideology analysts, among whom we would include de
Beauvoir and Millett, have demonstrated the significance of patriarchy and the pervasiveness of sexual distinctions as the basis for the
skewed distributions of valued goods in society. Eisenstein points to
the sexual division and the stereotyping of social, political, and economic roles as a root cause of women's subordination (1979).[21] We
would add that sexual hierarchies are both reflected in, and reinforced by, women's unequal participation in institutions that determine the distribution of valued goods and resources. From our
perspective, women are structurally subordinated to men by patriarchal mechanisms that link access to key institutions to sex role stereotyping and the sexual division of labor.

The social ideology approach gives a more central role to belief
systems and world views than the other approaches to women's subordination. At the same time, it examines those belief systems in the
concrete conditions of social life. This is a *grounded* concern with the

meanings of sex differences for the participants in a social and political system. An analysis that is not grounded would examine abstract images of the sexes in, for instance, religious belief. These images (such as Eve and the Virgin Mary in Catholicism) would be treated as central elements of symbolic systems which can be interpreted independently of nonsymbolic reality. In contrast, a grounded analysis requires the study of the ways in which images, stereotypes, symbols, and perceptions are historically and socially manipulated by people and influenced by the material conditions of their lives. The concrete conditions of social life, the institutional structures of society, and the context in which images are evoked are all relevant to this analysis.

The importance of studying both patterns of behavior and ideology is exemplified by Harris's analysis of an Andean community in Bolivia. Like Silverblatt (1978) for pre-Incan and Incan society and Núñez del Prado Béjar (1975a, 1975b) and Isbell (1978) for contemporary settlements, she is struck by the complementarity of male-female roles in agrarian households. Harris, however, further analyzes complementarity in terms of the meanings that the Aymara attach to their concepts of woman and man, the ideological uses of the images, and the social behaviors that conform to and contradict the cultural conceptions. She finds that the Aymara stress unity, complementarity, and egalitarianism when discussing their image of the marital pair in household affairs (chachawarmi). In contrast, their conceptions of "maleness" and "femaleness" emphasize differences and potential antagonism between the sexes and are used by men to exclude women from the broader community in which all households are embedded. Harris concludes: "Their characterization of women as weak and vulnerable has the explicit consequence of disqualifying them from participation in most collective activity" (1978, p. 37). Furthermore, in this community, wife beating during periods of ritual drinking was used to "ensure that women did not abandon their children or domestic tasks" (p. 37). Behaviorally, potential violence kept women at home so as not to risk problems with drunken husbands at community celebrations or to be found missing on the husband's return. By exploring multiple ideological levels and their social contexts, this analysis reveals the complexity of "complementary" sex roles in an Andean agricultural community.

The social ideology approach looks at belief systems as ideologies, as systems of ideas that deal with the politics of establishing and defin-

ing value in social and material realities. Individuals formulate their ideas about sexuality, sex roles, images of the sexes, and the politics of male-female relations by using the categories of their culture's social ideologies. Because ideological categories and values are embedded in the common sense reality of everyday life, they are often unquestioned and thought of as thoroughly natural.

In the United States we commonly use the biological and psychological vocabularies of instincts, hormones, dispositions, personalities, natures, physical qualities, and organic differences to give cultural meanings to sexual contrasts. In studying the patterning of the Western world view, historians have found important linkages between the prevailing scientific and social theory regarding sexual differences and the institutions (such as schools, legal systems, political, and economic organizations) which give these theories concrete meanings in people's lives. The social ideology analysis would trace the translation of scientific and social theory into public expectations and prevailing ideologies through institutions that govern access to resources and opportunities.

The transfer of nineteenth-century Victorian notions of biological differences between the sexes to theories of appropriate social roles has already received the attention of scholars such as Conway, who shows the use of biology to explain inequality and justify the maintenance of separate sexual spheres (1973). The power of stereotyped notions of feminine behavior in restricting women's opportunities and self-perception during the expansion of women's professional, public, and political opportunities has received renewed attention. These studies demonstrate the crucial link between prevailing ideology and institutional behavior in historically creating and perpetuating sexual inequity.[22]

The reoccurence of such biological explanations in the late twentieth century and the attempts by their proponents to link such theories to prescriptions for access and opportunity suggest the persistence and potency of this kind of explanation in American society.[23] Whereas the content of the biological explanation changes, the use of such explanations has a long history and continues to attract adherents. While biologically phrased stereotypes are not universally important in justifying sexual hierarchy, they figure prominently in the West and are common in rural Peru.[24]

The linking of sex role stereotypes, however conceived, to dif-

ferential access to resources and reality-defining institutions trans-
forms sexual contrasts into sexual hierarchies. The result is an uneven
distribution of power—as manifested in the control of social institutions, cultural attitudes and values—which further reinforces the
structural subordination of women to men.

The social ideology analysts do not assume that world views are
simply taught, absorbed, and lived, although, like language, these
beliefs are certainly learned and culturally perpetuated. Rather, this
perspective assumes a reflective, questioning participation of individuals in using, manipulating, and internalizing ideological portrayals
of their social reality. Clearly, ideologies may systematically misportray; they may be reworked to provide useful appraisals of alternatives; and they may justify or defeat institutional definitions of
social relations. The social ideology analysis asks for an examination
of the manipulation and grounding of ideology as well as the political
implications of the patterns found in a particular society.

Fundamental to many social ideology approaches is the view that
sexual distinctions persist over and above class, ethnic, and racial distinctions. Thus, even though both men and women find themselves
exploited by virtue of the unequal distribution of power along the
lines of class and ethnic identifications, within these groupings the
criterion of sex further subordinates women to men. This approach
argues that, while women's lives cannot be understood without reference to class and ethnic differences in state societies, one must examine these forms of inequality independently. As a result, social value
ideology analysts are more likely than class analysts to find patriarchy
in prestate societies, to see divergences between the political interests
of sex and class groupings in contemporary societies, and to point to
consistent patterns of sexual hierarchy in state societies despite great
differences in political ideologies. The social ideology and class
analysis perspectives are most compatible when researchers from both
viewpoints are willing to treat sex and class as potentially independent
and equivalently significant dimensions of social reality, at least for
analytical purposes.

It is our sense that a coordinated application of the social ideology
and class analysis perspectives reveals most accurately the complexity
of sexual hierarchies in state societies. While neither model can be
usefully reduced to the other, various useful syntheses are possible.

Hartmann's work on dominance-dependence relations of the sexes in industrialized England and the United States is a good example of an analysis which approaches a synthesis of the social ideology and class analysis models. Hartmann examines the industrialization of work such as spinning and weaving in rural England as a historical process that linked earlier forms of patriarchy to the later development of capitalism. She describes the differential impact of early economic changes on men and women in terms of work patterns, power relations, and social values:

> domestic industry, created by emerging capitalism, was later superceded and destroyed by the progress of capitalist industrialization. In the process, women, children, and men in the rural areas all suffered dislocation and disruption, but they experienced this in different ways. Women, forced into unemployment by capitalization of agriculture more frequently than men, were more available to labor both in the domestic putting-out system and in early factories. It is often argued both that men resisted going to the factories because they did not want to lose their independence and that women and children were docile and malleable. If this was in fact the case, it would appear that these "character traits" of women and men were already established before the advent of the capitalist organization of industry, and that they would have grown out of the authority structure prevailing in the previous period of small-scale, family agriculture. [Hartmann 1976, p. 149]

In studying later patterns of sexual hierarchy in eighteenth- and nineteenth-century wage-labor economies, Hartmann goes on to locate what we would term a patriarchal mechanism linking differential access to institutional resources to sex role stereotyping and the sexual division of labor. She argues that a key mechanism perpetuating sexual hierarchy in industrializing societies was the system of sex-based job segregation.

> In the labor market the dominant position of men was maintained by sex-ordered job segregation. Women's jobs were lower paid, considered less skilled, and often involved less exercise of authority or control. Men acted to enforce job segregation in the labor market; they utilized trade-union associations and strengthened the domestic division of labor, which required women to do housework, child care, and related chores. Women's subordinate position in the labor market reinforced their subordinate position in the family, and that in turn reinforced their labor-market position. [1976, pp 152-53]

Forms of job segregation that specifically disadvantaged women were favored by both male unions and factory owners, though for somewhat different reasons. Actions which fostered sex-based job segregation were patriarchal, according to Hartmann, because they flowed from social relations with a material base that involved "hierarchical relations between men, and solidarity among them, which enable them to control women" (1976, pp. 138n). Hartmann's analysis moves toward conceptualizing the historical interplay of capitalism and patriarchy. She finds that patriarchy has shaped the development of Western capitalism much as capitalism has created new institutional forms for patriarchy.

The strength of a combined social ideology and class analysis is its potential to achieve new precision and insight into the relations of economic change and sexual hierarchy. In the following chapters we will present another synthesis of the two perspectives. Our framework will be tailored to fit an agrarian society which has gone through the second wave of industrialization and integration into international economics. Peruvian workers in small rural communities are not factory workers or union members, though some of their coastal kin may be. Thus, the pattern described by Hartmann for the initial development of industrialization in Europe and the United States is not directly translatable to the Peruvian context.

In order to specify the mechanisms that perpetuate sexual hierarchy for rural Peru, we need to examine links between the sexual division of labor, rural institutions which regulate the allocation of resources and define values for the community, and social ideologies which give cultural meanings to sex differences. Because we are concerned with the meanings of sex roles for men and women we will pursue the analysis of ideologies in a much more explicit fashion than Hartmann. We will balance our ideological approach with an awareness of the impact of capitalist economics on class relations in rural society.

The class analysis perspective would hold that we must examine women's position in the context of Peruvian economic and political change. Rural settlements are not isolated remnants of traditional society; they are subject to state control and to international markets. Increasing national integration in this century has meant a continued weakening of local autonomy, even for relatively self-sufficient peasant communities outside areas of commercial development. Of course, neither sex in rural populations has significant influence over their country's political and economic policies. Nevertheless, within rural settlements important differences in power and influence originate from class relations as well as from relations between ethnic groups and between the sexes. In some dealings, women may be powerful because of their class position, but all women in these communities share one dimension of subordination by virtue of their sex. In situations where sexual identities are central, women are reduced to attempts to influence the exercise of power vested in men. The following chapters further develop and test our framework for analyzing the mechanisms that perpetuate and transform sexual hierarchies.

Notes

1. See Wilson (1978), Goldberg (1973), Divale and Harris (1976) for examples of biosocial explanations, and Callan's insightful critique (1978).
2. Chodorow (1978), Frieze et al. (1978), and Dinnerstein (1976) provide social psychological explanations.
3. See, for example, Chodorow (1978).
4. At their worst, biosocial and psychological explanations ignore or dismiss the culturally diverse organization and meanings of sex roles and, thus, are prone to serious ethnocentric biases. Both Ariès and Stone point out the historically bound nature of contemporary Western notions of the nuclear family and childhood (Ariès 1962; Stone 1975). To avoid reducing social, political, economic, and religious behavior to individual psychologies or to alleged biologically based sex differences, we would stress the independent analysis of social and cultural institutions as well as research linking the psychological and biological with the institutional realities in nonreductionistic ways.
5. Knaster (1976) and Saulniers and Rakowski (1977) are important bibliographies of Latin American materials.
6. In more recent work Jaquette (1976) recognizes that her initial analysis failed to treat class differences adequately. Even in the current work, however, Jaquette does not distinguish clearly between a group's exercise of power and a group's development of strategies to limit power exercised upon it.
7. The separate spheres perspective is a first cousin to the "complementary-but-equal" argument used by some anthropologists to argue for parity between the sexes among prestate societies such as the Hopi and Eskimos. Lamphere (1977) argues that this approach fails to consider women's restricted role in public affairs and the differential control of key productive resources by the sexes. Kelly (1978) has contributed an important critique

of the separate spheres models. She also argues for the need to understand "the *simultaneous operation* of relations of work and sex" in the context of race and class distinctions (p. 227).

On the other hand, in another cultural context the work of Fernea (1969, 1976) which describes women's sphere has been particularly insightful in that it gives us a new appreciation of the world Iraqi and Morrocan women inhabit and the skills which they have developed within their own sphere and their own perspective upon it. Fernea's approach never mistakes women's leadership within their sphere as an equivalent to the authority or power of men. Nor does she argue that one can separate the private sphere from public control. She makes clear the importance of women's spheres of activity without losing sight of the limitations inherent in them.

8. Scholarly work on the notion of women's separate sphere and its influence on American politics is especially rich. See for example Conway (1971–72), Sklar (1973), and the exchange between DuBois (1980) and Smith-Rosenberg (1980). For interesting parallels in Great Britain see Harrison (1978).

9. See Lefevbre (1971) for a full presentation of this position. For an analytically parallel argument in the case of ethnic subordinates, see Warren (1978).

10. For further discussion of the state's manipulation of the family and women's roles in it see Rupp (1978), Stone (1975), Douglas (1977), and Koonz (1977).

11. To explain specialized male work involvements, J. Brown advances the interpretation that men are the recipients of those activities found to be incompatible with the requirements of child care, such as herding large animals, hunting large game, deep sea fishing, and plowing fields. Such tasks are antithetical to women's child care duties because they require continuous attention, expose participants to special dangers, and require great geographical mobility (1970, p. 1076). Murdock and Provost (1973) add to this analysis the point of view that masculine specialization is favored by greater male strength as well as male mobility. On the other hand, they reason that women (who by definition have a smaller range outside home settlements) are more likely to specialize in technological tasks requiring continual, localized attention. Unlike more mobile men, they are not disadvantaged for these tasks by absences from home for hunting, warfare, and other distant specializations.

Recent analyses deemphasize differences in strength as a basis for sexual specializations in work and reaffirm the constraints of childbirth and nursing that are said to lead to "a tendency for women not to work at great distances from home and a tendency for women to avoid doing dangerous tasks" (Burton, Brudner, and White 1977, pp. 228–29).

12. For example, among the Maasai of Kenya either men or women participate in the milking and the butchering of cattle, depending on how far animals are from the homesteads and whether they are found in the safer grasslands or in the more dangerous forested areas (Burton, Brudner, and White 1977, pp. 229–30).

13. In synthesizing a "class analysis perspective" we are aware of deemphasizing the emerging differences and debates between Marxist and dependency theorists. Dependency theorists do not see the evolutionary transition to state society as the unit of investigation. Rather, they emphasize a country's historical embeddedness in the international economic order as shaping underdevelopment and class formation. Many class analysts dealing with Latin America find dependency approaches more useful. In our synthesis of the class analysis approach we have decided not to use the technical vocabulary common to those approaches. Readers interested in further pursuing the issues central to these perspectives should consult the scholarship of social scientists such as Saffioti (1977); Eisenstein (1979); Kuhn and Wolpe (1978); Deere and León de Leal (n.d.); Caplan and Bujra (1979); Sacks (1979).

14. See Leacock (1972) for this revision.

15. See, for example, Sacks (1975), Leacock (1977), Nash (1978, 1980), Etienne and Leacock (1980), and Silverblatt (1978, 1980).

16. See, for example, Leacock (1972), Sacks (1975, 1979), Reiter (1975*b*), Fee and Gonzales (1977).

17. See Fee and Gonzales (1977).

18. Deere (1977*a*), Stavanhagen (1975), Young (1978), Jelin (1976), and Safa (1974) analyze this process.

19. As our discussion of this approach shows, this perspective does not deal only with beliefs about sex roles. Rather, the social ideology approach is concerned with the patterned interconnections among sex role stereotypes, sexual divisions of labor, and institutional access to the total system that perpetuates sexual hierarchy.

20. The analysis of gender, social ideologies (or meaning systems), and behavior is currently being taken in a number of productive directions by anthropologists. For example, Magdoff (1977) examines the cultural construction of identities—including male and female—in a wide-ranging symbolic analysis of central Italian social ideology. Other anthropologists have begun to examine gender as a symbolic system providing fundamental categories for the metaphorical ordering of the natural and social universes. Along these lines, using data from highland New Guinea, Buchbinder and Rappaport (1976) make provocative arguments for a symbolic feedback of cultural meanings from other domains onto gender classifications, and Meggitt (1976) analyzes the symbolic expression of role conflicts which may mystify (for men, in this particular case) sexual hierarchy. Dwyer (1978*b*) has analyzed a single symbolic system (folktales) for images of the sexes in Morocco. She has also proposed that anthropologists study the fit between male and female ideologies in any given cultural system, arguing for a small range of possible types that may have different implications for women's attempts or lack of attempts to change sexual hierarchy (1978*a*, 1978*b*). From another symbolic perspective, Shirley and Edwin Ardener (in Ardener 1975, 1978) speak of the "inarticulateness" of subordinate women who are "mute" because their models for discourse are at variance with those of the dominant groups and so they are forced into a laborious process of translation between

models in order to be heard. Ifeka-Moller's analysis of the Women's War in Nigeria is an insightful, historically grounded analysis from this perspective (1975). From a conceptually insightful, neo-Marxist perspective, Bujra (1979) sees the interrelation of domestic labor and mode of production as shaping women's solidarity and a double consciousness, arising from class antagonism and sexual subordination.

21. Kanter (1977) combines aspects of the division of labor model with social value analysis in her examination of United States corporate life.

22. See Conway (1971–72), Conable (1977), Elshtain (1974).

23. See Goldberg (1973), Gilder (1973), Wilson (1978) for examples of variations in the sociobiology arguments, as well as an important critique by Green (forthcoming).

24. Bamberger (1974) explores a nonbiological ideology for the Amazon. Recently historians have done especially interesting work on the analysis of biology as a symbolic system through which Americans organized sex role ideologies during the Victorian period; see, for example, Conway (1973); Conable (1977); Cominos (1973); Fee (1974); and D. S. Smith (1974). See Hastrup (1978) and Callaway (1978) for anthropological approaches to the "semantics of biology." For biologists looking at the uses of biology, see Hubbard (1979).

IV

Childbirth, Marriage, and Family Politics

The cultural meanings and experiences of marriage, childbirth, and child rearing are shaped by local social ideologies and beliefs, by the social relationships mobilized to carry out and celebrate important life transitions, and by the material conditions of rural society. In this region of the Peruvian *sierra,* women are expected to give birth to children, to play a major role in the early socialization of their off-spring, and eventually to form a family unit independent of their own parents' household. In fact, the overwhelming majority of women fulfill these expectations, but the order of these events varies because formal marriage often follows the birth of children and a period of living with the future spouse. This chapter explores the life cycle of women in Chiuchin and Mayobamba, discussing patterns of change in childbirth, marriage, and family dynamics.

The picture that emerges is one of rapid social change in women's lives as they grow more involved in coastal institutions: in hospitals where they give birth, in schools where their children are socialized after infancy, and in legal marriages which fix rights and duties according to national law as locally administered by the police and courts. Whether such changes enhance women's status and the quality of their lives is the central issue with which we conclude the chapter.

Women's Fertility and Perceptions of Pregnancy

When Western urbanites discuss peasant women's fertility and their attitudes toward pregnancy and childbirth, two stereotypes emerge: one portrays the peasant woman as a buxom, fecund earth mother, giving a religious aura to women's fertility which is symbolically linked to the fertility of the agricultural fields. According to this stereotype, peasants believe that an abundance of crops and large numbers of children are equivalent blessings; the peasant earth mother welcomes pregnancy, gives birth in the fields, and returns to her agricultural labors after only a brief rest.

A second urban Western stereotype envisions the peasant woman as poor, perpetually pregnant, and victimized by her husband's *machismo*. This stereotype sees rural fertility as a prime cause of rural poverty. Men contribute by dominating women and giving them children as a sign of male virility; women comply because they welcome children as allies and hope that one among the many will support the parents in old age. The consequence of such values is a surfeit of children who deplete family resources, overburden rural economies, and further subdivide small landholdings.

Both woman as earth mother and woman as the victim of *machismo* misportray reality. For the most part, these images are inaccurate; to the extent that any aspects of these images ring true, they are over-simplifications. Both stereotypes assume that peasant women are un-conscious of the wider social and economic implications of their fertility and that they are either uninterested or opposed to limiting the number of children they conceive. These images portray peasant women as irrational and self-destructive in their attitudes and prac-tices. In this analysis we attempt to move past such stereotypes toward a more accurate understanding of women's fertility and attitudes to-ward pregnancy and childbirth.

Having children is very positively valued by both women and men in Chiuchin and Mayobamba. Both men and women say that children are the reason that people work. Family sizes vary substantially in Mayobamba and Chiuchin; the total births per woman (for women who have completed their childbearing years) ranges from 0 to 13 with an average of 5.8 births per woman in these two towns. A 22 percent infant and child mortality rate, however, reduces both the range and the average family size. In Chiuchin and Mayobamba the number of children surviving to early adulthood ranges from 0 to 10 per woman with an average of 4.5 survivors to late adolescence.

Women and men have strong opinions about family size. Childless individuals are described as sad cases or considered to be socially and psychologically marginal individuals by their fellow townspeople. Families at the other end of the spectrum with ten to thirteen children are also regarded negatively. In such cases, men are sometimes criticized for not showing enough concern about the number of children their wives have, while the mothers of unusually large families are thought to conceive more often because they fail to wash themselves after having sexual relations.

While women and men highly value children, there are limits on the number of children they see as desirable. Women admire other women who have had only two or three children, commenting that such women have "more pride and status" in the towns. Actually, less than a quarter of the female population past childbearing years has the ideal number of surviving children. The problem in most families is too many rather than too few children in comparison to cultural values. Women talk about the costs of high fertility and show great interest in controlling conception.

In Chiuchin and Mayobamba women do not have reliable ways of limiting the number of children they conceive. After the birth of four or five children, mothers lose their energy and vitality. At that point women say they become frightened and timid when they show signs of pregnancy, such as missing their menses. After four or five children women report that their husbands complain, "How are we going to support more children? *You* just want more children." Thus, women take the overall blame for a couple's excessive fertility.

Women have several birth control strategies.[1] Both men and women from these communities are aware of modern birth control techniques such as the pill. However, they lack both access to adequate information and supplies of such products. Consequently, they must rely upon their own techniques. Women believe that if they douche after intercourse, they will not conceive as often. While women comment that some coastal women drink strong herbal potions in order to abort unwanted pregnancies, there is no evidence that family size is controlled in these rural settlements by inducing abortion. In fact, women agree that this practice is very dangerous and may result in the death of the mother. Those women with several young children try to limit intercourse by sleeping in the kitchen or sleeping surrounded by their offspring. These women observe, however, that if a husband is determined to have intercourse with his wife there is little she can do to avoid it. Finally, women attempt to control fertility by the practice of throwing the placenta into the river after childbirth instead of burying it in the fields as is customary. While not everyone agrees this is an efficacious method, women who have given birth to only two or three children are commonly said to have disposed of the placenta in the river or waded in the river to cool their ovaries so that they will not be able to conceive.[2]

Social expectations narrow the scope of women's activities during pregnancy, but not in a rigid or inflexible way. Women engage in lighter aspects of agriculture, gather firewood, help with domestic animals, work in their businesses, and perform domestic chores. Women argue that continual activity throughout pregnancy results in smaller babies which are much easier to deliver at birth. In the event that a woman becomes especially large because she has not been active, others are quick to criticize her and predict a difficult and perhaps dangerous delivery. In fact, women in the agricultural community who engage in demanding rounds of domestic and agricultural activities are thought to suffer less in childbirth and to recover more rapidly because of the benefits of exercise during pregnancy. Work is also seen as a pain reliever. Women in both communities may go out to nearby fields to engage in light work when they become "tired" of prolonged labor pains.

While women are encouraged to work during pregnancy, there are some situations which it is thought women should avoid in order to protect the developing fetus. For example, women believe that they should restrict their activities so that they are not subject to fright (*susto*) or to lightning, common during the summer months. In effect, these beliefs limit but do not prohibit women's travel to the higher altitudes and distant fields during pregnancy.[3]

If a pregnant woman is subject to fright or struck by lightning, townspeople believe that her child may be born with deformities. In fact, these are explanations offered by parents and local healers for birth defects. Settling on an explanation is undoubtedly very important to parents who are especially saddened if a child is not born fully developed. How much these beliefs limit women's activities during pregnancy is open to question. Women who have given birth to healthy children recount escapes from lightning in a lighthearted fashion while noting that they took the threat seriously at the time.

Childbirth: Variation and Change in Women's Experiences

In her eighth month of pregnancy, Luz kept to her small compound on the edge of Chiuchin, hanging clothes to dry, feeding her household animals, and preparing monotonous meals of boiled potatoes for her children. Although she was only thirty-six she had lost her quick movements, her clear healthy complexion, and her energetic way of moving through the town to sell vegetables from her fields. Yet, it would have been a mistake to have blamed her slow movements, lack of energy, and increasing bitterness on the late stage of this particular pregnancy. Rather, Luz's youth had been eroded by a combination of five of her pregnancies within eight years and by her household's growing poverty. Poverty had become more of a burden because the family had only limited access to agricultural lands, because she had no close relatives in Chiuchin or the higher agricultural towns, and because her husband, a traveling merchant, contributed only irregularly to the family's finances.

Faced with the decision of where to have her ninth child in 1978, Luz said that she strongly preferred to give birth at home in the *sierra*. Her decision was based on past experiences: three of her children were born in urban hospitals on the coast. Luz found treatment in these public hospitals both demeaning and frightening.

> They leave you with nothing to cover yourself and they don't take care of you. You could drown in your own blood and they wouldn't change the sheets. They give you nothing to eat. Once when I was giving birth, all of a sudden I became very cold and asked for an herb tea to warm me. They wouldn't even give me that. They won't bring you a bed pan. The nurses sit in another room, laughing and gossiping. The doctor comes but he just looks at you and tells the nurses to carry on with the delivery. It [childbirth] is much better in the *sierra*. You have someone to help, to bring you something to eat and drink, to take care of you.

Luz's bad experiences in hospitals were due in part to the serious overcrowding and understaffing that occur in public maternity hospitals. These facilities are open to the public at nominal charge, providing basic services. Patients wait in crowded public rooms; later they are given closely spaced beds in rooms with minimal privacy. Rural women complain about the impersonality of these services and the lack of privacy during their brief stays. In Luz's case these feelings were heightened by the fact that she had no coastal relatives to visit her in the hospital. It is assumed that such relatives will care for the patient by providing moral support and by bringing favorite foods to make up for institutionalized care and feeding.

Luz hoped that she would find childbirth in the *sierra* an easier experience. In fact, her last child was born at home without complications. In this region of the *sierra,* ideally, women are waited on by their mothers and by older women who have reputations as successful midwives (*curiosas* or *entendidas*). As labor pains begin, the midwife feels the woman's abdomen, massaging it to position the baby correctly and to ease the pain. Relatives may also prepare oregano tea laced with a sweet liquor or a brandy punch to lessen labor pains. A sweet fruit pudding is given to the woman to provide her with extra energy in the final stages of labor. (This pudding is a counterpart of the glucose solution that coastal hospitals give women for strength during delivery.)

Just before birth women are said to often express the fear that they are going to die. Those who attend the birth respond with encouraging words, telling the woman to be brave. Many women note that at the moment of birth, they feel like urinating and squat only to find to their surprise that the baby is emerging. In the event that the delivery is difficult and prolonged, however, the midwife wraps a band of cloth around the woman's abdomen tightening it to force the baby downward as the mother crouches for birth.

After the child is born on a cloth, the midwife measures the umbilical cord and cuts it; she then bathes the newborn. Women believe that the passage of the placenta is just as difficult for the mother as the actual birth of the child. There are numerous accounts of difficulty with the placenta and the great dangers the afterbirth presents to women. A member of the family buries the placenta in a field near the town.

After the birth, the midwife receives a token payment in cash, a few gifts, and a loyal following of children who have been successfully delivered by her. At this point the mother is treated to a rest which may range in time from several days to three weeks. During convalescence, other children are kept quiet and at a distance. Community women visit the mother during this interval, bringing small gifts of food and chatting with the new mother.

In practice, however, Luz's situation departed from these ideals because her mother died many years ago, and she had no close female relatives. She asked a distant cousin to help and to arrange for a midwife to attend the birth, but knew that midwives would be difficult to find in Chiuchin. Whether or not one finds a skilled midwife, there are real risks in giving birth in rural towns. First, those who assist the birth may have problems removing the placenta. Women believe that if a woman gets cold before the placenta passes, she will close up, making it impossible to remove the afterbirth. In this event, the mother sickens and later dies. Second, women are concerned about the chance of a breech birth in which the baby emerges from the mother feet first. Such births are dangerous in Chiuchin and Mayobamba because more specialized medical attention is a day's travel away by bus or truck. In the event of a breech birth, the mother is fanned and told to keep her mouth open so the baby will get enough air. The greatest fear is that the baby will suffocate or strangle before emerging and that the midwife will be unable to deliver the dead fetus. In such an emergency, the family does everything possible to reposition the fetus for delivery. A man may be brought to hold the woman head down and shake her in a last ditch effort to right the child. Death in childbirth is a very serious concern for the women of these communities. Luz had survived two breech births, and the possibility of another was of great concern to her.

Luz's fears are shared by all women who give birth in these settlements. Yet, in other ways her circumstances were exceptional because she was so isolated in Chiuchin. Most women have networks of female relatives, friends, and even neighbors who help them in the later stages of pregnancy, childbirth, and recovery.

Childbirth practices in Mayobamba and Chiuchin appear to be very similar except for men's involvement. Women in Mayobamba tend to depend on female relatives, usually mothers, and on midwives for assistance. Some women describe the experiences of childbirth as embarrassing because others see them during labor and birth. Some prefer to let only their mothers attend; others reject the help of a midwife, giving birth on their own, and only allow their mothers to enter after the baby is born and they need assistance to cut the umbilical cord. Women who give birth without assistance are singled out by both men and women as being especially valiant. Men are brought in only if the mother begins to have serious difficulty. Generally, men are asked to remain outside the house during births because Mayobambinos believe that a male's presence might "suspend the birth," making labor more difficult for both mother and child.

In Chiuchin, however, men appear to be more involved at births, holding the mother when support is required and helping to bathe the baby. Male assistants may be husbands, relatives, or even close family friends who are called to help if a midwife cannot be located.

Often such men work alongside female relatives. One explanation for the greater involvement of men in Chiuchin is the lack of extensive kinship networks for many individuals in the town. Women who have migrated from higher agricultural towns may have few close relatives to call on for help. If a midwife is not available, these woman are dependent on husbands and even neighbors for assistance. Not all men are willing assistants, but Chiuchin women talk about those who do collaborate in very positive terms. Men recount successful efforts to help women give birth in positive, adventurous stories as well.

Childbirth gives rise to complex attitudes and generational differences among women. Those in their forties and above are much more likely to have given birth at home with the help of relatives and midwives. These women encourage their daughters to stay at home, or return to the *sierra* from Lima to have children so that the family can care for them during their recuperation. Younger women with coastal experience, however, often prefer to give birth in hospitals because they believe that modern medicine minimizes the risk of death in childbirth. Women who have had especially difficult pregnancies and dangerous childbirths attended to on the coast are among those who most strongly advocate hospital deliveries. Discussions between mothers who have lived primarily in the *sierra* and their pregnant daughters who favor coastal childbirth may be difficult for both parties. Mothers find it impossible to leave their agricultural and stock raising duties to make a long and expensive trip to the coast in order to visit daughters during their stays in the hospital. Cultural differences between the coast and the *sierra* make such trips all the more difficult for older women who have often had only limited contact with urban, coastal society.

Thirty years ago, women in Chiuchin and Mayobamba did not give birth in coastal hospitals. Before the late 1940s ground transportation did not reach from the coast to this part of the *sierra,* and the connection between Chiuchin and Mayobamba was a steep, rugged path. Before truck and bus service, it was simply not feasible for women in the later stages of pregnancy to make the 120 kilometer trip to urban medical facilities in Huacho or travel the 250 kilometers to Lima. According to older women, little thought was given to the notion of having children outside one's home community before the late sixties and early seventies.

Today the new generation of women in their twenties and thirties prefers coastal childbirth. Those who still have their children in the *sierra* do so for several reasons. First, when a woman already has a large number of young children or major responsibility in a local business, it may be very difficult for her to find someone to replace her for the several weeks she would have to remain on the coast. Second, a woman must have a network of relatives which includes coastal migrants so that she will have a place to stay while she recuperates from the birth. Finally, coastal childbirth is very expensive, an affordable luxury for local elite women and extraordinarily expensive for everyone else. In 1975 a hospital childbirth cost one local elite woman over $100.00 (that is the equivalent of four months of a wage laborer's earnings) in expenses for transportation, medicines, delivery fees, and diapers. Her expenses were lower than they might have been because maternity hospitals did not charge for hospital beds in honor of the year of the Peruvian woman. An earlier hospital birth in the late 1960s cost this woman a comparable amount of money.

In Mayobamba and Chiuchin there has been a general shift of childbirths to coastal hospitals, even for women who plan to live their lives in the *sierra.* Accompanying this shift is a decline in the number of women who are midwives, that is, who have the experience and facility to be asked to assist in childbirth. Chiuchin presently has only one midwife; Mayobamba has two women with reputations of being especially knowledgeable and efficacious as midwives. Local women say that this represents a notable decline from the numbers of midwives available in the past.

It is possible to argue either that increasing coastal births have contributed to the decline in women specializing in midwifery or that a local decline in specialists has contributed to higher levels of coastal births in hospitals. Whatever the causal connection may be, at present the two trends reinforce each other. Furthermore, these changes have similar consequences: the growing reliance of these women on coastal institutions. On the one hand, women are losing the sources of knowledge with which they medically treated themselves in the past as midwives die without passing on their expertise to daughters. The towns are also losing the publicly respected position of midwife, one of the few specialties open only to women in these settlements. On the other hand, younger women see these changes in a positive light to the extent that they have more confidence in surviving medically difficult births. At this point, most younger women feel that the benefits of hospital births generally outweigh the crowded conditions and impersonality of urban hospitals.

Attitudes toward Children and Young Adults

Women report that men prefer male children as opposed to females. In fact, many families in the agricultural community are said to petition San Juan, the town's patron saint, so that their firstborn will be a boy. Others hold that a firstborn daughter is a sign of prosperity for the family. Parents agree that daughters are very useful in the household and that it would be sad, especially for the mother, if a family had no daughters. Generally, boys are preferred and their births especially celebrated because they are thought to be less trouble and less cause for concern. Daughters are felt to require greater parental responsibility, and there is greater uncertainty about their futures.

Attitudes toward the sex of children at birth relate to parents' view of the contributions children will make to the household as they grow up and marry. Many parents assume that sons will make longer term contributions to the parental household because they do not definitively join another household with marriage. Sons, when they marry, are in a position to decide where their family will live and what kinds of social and economic ties will be maintained with close kin. In contrast, daughters fall under the authority of husbands and their in-laws at marriage. Husbands may or may not facilitate close ties with the relatives of their wives.

The relationships between parents, daughters, and sons-in-law often give rise to tension because of the conflicting demands placed on a woman as daughter and wife. In some cases, fathers have blocked their daughter's marriages and, in effect, forced them to become single mothers in order to retain their services and loyalty at home. In other cases, husbands have gone to great lengths to promote distance between wives and their families. Tensions between fathers and husbands can be fueled by class differences between families, by rivalries for local economic and political dominance, and by patterns of respect that call on husbands to defer to fathers-in-law. Brothers often become involved in disputes on the side of the sister. Brothers are often emotionally close to sisters and are very sensitive to their physical abuse and economic exploitation by husbands.[4] One result of the structural rivalry between natal family and husbands, however, is that daughters cannot be counted on to contribute economically to their parents, though a great deal of emotional support may continue to flow between daughters and parents throughout their lives.

Women are not passive actors in these family dramas. In fact, at least part of the father-husband tension is due to women holding firmly onto kinship ties with their natal families. Women understand that while parents may limit their investments in daughters, nevertheless, kin ties to blood relatives may be more enduring than relationships established through marriage. Such kin ties can be mobilized for moral support and for access to resources such as employment, education, and commercial and agricultural products outside one's home community. Women are reluctant to cut themselves off from such networks at marriage.

Conceptions of personality in Chiuchin and Mayobamba reinforce women's ties with their kin. Both men and women say that girls are more sentimental and more emotionally involved with close relatives than are boys. Women are said to be more person-oriented because of their "female character" and because they have greater opportunities to socialize while they work. Men are noted for "stronger characters" and are believed to be less dependent on others because their work and aspirations take them away from their families and often their home communities. In contrast, women are thought to have a much harder time away from relatives, worrying, "Perhaps my family isn't well, perhaps my child or my brother is sick." One consequence of these cultural personality traits (in addition to reinforcing a sexual division of labor) is that they can be used by women to maintain social and economic kin networks which are independent of their husbands.

While they are young, both boys and girls stay with their mothers. Children begin to share in household tasks by the age of five or six. They care for animals, carry water, mind younger siblings, and help gather brush for cooking fires. Fathers say they have little to do with the socialization of daughters: "What would we know about the things which concern women?" This comment reflects the sexual division of labor which assigns to women the responsibilities for cooking, harvest storage and management, clothing production, laundry, and child care. Housekeeping per se is at a minimum in these homes where conspicuous consumption and home decorating do not occupy people's time. There is nothing frivolous, no attempt at self-expression or fulfillment in the decoration of a house. There is no invented labor in household tasks. Given the general lack of mechanization, electric power, refrigeration, and running water, the performance of such tasks as cooking, laundry, and clothing production take awesome amounts of time, effort, and endurance. Little girls assist their mothers in lighter domestic tasks, in pasturing sheep, hauling water, and running errands. They are taught to serve their brothers at the table because they are boys.

Girls are thought to mature more rapidly than boys, and by the time they are fourteen, are said to be more socially developed, more experienced than boys of the same age who are more timid and less likely to act on their own initiative. At fourteen or fifteen boys are still considered to be children who have to be supervised, while girls are believed to have the maturity to set up their own households although they are considered too young to marry.

By eighteen or twenty, boys have gained independence and are thought to have a greater sense of responsibility in their work. At this point, young men and women change places in the social world of these towns; men emerge as individually dominant and women structurally subordinate. One woman described the outcome of this transformation in sex roles in the following terms:

> When a couple marries, the woman is under the disposition of the man. The woman is an auxiliary. What the man thinks is given value in the home. Women's opinions are not given the same value, they are not accepted by the husband. The husband gives his opinion and the wife agrees whether his opinions are good or bad. She just says, "That's fine."

With marriage, a new phase of women's subordination is crystallized. To understand the mechanisms through which women are subordinated in the domestic sphere, we must take a closer look at the variations in marital arrangements and the distribution of authority in the family.

Patterns of Marital Life

In the Andes, marriage is a particularly complex issue due to the diverse forms of marital unions and to the substantial change such unions have undergone in this century.[5] While it is evident that the vast majority of women marry, they do not all establish the same types of unions. In addition, women often move from one type of marital union to another during the course of their lives. The predominant types of unions have changed over time. From shortly after the Spanish conquest until the first part of this century, Catholic priests resided in the Mayobamba-Chiuchin region, and marriages involved religious ceremonies in addition to indigenous traditions regulated by community elders. For the last thirty years, however, the influence of the clergy has been in steady decline and a priest no longer resides in the district. Religious marriage in the Catholic Church is now infrequent, and elders do not play significant roles in arranging marriages of local youths. Today, Mayobambinos and Chiuchinistas find that civil marriage by the district secretary meets their needs for a publicly legitimized union.

In the Chiuchin-Mayobamba region, local communities regulated marriage practices in the past through mechanisms such as trial marriage, arranged marriages, and the use of powerful intermediaries for marital negotiations between families. In many areas, trial marriage practices (called *serviancuy*) died out in this century. Mayobambinos recall that a couple established a household together, usually in the home adjoining the home of the boy's family, after a period of courtship. The couple lived together for about a year and if all went well they officially married after this trial period. Children might result from the first years of trial marriage, but this was not a requirement for formalizing the union. The transition from trial marriage to formal marriage was controlled by community officials. It was their responsibility to periodically round up all the couples who had lived together for more than a year and hold them until their godparents arranged for the legal marriage of the young couples. These spring round-ups involved communal celebrations and resulted in high rates of formalized unions among townspeople. Some aspects of trial marriage are still practiced in neighboring Tongos and in towns to the north such as Vicos.

Townspeople of the great-grandparental and grandparental generations in Chiuchin and Mayobamba, however, do have detailed memories of arranged marriages because many of them were married this way. In arranging the marriages of their children, parents balanced local demographic realities with the economic benefits of strategic marital ties and a concern with finding hardworking partners for their children. Many older women portray themselves as the unwilling partners to arranged marriages. Some women remember the frightening experience of being locked in a house with a bridegroom who was a virtual stranger. Others recount stories of being carried off by a man who took advantage of a girl's youth and sought parental approval after the fact. Whether marriages were arranged beforehand or recognized later, these unions were initiated by men in their roles of godparents and parents or by the groom himself. Mothers are said to have had little influence on decisions regarding their daughters' marriages. (Only in the event of chronic physical abuse did older kinswomen intervene to punish the misbehaving husband.) Until relatively recently, young women themselves are not portrayed as having effective veto powers in the event that they did not care for a particular partner in an arranged marriage.

In the present, community control of marriages has weakened. Most marital unions now begin when a couple decides to live together, establishing an independent household into which children are born. These nonlegalized unions (known as *convivencias*) do not give parents or the community many formal opportunities to intervene in the domestic affairs of a couple. Most women begin their first union at about nineteen years of age and have their first child shortly thereafter. Young women agree that having children any younger causes the mother to suffer. While most marriages begin as consensual unions, there is a tendency for most to be legally formalized through civil marriage in later years. Some women, however, find themselves in a pattern of cyclical consensual unions, never marrying legally (Morris 1970, pp. 125, 150).

Our data confirms the findings of Morris that "*sierra* wives indicate a strong preference for [formal] marriage over consensual unions and strong support for the position that women have more family rights in legal marriages than in consensual unions" (1970, p. 160). The disadvantages of consensual unions for women are several. First, there is always the possibility that a woman will be abandoned with the added responsibility of children. Second, if the man should die, the woman and her children may not be able to inherit property or animals and may even lose possession of what she brought into the joint household. The husband's brothers often attempt to claim the deceased's property for their own children. Joint acquisitions from the period of *convivencia* as well as property brought into the relationship by only one partner may be difficult to disentangle. Finally, unless a woman's children have been legally recognized by the father, they too will fail to inherit. Thus, a woman in a consensual union runs the risk of spending her efforts to acquire and work property in which she and her children may never exercise a legal claim.

Women in Mayobamba know that this fate has befallen their friends. Lourdes lived with one of the wealthiest men in Mayobamba, Simon, for thirty years. She bore him three daughters and no sons. Simon, an irascible man, refused to marry Lourdes and denied recognition to their three daughters. After thirty years of *convivencia* with Lourdes, Simon fell in love with the young school teacher, recently posted to Mayobamba, and banished Lourdes from his home. She left, taking nothing with her but two cows he unwillingly relinquished. Mayobambinos, both men and women, viewed Simon's behavior as outrageous. One man commented, "How absurd to receive two cows for thirty years of work and three children." The marriage to the school teacher did not last; she left Simon after less than a year. He in turn divorced his bride for abandoning the home, thereby insuring that she could make no future claims upon his property.

Simon's three daughters were adults when he threw their mother out. Two of the daughters married; the third, Francisca, is a single mother with two children. Francisca has decided to care for her aging father, cooking and performing the other domestic tasks for him. Francisca's decision has not been without its costs; the father of her second child refuses to marry her, in part because he cannot tolerate her father and refuses to put himself in a deferential son-in-law relationship to him. In spite of this, Francisca has decided that her best option is to remain in her father's household. He has not recognized her, but she hopes that one day he will. He has made gifts of cattle and small plots of land to her youngest son and this gives her hope that his generosity will improve with age. Her mother, Lourdes, now lives alone. She has access to communal fields and is assisted by her daughters. She is relatively impoverished and stands as a commonly evoked example to Mayobamba women of the risks that *convivencia* entails.

When a consensual union, resulting in children, dissolves within a year or two, the woman becomes a single mother (*madre soltera*), like Lourdes's daughter Francisca. The single mother is disadvantaged in that she does not have the regular contribution of a husband's labor in her household nor the benefits of access to his land. Some single mothers never live in consensual unions, becoming pregnant without establishing a separate household and continuing to live in their parents' home. Other single mothers are widows who have children after the death of their husbands without remarrying or forming a stable consensual union. In Mayobamba roughly one-quarter of the female population has the status of single motherhood for part of their life cycles. The level of deprivation experienced by a single mother depends on the economic standing of her family and their attitudes toward her.

In these towns, men and women have different views of the desirability of marital forms. Some men, while recognizing that legal marriage gives women greater rights in the family, say that they prefer to remain single. By this, they mean that they prefer a consensual union, not that they want to live alone. Men want the services that a woman provides as a wife, and, like women, men desire children. Yet, at least in theory, a man can legally recognize his children and incur some responsibility for their support without contracting a legal marriage to the mother. (In this event, though, the father must be willing to go through complicated procedures to legally recognize his children and file a legally valid will.) This option is important to men who uniformly believe that "if one does not have children there is no reason to work. If there is no one to inherit the fruits of a man's labor, why labor?"

Men's reluctance to contract a legal union seems to be based on the sense that these unions give women more claims on a man and limit his access to other women. Yet, what a man wants for himself and what he wants for his daughters are often distinct preferences. For example, one older Mayobamba man described his emulation of an uncle who had managed to retain his single status while fathering a large family of children whom he legally recognized. While admiring the uncle as a masculine ideal, the Mayobambino eventually married the mother of the majority of his children and insisted that both his daughters contract legal marriages instead of consensual unions. He argues that he wanted his daughters to have more security, and legal marriage would give them that. His wife also demanded legal marriages for her daughters. One of his daughters added the following analysis:

> When two people decide not to marry legally but to live together, it's the man who makes this decision. When the man isn't very interested and

hasn't made up his mind, then they stay together as *convivientes* for a period of time until they decide to formalize and legalize the union. But lately people are marrying formally. They take the legal route. There is damage to both if they don't, especially for the woman. The woman must always look for security. The majority of men would prefer to just live with a woman because they don't want to take on the responsibility. But now a young man's parents will insist that he marry. When the parents aren't watchful, however, the couple may just continue to live together and not marry.

Marriages are no longer rooted in the customary law of these rural towns. In the present, legal norms and administrators come from outside the community, replacing traditional intermediaries. Civil marriage occurs at the district level, tying local populations to national legal codes as enforced by local governmental officials and by the national police. In both communities roughly three-quarters of the female population legally marry at some point in their life.

Today, both sets of parents may promote civil marriages. The woman's parents do not want to see their daughter mistreated with limited legal recourse for the support of her children if she is abandoned. Also, children born of consensual unions are illegitimate. Though there is no great moral stigma attached locally to this status, some parents worry that illegitimate children will suffer special difficulties when they register for school or look outside the region for work. The man's parents further fear that their son will tire of the woman and leave her for another. In this event, his parents grow concerned over the possibility of legal suits being filed against their family as a whole seeking recognition and support for the children.

One exception to the parental preference for civil marriage may be developing for single self-supporting daughters who work as merchants in Chiuchin. One mother objected to the marriage of her daughter who already had children. She reasoned that if her daughter legally married, she would be obligated to have more children by the new husband. In this instance, the mother felt that having a larger family would have been a serious mistake for her daughter, overtaxing her physically and economically.

Decision Making and Women's Influence in the Home

Our analysis finds that while women are generally successful in maneuvering men to marry formally, they exercise very limited influence once in these relationships. Women's contributions to the maintenance of the family are critically important. Whether or not a family eats, the level of its daily consumption, the care of children, and the production and cleanliness of clothing are all dependent on their managing abilities and daily labors. Both men and women may agree that women should have special responsibilities in the home and a degree of authority over those areas in which they are solely responsible, yet this level of specialization and responsibility is never intended to challenge male authority. Data from Mayobamba and Chiuchin suggest that women's decision-making power, while greatest in the home, is still severely restricted there.

Within a general pattern of male control, townspeople in Mayobamba and Chiuchin do talk about variations with regard to individual men's and women's participation in family decision making. Both sexes recognize a small but significant number of families in which women have broad influence in the family. An example of the forcefulness of a Mayobamba woman's personality is described by another woman in the following words:

> Because of her character, Mercedes [the successful co-owner of a Mayobamba restaurant] makes 70 percent of the decisions in the family. She's very influential, putting in orders for the store based on her suggestions. She decides whether to pursue business, how to buy products, whether to enlarge the stock. She's very dynamic and helps the family get ahead.

Mercedes takes an unusually active role in family finances. She is said to advise her husband about financial opportunities and to block unwise investments. Her husband is said "to accept this advice, taking it into account. He doesn't buy if she opposes a purchase. If she doesn't want to rent community fields, they don't." While Mercedes is admired as a brave, independent, energetic woman, her husband is soundly condemned for his lack of control in the family. One Mayobambina described his reputation in the following terms:

> Townspeople say that her husband is henpecked. Both men and women say, "He's a *saco largo* [dominated by his wife] and isn't good for anything."

Rough jesting among men about being a *saco largo* (literally, wearing a "long coat" which describes the dress of an older married man) indicates at least some public perception that marriage curtails a man's freedom, subjecting him to the attempts of a woman to control his behavior, attempts which he should resist. The force of the taunt suggests that women do try to exercise some control over men, that the exercise of such influence is associated with marriage, and that men use this form of teasing to reinforce male resistance to parity, or even negotiating decisions, with women. In this cultural system, authority in the family appears to be conceived of as limited in quantity. Thus, a woman's extension of competence in decision making is seen as inevitably challenging and undermining her husband's position.

Men are also subject to strong criticism for doing work that is culturally associated with women in the sexual division of labor. Men who carry babies or take care of the family's children by preparing them for school, who milk cows, or carry water from the town square are ridiculed. Each of these tasks is perceived as women's work. Men are considered to be weak, dominated by their wives, or unable to control women's behavior if they do women's work. Occasionally, a husband "becomes accustomed to this (i.e., helping with women's work) and doesn't complain much." More generally, men refuse to help their wives in order to avoid criticism.

Women's authority in the home is believed to increase in the couple's old age. Women make more domestic decisions and become more demanding of their husbands. Men are said to spend more time at home instead of stopping at local taverns after work. As men's physical strength wanes in their late fifties, they are said not to be "so proud and commanding any more." Even men who were especially dominant (*mandones*) in their earlier years are believed to mellow somewhat with age.

While dominance in interpersonal relations within the family may become increasingly negotiable with age, men retain their structurally powerful position in the community. In addition, if a couple has never married civilly or if a common-law husband has not legally recognized his children, the man may reassert dominance at any time by hinting that he might marry another woman or select other heirs for his homestead, land, and livestock. Community elders have in fact used just such tactics to maintain firm control over their families in their declining years.

To examine further the patterns of authority and decision making in the family, we now turn to problems that rural families commonly face: (*a*) decisions about the allocation of limited resources to children; (*b*) the impact of endemic male drunkenness on family income and savings; and (*c*) the structure and regulation of domestic disputes. In each case, power relations in the family are revealed through the definition of the problem, the ranking of alternative solutions, and the implications of solutions for men and women.

Within the family, mothers do not have the ultimate word on the allocation of limited resources for their children's futures. Generally, fathers take the responsibility for important educational decisions, believing that they are better able to judge alternatives. Girls frequently recall their efforts to convince their fathers to let them continue studies. This is not to say that mothers have no influence on such decisions. In fact, our data suggest that when there is a disagreement about the future of children, women are effective lobbyists for their offspring. Moreover, not all mothers are in favor of the higher educational aspirations of their daughters.

Women may also adopt strategies that minimize conflict, pain, or difficulties, which in some instances means adopting strategies that perpetuate rather than alleviate subordination. For instance, a mother may focus her encouragement and financial support on an elder son, at the expense of daughters (and younger sons), especially when the family's economic resources are limited.[6] The mother favors a boy child because, as she analyzes the situation, his chances are better than a daughter's in the economy. In fact, by virtue of being male, the son will undoubtedly have greater access to cash earnings, to capital through *comunero* status or inheritance, and to more lucrative occupations outside the community that require educational backgrounds. The daughters' opportunities are seen as more problematic and females are given lower priority. This strategy may increase the mother's chances of financial support if she is abandoned or needs help from her children in old age. Nevertheless, this ranking of priorities contributes to lower educational achievement and limited options for daughters, despite their individual talents or potentials. Such strategies clearly reinforce existing patterns of female subordination.

Another dimension of the very real differences of power within the family is reflected in women's continual concern with the effects of alcohol consumption on their husbands and families. Male drunkenness is a serious social problem, one which cross-cuts communities and differences of wealth within communities. Women are especially critical of the impact of drinking on the family economy.[7] Married women and those in consensual unions agree that whereas women may be given the temporary responsibility for guarding money, men can always demand savings and spend money as they wish. Women have little success in denying their husbands money, even when they fear that earnings will be squandered. A substantial part of family cash resources is lost to liquor consumption. Husbands confront wives who are reluctant to give them money for visits to local taverns saying, "Give me money, little child. I earned it and I want to spend it drinking it with my friends. Otherwise what is the point of my working?"

Some women say that a wife should attempt "to dominate" her husband. "Domination" in this context involves strategies that successfully get husbands to control drinking by appealing to the man's sense of responsibility to his children. Women say that a wife must attempt to control her husband from the beginning of the marriage. When asked if they have been successful in this, most women reply with resigned smiles that, although they have tried, they have not managed it.

A second economic consequence of drunkenness is the loss of male labor force participation as a result of alcoholism. Morris et al. (1968, p. 18) estimate that Mayobamba men spend up to one quarter of their time in some stage of drunkenness: either getting drunk, being drunk, or recovering from drunkenness. Women's inability to stop or to control this behavior is a reflection of male-female authority patterns within the home. Women try to convince husbands not to go off to situations where they are likely to drink, because once the men start there is no stopping until everyone is drunk. Men on the other hand say that they drink because it is the only way they can fully relax, the only time they can be emotional, joke, laugh, and enjoy other men. In these towns, once a man has begun drinking he is obligated to remain until everyone has treated the assembled group to a round of beer or rum. Reciprocal invitations are an important expression of friendship, and some tavern owners in Chiuchin play on this value by treating patrons to a round in order to spur them on. Women are not a part of these reciprocal exchanges, and if a woman interferes and attempts to get her husband away from the group, the other men will taunt her husband, calling him henpecked.

Women associate male drinking with wife beating and family violence. According to Mayobamba women, when men get drunk they are likely to behave aggressively, sometimes beating their wives. After sobering up these same men are said to deny violence or to suggest that when they drink they lose awareness of their actions.

Wife beating is the primary reason women give for wives' leaving their husbands. Few women, however, actually leave their homes permanently. It is much more likely, according to Mayobamba women, that a man leaves a woman, usually for another woman. Wives rarely leave their husbands because their alternatives outside marriage are so few, especially in agricultural communities. If forced to leave without her children, a mother would be disconsolate and strongly criticized as an irresponsible woman who abandoned her family. But if a woman decides to take her children with her, she will have a difficult time finding work. The only employment that she is likely to find would be outside the community as a domestic servant in an urban center. Yet, few employers will hire women as servants if they have children living with them. Moreover, life as a domestic is viewed as inferior to life in the agricultural communities by women who explain that at least in Mayobamba one has a home of one's own. If a woman attempts to remain in her home community, her parents may not be anxious to take her back because of the financial burden this will impose. Parents may argue that it is the husband's responsibility to maintain his wife and children. Apparently, some parents feel that a woman without a husband will eventually take another man as her lover, causing additional criticism of the family. Thus, parents may try to send their daughter back to her husband in the event of domestic disputes.

When a man's treatment of his wife is flagrantly abusive, mechanisms of social control may intervene. For instance, it is possible for older women to take on a man who has truly and outrageously gone beyond acceptable limits. The older woman punishes the erring man with a beating. Since the differences in their strength are considerable, the mock beating has symbolic value.[8]

Family violence and other domestic problems can also be called to the attention of the national police who have a regional post in Chiuchin. Police officers carry out a broad range of duties as official message carriers, election monitors, and investigators of complaints filed against townspeople. They investigate charges by interviewing all concerned parties, drawing their own conclusions about the guilt or innocence of the parties involved, and sending reports on to the courts. Wife-beating cases are considered to be less serious offenses, and are generally handled by two regional justices of the peace. More serious crimes against property and persons are sent on to coastal courts in Huacho.

Wives file legal complaints against husbands for beatings or for failure to support children. In the case of physical abuse, the legal system allows women to seek medical expenses or to argue physical abuse as a ground for legal separation. It is not clear that the potential of such judgments deters husbands or that wives see the courts as successfully representing their interests. With no local medical facilities, medical expenses are not meaningful judgments unless a woman is so severely beaten that she must seek professional help in a larger town. Separation and divorce are options seldom exercised because they present women with the added burden of seeking employment elsewhere and leaving children with relatives, or moving back into their parents' homestead.

Other domestic legal cases involve single mothers or secondary wives who seek economic support as well as legal recognition of their children by the father. While fathers socially acknowledge paternity and all children are told who their fathers are, unmarried mothers' claims on the fathers of their children are very limited unless legal paternity is established. Generally, fathers are able to avoid suits by occasionally contributing to their children's economic welfare or by helping older children find employment. When mothers subsequently establish stable *convivencias* or marry other men, earlier claims are suspended and economic support dries up quickly. In any event, these children stand almost no chance of inheriting from their fathers because of the competing claims from legitimate members of the immediate family.

The women most likely to attempt to force legal recognition and support of their children are abandoned secondary wives who have had large numbers of children with the same man. Locally, both men and women agree that such women are fools. One woman summarized community sentiment directed toward these women:

> Anyone can have one child and claim that she was deceived by a man. A woman could even have a second child just to compel the man to recognize his children. But a third child [outside a stable *convivencia* or a marriage] . . . then, you are asking for trouble.

While local police officials see their duty to investigate the charges in these cases, by and large they find themselves in agreement with the general sentiment regarding the women. Undoubtedly their attitudes are shaped by their own domestic situations. Members of the national police are notorious for having multiple families, the result of frequent moves to different parts of the country.

Returning to the Western urban stereotypes of peasant women, it should now be clear that the women of Chiuchin and Mayobamba are neither earth mothers nor self-destructive victims of male virility. Such stereotypes oversimplify and distort reality, portraying women exclusively as biological creatures who fulfill their destiny through the physical acts of conception and childbirth. Those who hold images of women that focus on biology may be blinded to the historical dimension of women's activities in childbirth, marriage, and the daily round of family life. Certainly these images fail to capture the complexity and variability of social values and cultural beliefs, patterns of decision making in the family, and people's knowledge of and access to options in the broader society. Only by examining changes in belief and behavior from the perspective of the inhabitants of rural communities can we break through the stereotyped assumptions that peasant women are irrational, self-destructive, and fatalistic.

Women's and men's activities surrounding childbirth, marriage, and family life have changed with time as have the social and political implications of these activities. In the not too distant past, these peasant women gave birth at home in the *sierra* under the care of local midwives. They participated in arranged marriages which were formalized in local celebrations and Catholic rituals. Older female relatives and godparents intervened in the event of domestic troubles, and customary law regulated legitimacy and inheritance. We can still see the imprint of the past on these towns, yet much has changed in women's lives.

Perhaps the most significant change has been the increasing penetration of national society into peasant women's lives. Childbirth increasingly takes place in urban hospitals, *convivencias* are formalized by civil marriages, family disputes may be taken to the national police for adjudication, and national legal codes define legitimacy and inheritance. These changes have undermined the position of local midwives, marriage intermediaries, and elder women who ritually punish violent husbands. In their place, new local officials—such as the regional secretary who marries couples according to national law—link local populations to national society. Other officials such as the national police or an occasional practical nurse are brought from outside the communities as rural extensions of national bureaucracies. The legitimacy of all these officials rests firmly outside the towns in the national bureaucracies that sponsor them.

When forces outside the community set up legal standards to which the family must respond, women cannot be said to be in control of a separate sphere in the home. In much the same way as it would be inadequate to characterize peasant women and men as members of closed corporate communities operating within their own separate sphere of control, so too the analogy stressing domestic autonomy for women breaks down.

Inheritance, property, and legitimacy are defined by the legal system and interpreted in light of local practices. National policies are manipulated and transformed both by coastal intermediaries and by local populations.[9] Individuals have learned to use national law to regulate interpersonal relationships in order to cope with change and to assert a measure of control over their own social positions. For instance, parents now attempt to use the threat of civil suits to promote the legal marriages of their children and to avoid the legal conflicts arising from unstable *convivencia* arrangements. On the other hand, older men may attempt to maintain an upper hand in the family by never completing the legal paper work to legitimize their children or name them as heirs according to national law. In both cases, the frame of reference for structuring interpersonal rights and duties has shifted to an external legal system. Rural inhabitants have become specialists in controlling family behavior by evoking the *potential* of the law to define social relationships.

Looking at the changing pattern of interpersonal behavior in the *sierra* towns, one sees that in some instances increasing national integration has reinforced existing sexual hierarchies in marriage and the family. In addition, integration has weakened women's traditional sources of influence and knowledge; older women have lost influential and prestigious roles as midwives and as punishers of violent behavior. At the same time, women have gained some measure of access to modern medicine which has the potential to reduce substantially women's mortality and their fear of death in childbirth. Increasing contact with national institutions such as hospitals has not been universally positive as the case of Luz demonstrates. Nor are women in the position to regulate their own access to modern medicine as in the case of badly needed birth control measures which rural women know are available to some families in the broader society. Marriage and family politics suggest that the relationships between men and women undergo change due to the integration of coastal and national institutions into rural life. However, the full significance of the changes occurring in women's lives requires a frame of reference that incorporates additional data from economics and politics.

Notes

1. Remarkably little is known about the reliability of indigenous birth control techniques, particularly with reference to Latin America. The *Population Index* from 1976 through 1979 cites only four studies, two done in Africa and two in Asia. Leading specialists in Latin American population studies point out that this is a serious gap in the literature that affects our understanding and the quality of population policy directed at these groups (Iëda S. Wiarda, personal communication). For the Aymara of Bolivia, Buechler and Buechler (1971, pp. 20–23) report practices of induced abortion and infanticide to limit family size.

2. Water is a recurrent symbol in *sierra* beliefs concerning women. Water appears to represent the neutralization of women's fertility. For instance, menstruating women are warned not to pass the river at the access to a large section of communal fields in Mayobamba. If a woman does wade across, it is believed that she will stop menstruating, her stomach will become bloated with water, and she might die. Women are said to be frightened of crossing the river during the first day or two of their periods and to work primarily at domestic tasks rather than in the fields. Additional water symbolism associates the death of premature babies or babies who die in childbirth without being baptized with the river. These unbaptized creatures cannot be buried in the holy ground of the cemeteries. Rather, the bodies are buried in deep pools of water in the river. Women's actions during menses, pregnancy, or childbirth, however, are not believed to affect the fertility of agricultural lands.

3. Locally stories are told which demonstrate the dangers of wandering. For example, one woman was said to have suffered from magical fright after she went to a high ravine outside town and heard strange sounds. Townspeople interpreted this fright as an arbitrary punishment from the *abuelos,* or ancestor spirits, who were said to have penetrated the woman as she was startled. Other stories are used to show how lightning pursues pregnant women who go out to the fields during the rainy season from November to February. Women fear that the energy from lightning bolts will penetrate them if they are unable to flee a storm in time.

Women are also expected to avoid actions during pregnancy which are believed to result in children that are difficult to handle in infancy. For example, pregnant women are cautioned not to become attached to young animals, like baby pigs or lambs. Otherwise, it is believed that their newborns will display the characteristic gestures of these young animals. Little pigs are thought to be very nervous and bothersome. When a baby is nervous, continually turning its head from side to side, it is likened to lambs. When infants behave in these ways, their mothers' actions toward domestic animals during pregnancy are said to have influenced the child. Once again, these seem to be standard explanations for later events rather than strongly held prohibitions for women.

4. Lambert (1977) notes the dual allegiance to siblings and spouses as a general Andean pattern. Cornejo (1978, pp. 4–6) discusses the preference for male children and the respect to be accorded males.

5. Most studies of the Andes stress different forms of marriage and protracted stages leading to formal marriages. See for example, Buechler and Buechler (1971); Hardman (1976); Isbell (1978); Bolton (1977). In very traditional, precapitalist communities some authors stress extremely high rates of marital stability after marriage; for example, O. Harris (1978) and Lambert's discussion of variations (1977).

6. For Vitocota, Bolivia, Hardman (1976) also finds that women stress formal schooling for sons. Her explanation appears to differ from ours in scope: "If a family cannot afford to send all its children to school, preference will be given to the boys; the choice, however, reflects attitudes in the dominant culture, not among the Aymara" (page 6).

7. See also Harris (1978).

8. Davis (1975, pp. 124–51) makes a similar point about the symbolic use of beating in early modern France. Isbell reports that for southern Peru, women jointly attack violent men, especially if they are outsiders (personal communication). Babb, however, notes that for Vicos, women were badly victimized and without effective recourse, by *hacienda* owners and a notorious *mestizo* from a neighboring town (1976).

9. Cole and Wolf (1974) discuss the local-national interaction concerning inheritance in their study of an alpine valley. See Bourque and Warren (1980) and Bourque and Palmer (1975) for variations in local responses to national policy.

V

The Sexual Division of the Economy

Sexual divisions of labor are not given in nature. Rather they are historical and cultural constructs that lead to patterned specializations in work and economic involvements. The importance of sex—as opposed to age, kinship, class, or ethnicity—as a way of organizing work varies greatly from society to society. In this region of rural Peru if one were to observe people's economic activities throughout an annual cycle, one would conclude that there are remarkable overlaps in women's and men's work and, thus, only a minimal sexual division of labor. Virtually none of the tendencies for sexual specialization would appear to be obligatory, monopolized by a single sex, or without important exceptions.

Nevertheless, in talking with Mayobambinos and Chiuchinistas, one discovers that these populations perceive important differences in the kinds of work associated with each sex and in the value given to sex-specific work. Clearly, in these cases, people are focusing their attention on those tasks in which the tendency for sexual specialization is strongly marked.

In this chapter we explore both the overlapping and specialized economic involvements of women and men in Chiuchin and Mayobamba. We will analyze observable patterns of economic participation as well as men's and women's perceptions and evaluations of the sexual division of labor. As our analysis will show, the exceptions to joint participation in economics are not random, though at first they may appear to represent an odd combination of seemingly unconnected activities. Our analysis finds that women are excluded from crucial resources and from the full economic benefit of their work by a strong sexual division of labor at a few key junctures and by a social ideology which justifies such specializations.

The mechanisms which exclude women from key tasks and resources vary significantly between Chiuchin and Mayobamba because of the different economic bases of these two communities. By concentrating on broader mechanisms and social processes—rather than focusing solely on tasks from which women are excluded—we are able to show much more comprehensively how women's status is perpetuated in rural communities. In comparing the two settlements, we find that women have broader access to crucial resources and occupy a wider range of class positions in the commercial town. In other words, although there are still significant sexual differences in access to resources and economic participation, the mechanisms which foster the economic dependency of women on men are, at this time, weaker in the cash economy. Our analysis leads us to ask if women's generally greater access to capital and cash earnings in Chiuchin translates into a broader social and perceptual parity of the sexes in the commercial settlement.

Women's Participation and the Issue of Control in an Agrarian Economy

In Mayobamba, agriculture and stock raising are labor intensive, requiring the coordinated efforts of extended families, of cooperative work groups, and, on larger fields, of wage laborers. While some townspeople wonder if rototillers someday might be brought into the community for more efficient field preparation, at this point agriculture has not been mechanized. Most tools that peasants use in cultivation, however, are purchased from coastal sources. Agriculturalists use a wide range of hand tools: store-bought shovels, machetes, axes, hand hoes, metal digging sticks, as well as locally made wooden plows. Draft animals are used to plow the fields and burros to transport harvests back to town.

One should be careful not to project an image of an unchanging ecological balance onto Mayobamba's labor intensive agriculture. In the past, Mayobamba's peasants specialized in agriculture for subsistence and exchange with those neighboring communities that exploited contrasting ecological zones. Potato surpluses were bartered for wool and other animal products offered by herders from the nonarable altitudes above the arable zones of Mayobamba. Herders brought llama pack trains to the town, assisted in local harvests, and engaged in trade. Although some of these earlier forms of exchange

are still practiced, in this century Mayobamba's economy has undergone a substantial shift away from production for subsistence and
interzonal barter. This shift has been marked by important changes in
land tenure patterns and by a reorganization of agricultural production by Mayobambinos to respond to trading possibilities with the
urban cash economies.

According to local oral histories, townspeople began a local transformation of production by expanding private landholdings in
Mayobamba earlier in this century. Traditionally the community gave
all households equivalent rights to communal lands on which to cultivate subsistence crops of potatoes. Such land was controlled and allocated by the community; individuals could not barter or sell these
parcels. Below the areas of communal lands were parcels appropriate
for a wider variety of crops due to their warmer microclimates and to
their access to irrigation canals. Mayobambinos say that these parcels
were transformed into private landholdings by individual appropria-
tion followed by the construction of stone boundary walls and the
extension of irrigation canals. Unlike communal lands, private parcels
could be bought, inherited, and sold. The division of alienable agricultural lands into private holdings was well established by the early
decades of this century. One result of private ownership has been the
institutionalization of differences in wealth among townspeople relating to the quantity and quality of private lands which have been retained or successfully accumulated in their families.

As Mayobamba moved toward greater integration with the national
cash economy, livestock and fodder became increasingly important in
local production, and sheep and cattle gradually replaced plant products as the chief source of individual wealth. This change in production is a direct result of closer ties with coastal markets such as the
capital city, Lima.

While certain sectors of the local economy expanded, participation
in coastal markets undercut the production of other subsistence
crops, especially grains such as wheat and corn. Once grown in abundance, these grains are cultivated now only in limited quantities. A
local mill formerly ground corn and wheat but no longer functions;
flour now arrives from coastal suppliers and is purchased for cash.
Adobe ovens, which all highland communities maintained earlier in
this century, are now in disuse and centralized bakeries in Chiuchin
supply the region's bread made from flour brought from the coast.

These changes fit an overall pattern of increasing integration of peasant and urban economies. As the local production of subsistence crops narrows, continued access to communal lands has become important to Mayobambinos. In addition, access to cash—with which to buy agricultural implements and bread, to transport harvests to the coast, and to acquire land and livestock—has become critical for all townspeople. Our examination of women's and men's economic participation in Mayobamba will be situated in the context of these broad changes in rural economics.

Work in an agricultural community such as Mayobamba is demanding and diverse. Seed must be selected and stored, fields prepared, and plantings coordinated with the rains and the availability of irrigation waters. Potatoes, broad beans, corn, barley, and alfalfa require careful planting, watering, weeding, and protection from animals until the harvests. Sheep, cows, pigs, chickens, and guinea pigs need to be cared for, bred, slaughtered, and sold or preserved for consumption. Houses, irrigation canals, terraces, and corrals must be built, repaired, or extended. Firewood and dung need to be collected for household cooking fires. Staples must be effectively stored, allocated, and prepared for family consumption in order to last to the next harvest. Wool must be cleaned, spun, and woven into cloth and blankets. Agricultural surpluses must be strategically traded for the products of higher and lower altitudes as well as for the necessities and luxuries of the industrialized economy on the coast.

The list of economic activities crucial to daily life and survival in the *sierra* is extensive and the patterning of women's and men's labors to accomplish these activities is complex. In Mayobamba, the nuclear family composed of parents and their children (and sometimes extended to include grandparents) is viewed as the critical unit of production. Within the family, each member has important functions. Families are marked by the interdependence of the sexes, by broad areas of overlap between the work that men and women perform. While sex specific behavior exists in the home, most economic activities including agriculture and stock raising are shared by men and women with varying amounts of assistance from children. Most commonly, men and women work side by side or divide an activity into complementary parts which they complete in a coordinated fashion. Sometimes no one cares which sex engages in a particular kind of work. On other occasions, as we will show, one sex avoids or is excluded from a particular task deemed the specialty of the other sex.

Despite the broad overlap in the work that men and women undertake, there are culturally important differences in men's and women's patterns of economic participation. First, women believe that they are centrally involved in agriculture while men tend to see female involvements as peripheral. Second, men's labor is valued more highly than women's. Both sexes explain this difference in value largely as a result of men's ability to work with heavier tools and to engage in more strenuous labor. Third, women are effectively barred from such agricultural tasks as plowing by their lack of access to tools and draft animals. Fourth, there are some types of labor such as clearing the fields, irrigation, and fixing loads on burros that women traditionally do not do for social and cultural reasons. Fifth, in addition to their agricultural involvements, women work a double day in Mayobamba. They are responsible for child care, cooking, spinning, and care of the home. By any standards, these tasks are especially laborious in rural society. They contribute to longer work days for the women than for the men of all social classes.

In Mayobamba, women recognize a sexual division of labor, marked by differences in strength and in the tools appropriate for each sex, but they indicate their own full range of involvement in agricultural tasks. One woman described women's work in the following words:

> We cook, we wash, we go to the fields, collect wood, harvest beans and potatoes. Women earn less than men because the work is less. Men have shovels and picks. Women aren't going to use shovels because it can't be done. We don't have the strength; we would become ill with the exertion. We cultivate beans and corn with smaller tools collecting the earth and turning it over. Men use the shovels and picks.

Here is an account by another Mayobamba woman:

> Women don't participate in rotating and aerating the soil before planting [called the *chakmayo*]. That is men's work. The women don't go. They prepare lunch for the work crews and stay home to prepare the afternoon meal. There is no need for women to participate in the *chakmayo* because it is men's work. There's nothing a woman could do. Women don't use those tools; they're too heavy. But they say in other places that women do this. In Santa Cruz, located in the [neighboring] Leoncio Prado district, it is the custom that women work with shovels and picks. Perhaps this is because of necessity or perhaps because of

custom. But here they don't. However, in the harvest, we do the same thing as men. Women also participate in the planting. The men just leave the rows, and the women plant. In the planting of corn it's the same as potatoes; the women plant after the men have made the rows. The only work in which women don't participate is the *chakmayo* and that lasts about two days.

Men, on the other hand, tend to locate women's primary activities in the domestic sphere and to minimize women's contributions when describing work in the fields. For example, while women do not differentiate men's and women's work at the potato harvest, men report that harvesting potatoes is a masculine activity. In fact, in our observations of a series of harvests, we found that as many women as men involve themselves in the exhausting work of digging up the potatoes with short pointed hand hoes. Both sexes move along raised rows of earth, dig under the dried plants, extract the potatoes from the soil, and haul loads of the harvest to a central area for sorting. Only in the harvest of the community fields for the town's treasury do men significantly outnumber women. In this case, officially recognized heads of households are required to harvest the community fields as a communal labor project. As men are designated as heads of household in disproportionate numbers, they are overrepresented in the one-day community harvest. Widows and older single mothers who officially head families also participate. These women are given precisely the same amount of work as men during the community harvest.

In general, men's misperceptions of women's economic involvements in the fields appear to be a strategic and patterned form of cultural blindness. These perceptions help to legitimize the masculine view that men should control agricultural activities and public decisions regarding agriculture.

When abstractly defining work, men and women often describe clearly differentiated sets of tasks which locate men's primary responsibilities in the fields, and women's duties in the domestic scene with secondary activities in agriculture. In talking about work such as irrigation, which integrates tasks from the domestic and agricultural spheres, men and women perceive work in different ways. Women, who prepare meals for workers and bring burros as transportation between the fields and town, perceive these tasks as part of an integrated whole called "irrigation." In fact, women speak directly of being involved in irrigation when they carry out tasks that complement men's work in the fields. Men, on the other hand, more narrowly define irrigation as the work they perform in actually opening the channels with shovels so that water flows into the fields. Watching over the channels during irrigation is tricky work because the volume of water entering the field must be regulated so that the entire terrace is watered without eroding the top soil. The work is not physically demanding but rather requires patience and skill in directing the flowing water. When men claim that women are not included in agricultural tasks such as irrigation, they are stressing a more restrictive definition of the tasks involved in a category of work.

In Mayobamba, the male-controlled community government enhances the significance of men's contributions to work such as irrigation. The community government reaffirms that the crucial aspect of irrigation is the task of opening up the channels. A community official (*el juez de agua*) determines the order of rotation for heads of households (*comuneros*) to irrigate their fields. Access to water at the appropriate intervals is crucial for the successful production of cash crops and fodder, and can only be gained through the community. One consequence of the singling out of the opening of channels as a task open to public decision making is that the narrow, masculine definition of work is emphasized and women's contribution to an integrated set of tasks involved in irrigation is deemphasized.

One might ask why women do not open irrigation channels. Townspeople's explanations emphasize women's alleged fears of being alone in the dark during occasional all-night irrigation. When many *comuneros* petition for water at the same point in the cycle, some must be prepared for assignments to irrigate the fields during the night, when the demand for water lessens. However, women's fear would seem to be an ideological pretext for legitimizing female exclusion since older widows often stay alone at night in the fields to guard their harvests until they can secure transportation to town. What appears to stand behind this justification is the fear on the part of husbands, that their wives will sexually wander if alone in the fields. Also, men demand that their wives be home to serve them.

Thus, while men and women may have different perceptions of work, crucial tasks are defined male-centrically and justified by emphasizing stereotyped images of the sexes. Male dominance in government, which allocates scarce resources, as well as in the household, where men are waited on by women, reinforces the disproportionate value placed on men's work. Cultural values limit women's access to crucial tasks, making women dependent on men for the accomplishment of such tasks.

The opening of irrigation channels is not the only set of agricultural tasks which is defined by the community as exclusively masculine. In addition, the preparation of fields before planting and the loading of harvested crops on pack animals are tasks which both sexes agree are inappropriate for women to undertake.[1] A closer examination of these tasks shows their broader implications for the sexual division of access to crucial economic resources.

For example, plowing is a stage in the preparation of fields from which women are excluded by beliefs that reinforce sexual specializations in certain tasks and access to tools and animals. In Mayobamba all fields are plowed before the plantings. Plowing is strongly identified as men's work. In fact, plowing is highly skilled labor which requires a great deal of strength and experience to do effectively. Few men actually engage in this "masculine" work. Some male employers attempt to show that they, too, can handle the oxen and heavy wooden plows. They are quickly put in their place by the teasing of those laborers who are especially skilled in plowing. Four or five men in Mayobamba are recognized plowmen. All are poorer townsmen who have access to plows although they do not generally own oxen. Landowners must hire a skilled laborer and rent oxen from one of the three wealthy families in town who own sufficient pasture lands to maintain draft animals. Plowing involves the cross-class collaboration of men as owners of oxen, plows, and technical skills. Women are uniformly excluded from the tasks associated with plowing. Women do not possess the animals, technology, or skills for this task. Culturally the work is considered "too heavy" for women. In addition, to further reinforce the sexual specialization of plowing, women are taught to avoid contact with wooden plows because townspeople believe that female contact causes plows to break in stony fields.[2]

Another example of tasks deemed inappropriate for women occurs at the end of the agricultural cycle, when families generally participate jointly in the harvests. Both sexes agree that women are unable to carry out one crucial aspect of the harvest: the loading of burros for the trip back to town. Loading and tying sacks of potatoes is felt to be difficult not only because of the strength needed to lift heavy sacks, but also because of the skills required to tie the sacks so that the loads are securely balanced. The concern expressed about the tying of sacks on the animals is entirely justified given the narrow trails and precipitous drops on route to the settlement. Both men and women pay close attention to shifting loads on the animals and to the pace of the group when the trails cross sharp cliffs. Burros are occasionally killed when they lose their balance on narrow trails and plunge down steep gullies. In Mayobamba, the task of securing 100 to 150-pound-sacks of potatoes on the burros is performed only by men. Women worry that, if they were to attempt this task, they might lose the sacks of potatoes if not the burros on the return to town. Women anxiously solicit help from male relatives as the day comes to an end. The economic significance of knowledge about loading and tying is clear: in 1975, for instance, potatoes were worth 5 *soles*/kilo in the fields and 7 *soles*/kilo in the town. Men's labor is a necessary component in this added value for the harvest. Additionally, men control the transportation of potatoes from the town to the coast, increasing their value from 7 *soles* to 12 *soles*/kilo or more. Thus, the potato harvest is an example of a category of work in which the single masculine task of loading burros takes on disproportionate importance given the fact that virtually all other tasks are shared between men and women.

In our discussion of men's and women's participation in agriculture, we have documented the ways in which a seemingly minimal sexual division of labor contributes to broader patterns of sexual hierarchy. Women participate in a broad range of agricultural activities, sometimes side by side with men, on other occasions in a fashion that complements men's work. Yet women's status appears to be more clearly shaped by those tasks from which they are excluded. Women plant, irrigate, and harvest; they do *not* break up hard earth with pointed metal rods, plow fields, open irrigation channels, or tie sacks of the harvest on burros. Because women are excluded from tasks such as soil aeration and plowing, they cannot directly open up new private landholdings or extend communal fields. Nor can they begin the agricultural cycle on old fields without assistance. Because women cannot load the harvest on pack animals, they are dependent on men as a link in the chain of events which establishes the value of crops women produce alongside of men. The reasons why women are unable to carry out these small but disproportionately significant tasks are multiple and reinforcing. The differential access to skills, tools, draft animals, and natural resources is legitimized by sex role stereotypes, social ideologies, and pollution beliefs. Our analysis also suggests that community government reinforces patterns of access and sex role stereotypes. (Chapter 7 presents a fuller analysis of government and its role in shaping sexual hierarchies).

The Mechanisms of Economic Subordination in Mayobamba

At this point, it is appropriate to speak more abstractly about our analysis of Mayobamba's economic system as it relates to men's and women's relative status. From the analyst's point of view, this social system has elaborated a series of what we will call "mechanisms" that define women's subordination to men and perpetuate structural differences. The notion of cultural mechanisms is our analytical construct for those *linkages* between economic, political, social, and symbolic systems that shape patterns of social organization and interaction. The concept of mechanism is a construct to explain the ways in which the varying rural points of view, perceptions, and values fit together along with behaviors and institutional organizations to maintain structural relations between the sexes.

In Mayobamba women's status relative to men's is defined and perpetuated by mechanisms which link

1. *Key tasks* within broad categories of work which serve as gateways to critical resources.

2. *Sex role stereotypes* which guide the ways individuals are characterized and their behavior is anticipated, organized, and evaluated.

3. *Larger institutional structures* on the local and national levels which define agrarian politics and economics.

Thus, while mechanisms that shape women's subordinate status involve both the sexual division of labor and economics, these mechanisms also incorporate ideological and political aspects of Mayobamban cultural reality into the equation that perpetuates sexual hierarchy.

In Mayobamba those mechanisms which are moored to the sexual division of tasks in field preparation, irrigation, and crop transportation have wide reaching consequences for women's lives. Women are constrained from opening up new agricultural lands, from plowing fields, and from the transportation of crops to town. First, because women do not have equivalent access to key tasks, resources, and social institutions, they are dependent on men in the roles of fathers, brothers, and husbands to carry out these activities and to gain rights to important resources. Second, women's dependence is linked by Mayobambinos to social values which explicitly and generally devalue women as inferior, incapable, and limited in knowledge and intellectual capacities. Third, these mechanisms seriously limit women's alternatives in times of family conflicts or in situations where families must make choices about the allocation of scarce resources such as private lands or money to educate children.

We would emphasize that the specific linkages between key tasks, sex role stereotypes, and social institutions do change over time just as they vary from settlement to settlement, especially when economic bases contrast. For instance, Isbell argues that in the traditional Quechua community of Chuschi men's monopolization of plowing is counterbalanced by women's specialization in the activity of placing seed in the ground. Others might argue that men's control of loading burros is counterbalanced by women's monopoly of the storage and allocation of crops. This variation in Andean communities is probably a function of the degree of traditional Quechua sexual complementarity which survives (Isbell 1976, 1978) and the rate of coastal integration. In present-day Mayobamba, we have looked for and found little evidence for complementarity in the sexual division of labor. If Mayobamba was characterized by greater parity between men and women in the past, this equivalence has been erased by the impact of the national cash economy and political systems on this peasant community. Most importantly, the complementarity of male and female tasks must be perceived as equivalent in status, if we are to find parity. This perceived equality of status is not found in the social evaluation of women's tasks in Mayobamba.

For example, women's specialization as the manager of subsistence production does not counterbalance male specialization or translate into a broader parity with men in family or commercial affairs. Women oversee the sorting and storage of the family's harvest, the selection of seed potatoes, and finally the consumption of the family's stores from one harvest to the next. This management function retains importance to the extent that the family is dependent on this production for consumption throughout the following year. However, as a family increases the cultivation of cash crops and gears consumption to commercial products, women tend to lose their control over the management of family resources. While it is true that many men give their wives money, an action consistent with a woman's role as financial administrator of the household, both men and women report that men ultimately maintain decision-making power over the use of money (cf. chapter 4).[3]

In fact, despite women's roles as household managers, Mayobamba men characterize women as frivolous in some of their trading decisions. The men say women are susceptible to the offers of coastal fruit traders who come to the highland communities during the potato harvest to barter fruit for potatoes. Mayobamba men complain that local women are deceived by the traders, giving them more potatoes than the fruit is worth. This is an example of how women's role as household manager does not free them from stereotypes which mark them as less sophisticated than men in dealing with the world outside Mayobamba.[4]

Women are not the equivalents of males in organizing agricultural work through labor exchanges (*washka*) or wage labor. In *washka* agriculturalists take turns in performing similar tasks on one another's fields in groups of relatives, ritual kin, and friends.[5] It is very difficult for women to secure continual agricultural assistance through reciprocal labor exchanges because women cannot directly exchange their labor for a man's. Thus, when we asked one Mayobamba woman if women could independently support themselves she replied:

> It would be very difficult, because it is the men who must participate most in the fields. It would be especially difficult for a woman without economic resources. She would have to find the money to pay for men and a bull [for plowing]. But, for a man, he would not have to use money. Take for example Marcelo, even without money he can still get help through labor exchanges (*washka*). There are some men that a woman alone could hire for payment, but this is much more difficult. Everyone is so busy that labor exchanges are preferred [over cash payments for day labor]. Thus it is much easier for men [to gain assistance in the fields].

If women need additional assistance in masculine tasks, they must rely on paid day labor. Yet in order to pay laborers a woman must have access to cash. This is a major obstacle, as one woman pointed out in describing where women get money for paid labor: "The husband gives her the money. She doesn't have her own money. What kind of businesses do we have? I don't have money when my husband doesn't give me any. Where am I going to get money? What kind of job could I have?" Women's access to cash is severely limited. They are only infrequently sought as agricultural laborers and then paid substantially below the going rate for male laborers. In addition, there are few opportunities for nonagricultural economic involvements in the community. The town supports a few marginal storefront bars, but no one makes a living from these, and the chief proprietors are men. This is especially true when the most lucrative item, liquor, is sold. Even in the event that a woman earns money from intermittent day labor, such as in the harvest of broad beans, she has special problems hiring workers. Both men and women agree that "women are without authority" meaning that men have "less respect" for them and may refuse offers of work, or break contracts for work. In the case of a man contracting labor, Mayobambinos feel that he is in a better position to insist that workers show up. It is said that he may "put a little fear" into the recalcitrant worker.

In short, as agriculture has turned from subsistence to greater integration with the coastal economy, women in the agricultural community are disadvantaged because of their limited access to cash. We are not arguing that parity existed in the community when subsistence agriculture was the norm. Rather, we are suggesting that the penetration of the cash economy has undermined those few roles in which women exercised control.

In Mayobamba, women's access to crucial resources—such as land, water, transportation, and cash earnings—is almost always mediated by fathers, husbands, and brothers. In contrast, Chiuchin's economy has what initially appears to be more flexible sexual divisions of tasks and access to local resources. In this commercial settlement, women are involved in all aspects of the cash economy.

Women's New Patterns of Participation in a Commercial Economy

In contrast to Mayobamba, Chiuchin is a commercial center with very limited agricultural and pasture lands in the valley bottom. Large extensions of the best land belong to outsiders who play no role in the town. Businesses in Chiuchin cater to the agricultural communities, providing them with staples not produced in the region as well as with housewares, clothing, and liquor. With the exception of bread, which is baked in Chiuchin, all commodities are brought into the town from the coast by bus and trucks. Boardinghouses and small restaurants serve visitors from the high towns; students continuing their education in the regional school; teachers, policemen, and extension agents who are stationed in the region; as well as Peruvian tourists visiting the thermal baths.

Most hotels and restaurants are incorporated into people's homes, although the growing tourist trade has sparked second-story additions built expressly to meet the growing demand for rooms. Agriculture and stock raising are clearly secondary activities in Chiuchin because landholdings of the high towns extend to just above the town, leaving very little land for noncommercial use. Most families own small plots of land below the town, which are used to grow corn, wheat, beans, and to pasture small numbers of dairy cattle, sheep, and horses. In some cases Chiuchinistas rent land from the high towns or manage to retain *comunero* status in other communities so that they have rights to communal lands. Commerce, however, remains the principal economic activity of almost all inhabitants of Chiuchin.

Relative to Mayobamba, Chiuchin offers an expanded set of occupations to women. Given the commercial nature of the town, women have established themselves as rooming house operators, shopkeepers, and restaurant owners and managers. These specialized commercial activities simply do not exist as options for either men or women in agricultural communities like Mayobamba. In Chiuchin, women work full time in the six major commercial enterprises in town. Each of these businesses operates a store, rents rooms, and, more often than not, serves meals. In the case of the two enterprises with the highest capital investment, men established the businesses and have expanded them over the past ten years in response to the opportunities offered by tourism. In both cases, wives are thoroughly involved in all local aspects of the establishments. Men play a much larger role in the running of these stores and hotels than in the establishments where women are the proprietors.

In four other major businesses, women are the sole proprietors who make all financial and management decisions, regardless of whether or not they are married. In three of these cases, women are directly assisted by adult kin, generally a mother or a brother and his spouse. In addition to women directly involved in major businesses, the entrepreneurial nature of the town has generated employment for other women as cooks, kitchen assistants, waitresses, and launderers.

Women in Chiuchin often compare their business ability favorably with that of the men they know. They will claim that they are now more worldly wise than when they first began their businesses and that they are less likely to be deceived by coastal suppliers. Moreover, they feel that they are better prepared than their husbands and brothers to strike fair bargains in local trade situations. For example, here is a typical comment by a Chiuchin woman: "My brother is impossible. It is a mistake to send him for purchases. He doesn't know how to bargain. He will pay any price the merchants ask. Even the taxi drivers [on Lima buying trips] take advantage of him. He's embarrassed to haggle over the costs." Women's economic involvement in Chiuchin varies dramatically in comparison to Mayobamba. In Mayobamba, the community defines the household in naming the adult male of generally nuclear units as a head of household with rights to communal land. Economic roles in the family follow from members' relationships to the *comunero*. The result is that women depend on men in order to gain access to communal land where potatoes are grown and to arrange for male assistance in the fields and the transportation of crops. Even when widows or single mothers establish independent rights to communal lands, they are still dependent on men for crucial tasks in the agricultural cycle. Men can acquire such help through labor exchange or by hiring laborers. Women are disadvantaged because they do not have the same access to labor exchanges as men. Even if they are able to secure funds to hire laborers, women have special difficulties as women in making sure that laborers will honor agreements. Furthermore, inheritance patterns which favor male children and the difficulty for a woman of assuring reliable sources of agricultural labor make it almost impossible for an unattached widow or a single mother to gain more than bare subsistence in the agricultural community.

In Chiuchin the patterns of economic involvement for women present a sharply contrasting picture. Rather than the *comunero*-centered family defining the economic unit, in Chiuchin the business delimits the household. Widows, single mothers, and married women (whose husbands work outside of the town) may set up economically independent units with the assistance of kinsmen and kinswomen who join the household. In maintaining a large labor pool, such households are able to diversify their businesses.

Of course, diversification is also a response to the economically difficult circumstances in which under-capitalized enterprises are forced to operate. Businesses are vulnerable to strong local competition, to changeable markets in the agricultural towns, and to the vagaries of the national market where government policy fixes prices of commodities such as flour and gasoline. Unable to count on agriculture for subsistence, the businesses of Chiuchin tend to incorporate several income-generating activities.

Chiuchin women appear to have more opportunities than Mayobamba women both to hire laborers and to work for others. Businesswomen in Chiuchin have access to earnings with which to pay laborers, in addition to any assistance they may receive from the extended household. Where agricultural divisions of tasks are maintained, hired help fills in the masculine roles if there are no men in the family. Chiuchin women who need the help of male day workers confirm the problems that Mayobamba women detail of male laborers' unreliability in meeting their obligations to female employers. However, they are able to count on the regional police, centered in Chiuchin, to make workers come through on agreements. In addition, women as employees have more opportunities to enter the cash economy and work for others.

These observations do not imply that the cash economy in Chiuchin is sexually neutral. In fact, women in Chiuchin (as in Mayobamba) are paid about two-thirds the typical male wage for day labor. This difference in wages is explained by men and women in terms of the different tasks that men and women perform. Men earn money by working in the fields or in construction, while women generally work washing sheets for hotels and cooking for restaurants. Townspeople observe that since men's work is "heavier," they should be and are paid more. Local employers in the commercial settlement use the same values regarding the differential worth of the work done by each sex that are found in the agricultural community.

For Chiuchin, one could argue that the sexual division of labor appears to be more flexible, though some tasks within broad categories of work are considered to be sex specific. Both sexes run stores, wait on customers, engage in economic transactions, and purchase stock from wholesale merchants who visit the town. In local restaurants and rooming houses, however, women proprietors or the wives of couples who own businesses specialize in the supervision of cooking and domestic maintenance for guests. Men never work in restaurant kitchens as cooks or supervisors. In fact, wives of store owners have effectively blocked their husbands' desire for an expansion of the family businesses to incorporate a restaurant by simply refusing to organize or involve themselves in food preparation for customers. In addition to their commercial ventures, Chiuchin women accomplish the full spectrum of agricultural activities if men are unavailable. While men generally follow the sexual division of tasks common in agrarian communities, women will stand in for a missing man to accomplish tasks such as loading burros or opening irrigation channels, often with the assistance of their children or a paid laborer.

Women in Chiuchin retain their domestic duties. One Chiuchin woman explained to us that she bought the shawl she was wearing because she did not have the time to make one. She had too much else to do because, over and above her commercial responsibilities, "a woman must wash, iron, spin, and cook. Amidst all this if she has children, she must be responsible for them as well." This businesswoman is assisted in her household tasks by permanent laborers, fictive kinswomen, and students who take board and room in her home while they study at the local high school. Other women find help with domestic chores through the extended nature of business-focused households. One member of a successful Chiuchin network observed, "When I'm in the house with my mother-in-law we help each other in the kitchen. When she's washing, I cook; when she's ironing, I wash. While we are united, we have help."

Women's access to local tools, skills, and sources of energy in Chiuchin is greater than women's access to critical resources in Mayobamba. Yet, even though women in Chiuchin have more work alternatives, it is evident that they suffer some special disabilities as women. Access to wages and education is not equivalent for men and women in Chiuchin. Moreover, in the context of regional economics, which depend on profitable contacts with the coast, men benefit from their monopoly of two critical tasks: wholesale purchasing and the transportation of goods from urban centers to Chiuchin. Regionally, men are the truck and bus drivers; locally, men have higher levels of experience with coastal society than women. Thus, despite the fact that women perceive themselves as more competent than their fathers, husbands, or brothers to bargain and assess local demands for coastal products, family businesses are often represented by men on the coast. All larger businesses send representatives to urban centers for buying expeditions instead of waiting for wholesalers who may attempt to get rid of slow moving merchandise on their visits to rural towns. Men control what is brought into town and thus decide what stores will be able to offer to the public.

The apparent paradox between women's perception of their greater business acumen and men's ultimate control of trade is explained in part by the fact that these activities involve contact with urban *mestizo* society. Successful interaction with national society requires articulate and literate Spanish as well as knowledge of the hidden agendas of police inspectors and wholesalers. Town sex role stereotypes hold that men will be most successful in dealing with coastal officials and urban merchants. Interregional trade and transportation involves skills which men designate as masculine. Moreover, sex role stereotyping and attitudes toward the education of daughters and potential wives restrict female access to those arenas where the skills can be acquired. Some men justify their resistance to educating daughters by claiming, "It will only allow them to write love letters to other men." Such judgments are examples of sets of values that restrict women's future patterns of participation, reflect sex role stereotyping, and feed into a division of tasks that insures dependence on males who have such skills.

Additionally, businesswomen are reminded of the special status of their sex by male customers' behavior toward them. Single women, particularly, must place limitations on the male customers that male proprietors do not have to face. These women feel they must be friendly to encourage the patronage of their businesses, but "wear a serious face" to ward off sexual misunderstandings. They observe that men enjoy doing business with unmarried women, but that customers often attempt unwanted advances. As a precaution these women send clear signals that they define men as purely business clients. They do not feel that married women proprietors suffer from these problems as much as unmarried women.

Some Chiuchin women, like their counterparts in Mayobamba, have had coastal experience. A few have had exposure to specialized training in sewing or have attended the training courses for women sponsored by a peasant organization related to the Catholic church. Yet most women who own businesses or engage in day labor in Chiuchin express their preference for the *sierra*. Some are highly enthusiastic about the quality of their lives and its superiority over what they see as their options in Lima. In short, these women are not in an intermediate stage of migration, where the final stage is settlement in Lima. Rather, knowing the alternatives that coastal urban society offers they have opted for life in Chiuchin. This suggests a conscious assessment of their opportunities and life chances at this intermediate stage where commercial opportunities exist, and increased dependence on cash is matched by greater access to cash or cash earning opportunities.

Economic Mechanisms in Chiuchin: Changes in the Center of Gravity of Subordination

Let us stand back for a moment from the details of economic participation and sexual divisions of labor in Chiuchin to consider the consequences of the patterns more abstractly. Do the more flexible patterns of labor force participation in the commercial town signify that women are less subordinate, that they experience greater parity? Has there been a substantial transformation of the mechanisms that shape women's structural position as one moves down the mountain from an agrarian community to a commercial town with much stronger coastal ties? To address these issues we will look for patterns in the linkages between the sexual divisions of labor, sex role images, and institutions that regulate access to critical resources in Chiuchin.

In the case of Chiuchin the positive effects of expanded economic options manifest themselves in women's self-perception as efficacious individuals and in their actual patterns of participation. Full parity with men has been constrained by the social and cultural mechanisms which continue to subordinate women to men despite increased economic status. In Chiuchin women's status relative to men's is shaped and maintained by mechanisms which link:

1. *Key tasks* connecting local commerce to the national economy.
2. *Sex role stereotypes* which legitimize the double standard in wages for laborers and cause parents to anticipate higher returns on the education of boys than girls.

3. *Larger institutional structures* such as the school system, regional transportation companies, and the national police which channel contacts with coastal economics.

In Chiuchin the center of gravity of the mechanisms that define women's status relative to men's has shifted more definitively to non-local factors. In the commercial town, the sex of individuals who open irrigation channels or load burros is much less important for commercial success than access to good business ties on the coast. Of course, in Chiuchin those merchants without strong ties to the coast may prefer to hold down stocks in their general stores and concentrate on restaurants and boarding houses which primarily utilize local resources. In fact businesses run by women are much more likely to be labor intensive rather than focused on successful turnovers of broad ranges of coastal products.

In Mayobamba and Chiuchin patterns of work do not sharply segregate men and women. Women are actively involved in agriculture in Mayobamba and in commerce in Chiuchin. It is not so much broad divisions of work that are most important in these cases. Instead, within a broad category of work such as the harvest or local trade, those tasks which are defined as exclusively masculine take on disproportionate importance in the production process. These tasks stand at the gateways of critical resources and marketing opportunities. They contrast in the two settlements because of the different productive bases of these interdependent economies. Yet, the structural form of economic subordination through male monopolies and female exclusion is strikingly parallel in the two settlements. The next chapter widens our examination of economic life by analyzing women's and men's positions in the agrarian class system.

Notes

1. In some Andean communities, burros are not always available as beasts of burden; rather peasants carry the harvest back to town or to market on their backs. See, for example, the sexual specialization of transportation in Hualcán as reported by Stein (1961, pp. 220–21). Our argument, however, is a *structural* one; we do not assume that the identical set of key tasks is monopolized by men in each community.

2. For examples of beliefs about plowing and variations in the sexual division of plowing, see Harris (1978) and Adams (1959).

3. Morris et al. (1968) also found that Mayobamba men were reluctant to recognize women's role in managing the family's financial affairs.

4. Women are active (often with other women) in *regional* trade, as we discuss in chapter 6. Mayobamba women, however, do not travel to the coast to sell agricultural surpluses and cash crops. For variations in rural Andean women's participation in regional and urban markets, see Buechler and Buechler (1971), Flores-Ochoa (1979), and Deere and León de Leal (n.d.).

5. Reciprocal labor exchange has received great attention in Andean scholarship (see Alberti and Mayer 1974). Mayobamba's economy is similar to the mixed exchange and wage labor patterning that Mayer (1974) reports for Tángor. This contrasts with communities like Chuschi where reciprocal exchanges are employed by *comuneros* and wage labor by *mestizos* (Isbell 1978).

VI

Women's Positions in the Agrarian Class System

Up to this point we have questioned the implications of the *sexual* division of labor in the two settlements. Now we turn to a second dimension of social inequality: the economic division of the labor force into strata with differing relations to agrarian production and commerce. Townspeople in Chiuchin and Mayobamba are well aware that individual families occupy distinct positions in the economic systems of the towns. Variations in family incomes and access to capital are significant. In this chapter, we want to show the interworkings of the agrarian class system and to present data on the impact of economic stratification on women's and men's economic positions and options.[1] Our analysis suggests that men and women experience the impact of economic stratification distinctly and that the sexes develop somewhat different strategies for coping with the implications of economic inequities. By bringing together the analysis of class and sexual inequities, we hope to create the basis for understanding the economic strategies—including cross-strata networks—that Andean women have developed for coping with sexual subordination and social change.

Rural Perspectives on Class Differences

Unfortunately, the generalized use in social scientific literature of the term "peasants" for rural populations has often hidden the complex class structures and the important differences of wealth characteristic of these settlements. As in most rural societies, in Mayobamba and Chiuchin there are great differences in individual incomes drawn from the mixed agrarian and commercial economy. In 1978, incomes

135

varied from S/2,500 ($17) per month for the lowest paid laborer to approximately S/20,000 ($130) per month for the highest paid, salaried government employees and the most successful merchant-farmers. In other words, while no one is particularly wealthy on a national economic scale, the gap between the lowest and highest incomes in the rural area is on the order of an eight-fold spread.

It would be a mistake, however, to understand "local elite" in any but relative terms. The elites of both towns are continually reminded that they are low status members of the national society which sees the *sierra* as the cultural and economic backwater of the country. Neither members of the local elite nor laborers have electricity in their homes. No one in either town has been able to afford to build a home or a business of earthquake-resistant brick instead of adobe. All townspeople use the second-class thermal baths with occasional forays by youths into the first-class sections which are frequented by coastal tourists.

When they describe economic strata, Mayobambinos and Chiuchinistas distinguish four groups: salaried professionals, wealthy merchants and farmers, self-employed merchants and farmers, and wage laborers. Members of each of these categories have a different relationship to the total economic system of which rural communities are a part.

Salaried government employees, the educated specialists who locally represent national bureaucracies, are considered "professionals." Not only do they earn the highest wages by far, but professionals also have the greatest economic security. One Chiuchin businesswoman talked to us about the differences between professionals and other workers.

> You are a professor and are paid monthly for your classes. Whether it rains or not, whether the dry season comes or the wet season continues, you are still paid. A policeman or an employee of the Ministry of Agriculture [i.e. an agricultural extension agent] also collects his pay monthly. For them, the weather does not matter. Nor are they affected by variations in business as are merchants. Merchants may do well today and tomorrow do poorly. For instance, the owner of a bakery may experience months or weeks when the demand is high and he earns a great deal. Then a slow period comes during which business declines. A professional collects a consistent salary every month.

In both communities, salaried professionals are outsiders posted to the rural area as teachers, agricultural extensionists, and national police. Professionals bring significant business to the region since most of them rent rooms and take their meals at local restaurants. Townspeople discourage further economic involvement of outside professionals, and few engage in commerce or agriculture. Local resistance is most obvious in the case of those school teachers posted to the agricultural communities who attempt to acquire *comunero* status and to purchase agricultural lands. On the whole, salaried professionals have no intention of making the *sierra* their permanent home. Most grumble about being posted to an isolated area, look for excuses to make trips to the coast, and send repeated requests for transfers to larger urban centers.

While local people may resent the steady salaries of professionals and attempt to block any moves they feel would result in economic dominance of outsiders in local affairs, they also aspire to professional status for their children. Families who can afford to send their children to high school, and perhaps beyond, direct their children toward professional careers. Such aspirations can only be realized by leaving the community and by seeking training and employment elsewhere. While rural citizens would oppose any further encroachment from professionals, they are also aware of the potential to use good relationships with professionals to maximize one's ties with the coast, or expand the options for one's children.

Unlike professionals, wealthy merchants and farmers must cope with variations in commercial demand and the agricultural productivity of the *sierra*. These second strata of rural elites are composed of individuals with substantial (in local terms) capital investments in agricultural lands, livestock, and/or local commercial establishments. The financial success of these local business people depends on a wide range of factors including the national market, the amount of capital to which they have access, and their willingness to put in long hours working in their business and organizing the labor of others. These local elites are seen as a distinct economic category and are referred to as "people with possibilities," "people with their own capital," "the property owners," and "those who employ others." A few merchant-agriculturalists who have good coastal contacts, sufficient capital, and access to reliable labor may earn as much as locally based professionals. For the most part, merchant-farmers have lower incomes than professionals though they have sufficient capital investments and business to employ laborers on a continuous basis. In either case, elite status in agriculture or commerce carries none of the benefits, such as sick pay and social security pensions, that are given to bureaucrats and teachers.

A third position in this economic system is occupied by independent farmers and petty merchants who manage to maintain enough capital to be fairly self-sufficient. These individuals are neither consistent employers nor wage laborers for others. Rather, they are self-employed farmers and businesspeople. In Mayobamba some independents are hard-working, younger agriculturalists who have inherited land and may be able to consolidate positions as employers later in life. In Chiuchin the independents are older businesspeople who have already distributed capital holdings to their children or have retired to the *sierra* after spending most of their careers working on the coast. Increasingly, the status of independent farmers and merchants is a transitional stage in individual life cycles. The economic structure in this region tends to favor the formation of elite and laboring strata rather than a large intermediate class of independent farmers and petty merchants.

The fourth class position in this economic system is occupied by workers lacking capital who engage in varying amounts of day labor. Generally workers have some capital in the form of small landholdings or, as in the case of Mayobamba, access to communal lands. Laborers gain access to land through community membership, through inheritance, through sharecropping, or, occasionally, as a benefit for long-term employment for a particular landowner. Laborers engage in subsistence agriculture and minor stock raising on these lands.

To a greater or lesser degree, workers are dependent on the wealthy local merchants and farmers for wage labor in order to gain subsistence on a year-round basis. In some cases, workers have specialized skills such as preparing fields with a team of oxen and a wooden plow. In other cases, workers help with the regular cycle of agricultural activities, with construction jobs, or with the business opportunities generated by tourism. Wages for workers are paid on a per day basis and are maintained at a minimum level. Daily earnings in 1978 were between S/100 and S/250 (between $.66 and $1.66 a day). This represents a very serious decline, due to high levels of inflation, from wages in 1975 when workers on the average earned an equivalent of $2.00

daily. Clearly workers have not ridden the crest of the disastrous inflation in Peru. In addition to their wages, laborers are given rum, cigarettes, and coca during work breaks. Their employers also provide the noon meal. While particular employers may help laborers in times of trouble, there are generally no formal benefits such as vacations, sick pay, or pensions associated with wage labor jobs.

In both Mayobamba and Chiuchin, four economic strata are recognized: one national stratum of coastal professionals and three local strata defined by levels of access to capital with which to farm and engage in commerce. The different productive bases of the two towns, however, are important to distinguish in order to further discuss local class formation and to pinpoint women's positions in the agrarian class system. Agriculture in Mayobamba combines the original subsistence economy, based on access to communal land, with the more recent expansion of commercial agriculture, based on private property and tied to coastal trade. Agricultural surpluses and cash crops are given value by the national economy. In turn, townspeople are dependent on the larger market for commodities not produced locally. The merchants and laborers of Chiuchin are even more oriented toward the role of bridging the gap between coastal and *sierra* economies through commerce. These individuals are further removed from subsistence production and more dependent on the cash economy.[2]

Class Membership and the Female Underclass in Mayobamba

Mayobamba households—be they nuclear or extended families—gain their economic standing through the occupational position of the head of household, as a wealthy commercial farmer and stockraiser, an independent farmer, or a laborer. According to townspeople, strata membership is determined by a householder's access to capital and position as either an employer or a worker for others. The key factor in determining wealth is the amount of private land an individual possesses. Private land is the basis for accumulation; without it a householder is dependent on communal land for subsistence and day labor on others' land for access to cash. With private land, a householder can meet subsistence needs on communal land and increase income by planting a cash crop or maintaining a private dairy herd.

Access to capital is usually acquired by membership in a wealthy family and by inheritance. Those from poor families do not inherit significant landholdings or livestock. Rather, they are more likely to inherit the position of laborers for the same families as their parents. "The Vásquez, Díaz, and López families have always worked as peons and wage laborers for the Cuevas and Clementes," exemplifies townspeople's perceptions of the continuity of class positions through the generations in family lines. According to oral history, the broad outlines of stratification have remained remarkably constant in Mayobamba throughout the twentieth century. Marriage and inheritance practices have perpetuated the stratification of this rural population.

Mayobambinos comment that families and their children are very conscious of the local elite's preference for marriage on the same economic level. One female member of the wealthy farmer strata made the following observations about marriage patterns and economic strata in Mayobamba:

> It is very rare that a Díaz, a Rosas, or a Clemente marries a Vásquez or a Valerio. None of them would because they are not of the same economic position. The Rosas marry the Clementes. They only marry among one another, not with other families. There is a group of families that make themselves different, more distinguished in education and wealth. They would never marry a Valerio.

Mothers from the wealthy farmer strata are quick to criticize sons who find themselves attracted to women from poorer backgrounds. Both men and women indicate that part of the success of the local elites has been due to their ability to find women from wealthy families for formal marriage. Since inheritance is channeled through families from parents to their legitimate children (or lacking children to legitimate nephews and nieces), marriage within one's social class tends to maintain capital within the same range of families. Furthermore, sons are favored over daughters in the distribution of inheritance. Fathers and sons assume that women in the family will lose control of inherited lands to their husbands. As a result, sons are generally given the choicest land in central locations for irrigation and transportation to town.

In our survey of Mayobamba, we found that 16 percent of the households were recognized as economic elites, including both older men who have consolidated their wealthy positions and *comuneros* in their thirties and forties who have been financially successful and show economic promise due to the effective management of inheritances. Typically, members of the upper strata own eight to twelve or more private, irrigated parcels, maintain herds of ten to fifteen improved dairy cows (and additional sheep), and gain income from occupational specializations like politics and commercial activities, such as the sale of cheese and cash crops. All elite households are headed by male *comuneros;* several include sons who are gradually taking over their fathers' economic and community responsibilities.

The middle stratum, representing 32 percent of the households, is composed of independent agriculturalists. All own some private land (in the range of three to six parcels, though this varies with the location and quality of the land). Land is inherited from the householder's parents, brought to the marriage by the wife, or purchased from coastal earnings. The middle stratum own smaller herds of cattle and sheep. Most of these economically self-employed families are headed by male *comuneros,* although four older women, as widows and single mothers, head middle-level households.

Over half (52 percent) of Mayobamba's population is poor. Poor households have little or no access to private land and work for the upper strata for wages and agricultural products. Impoverished *comuneros* have not inherited land often because their parents were impoverished migrants from other towns or because they were illegitimate children. Poor families are often described as "precarious;" some own a few cows or sheep, others do not even own the house in which they live. Most families are headed by male *comuneros,* although six widows and single mothers head impoverished families, several of which include adult daughters who will take on their mother's responsibilities in the community as she grows older.

In Mayobamba men occupy the full spectrum of economic positions independently of their marital status. Women, when their economic position is not defined by legal marriage, are most likely to be marginal members of the laboring stratum. The combined impact of sexual hierarchies, the sexual division of labor, and economic stratification creates an underclass of women who have a more precarious economic position than wage laboring males. Thus, while economic stratification shapes differential access to crucial resources for Mayobambinos so that over half of them are impoverished laborers, we argue that sexual hierarchy intervenes to further marginate laboring women who are not attached to men. The difficult economic position of these women is due to a series of impediments which make the accumulation of even minor amounts of capital difficult for them. Members of the female underclass are impoverished widows or single mothers who have never accumulated private land or livestock and have no access to capital through kinsmen or husbands. By virtue of their membership in the community of Mayobamba, these women are given small plots of communal lands on which to grow subsistence crops. Yet bare subsistence is all that can be reaped from communal lands without supplementary wage income. Women are recruited for wage labor only a few times each agricultural cycle, and then they are paid only two-thirds the minimum male wage for a day's work. In 1978, women in Mayobamba were paid $.66 a day for their labors in the harvest of broad beans; men were paid between $1.00 and $1.66 for a day's labor.

Some Mayobambinos recognize women's special position by talking about impoverished, unattached women as if they were a fifth economic stratum below the category of wage laborers. Structurally women in the underclass are doubly disadvantaged. They need access to cash with which to pay laborers for "men's work" in their communal fields. Yet, they have extremely limited access to cash earnings themselves because they are solicited less frequently and paid less than male laborers. In Mayobamba some crucial agricultural tasks involve major expenditures which are especially taxing for impoverished women. For instance, one married woman discussed the problems that widows have in plowing their fields.

> There are widows who must rent oxen and a plow. But it's difficult. They have to anticipate when they will need this work [done to their fields]; they have to beg ahead of time. The charge for the oxen is S/500 a day; for the plow itself they don't charge much. Or one can pasture the oxen for a period of time instead of paying money. But oxen eat a great deal of alfalfa.

Widows are unlikely to own extensions of private land on which to plant alfalfa. They are dependent on their own earnings or on economic assistance from children on the coast for the money to rent oxen and pay laborers.

Women are able to compensate for limited access to laborers and gain agricultural assistance outside their families by organizing traditional cooperative work groups for reciprocal labor exchanges. For tasks such as weeding, groups of women work on each other's land. They take turns working on one woman's land at a time until they have completed a task for the entire group. No cash is involved in these cooperative work groups, though each day's host provides a snack of fruit pudding for her companions to spur their efforts. These labor exchanges occur most commonly among the women of the lower strata and much less frequently among wealthier women. Labor exchanges are not organized to cross-cut strata unless the individuals concerned are very close relatives.

Actually, sexually segregated work groups are organized both by women and men to secure mutual assistance in agriculture without paying wage labor. On the one hand, labor exchanges are a class phenomena by which poorer laborers compensate for their limited access to cash incomes through working outside the cash economy. On the other hand, these groups observe the community's sexual division of labor in agricultural tasks. Thus, while women gain important assistance in their fields through cooperative work groups, they are still dependent on men for the heavy work of clearing and breaking up the earth in fallow fields as well as plowing before plantings.

Not all women fall in the female underclass. Women married to or born into the higher economic strata have access to capital through husbands and fathers. They enjoy a higher standard of living, consume more coastal products, and have very different patterns of economic participation than poorer women. Women in the wealthy farmer strata work at home cooking for the family's laborers. They also assist in the fields during plantings and harvests. They tend to avoid unpaid traditional exchanges of labor with the poor and engage in few labor exchanges with the other elites. Nor do women in these strata work for pay in the harvest of cash crops. In general, elite women engage in less agricultural work in the fields than poorer women, though their contribution in the fields at busy times such as the harvest is substantial. Poor women engage in the most diverse range of tasks in the agricultural community. They work in all aspects of the agricultural cycle; organize labor exchanges with other poor women for tasks like weeding; seek wage labor for the harvest of corn, potatoes, and broad beans; and maintain their homes and children.

Access to capital for high status women is almost always mediated by a male just as it is for lower status women. As a result, women's strata position as wealthy or independent farmers is much less stable than their male counterparts. If abandoned by their successful husbands or *convivientes,* such women will most likely drop in position because of narrowed access to crucial resources. Men, in the unlikely event that they are left by women, do not suffer this change in economic position because they maintain direct access to capital, *comunero* status, and wage labor.

Although we have noted that women in the upper strata in Mayobamba enjoy a higher standard of living, they also experience a loss of control and a restriction of economic participation which have accompanied increased family involvement in the cash economy. While upper strata women still contribute to the total economic function of the family enterprise by cooking for laborers, they are further removed from cash producing work than are women at the lower end of the economic scale. In addition, they work in increased isolation in the home with fewer cooperative ties with other women and an accentuated sexual division of labor.[3]

Class Membership, Female Employers, and Female Laborers in Chiuchin

Like Mayobamba, Chiuchin is a highly stratified town with broad patterns of economic participation for both sexes governed by a minimal sexual division of labor. In contrast to the agricultural community, however, Chiuchin's commercialized economic base offers women the opportunity to accumulate capital or engage in steady wage labor. Thus women are independently represented in the wealthy, self-employed, and wage laboring strata in Chiuchin, which make up, respectively, 31 percent, 17 percent, and 51 percent of the local households. Their economic standing is not always dependent on marital status or their husband's economic position. In fact, in Chiuchin single mothers, single women without children, long-term *convivientes,* and married women appear in all local economic strata. Single mothers and widows do not form an especially impoverished underclass as they do in Mayobamba. Again, because of their status as outsiders, we will not consider professionals in Chiuchin except to note there are more of them, and because there are female school teachers some of the professionals are women.

Chiuchin is a commercial settlement which lacks a tradition of labor exchanges. Certainly, within networks of immediate relatives, mutual assistance is an everyday occurrence in child care and business. Most other labor, however, is compensated by wages or payments in commercial goods. In Chiuchin women are employers as well as laborers. Unlike Mayobamba, where women are solicited for work only occasionally, the businesses of Chiuchin provide stable wage labor for local women. Thus, women who are abandoned or widowed without capital for a business can find steady employment with which to support themselves. Their position is seen as less marginal than that of single mothers and widows in Mayobamba who have very limited access to cash incomes.

Women are the primary employers of other women in restaurant kitchens and local hotels where employer and employee often work side by side. In analyzing the implications of women's economic relationships in Chiuchin, one might stress that the wages paid to laboring women by local female employers remain at two-thirds the male wage. Alternatively, one might point to the cross-strata work arrangements between Chiuchin women as a case of women's responsiveness to the specific problems and needs of other women.

In both action and words the female employers of Chiuchin express a strong sense of responsibility to insure that impoverished wives, single mothers, and widows are given steady employment. This sense of responsibility is undoubtedly shaped by the economic interests of the wealthier women who need the assistance of other women to run their businesses. Yet the relationships between women employers and women laborers appear to be more widely defined than just the pragmatic concern of insuring adequate laborers. For instance, women employers invite female workers to major family events where they participate in all facets of the celebrations. After feasts, leftover soups and meats are divided by the women for the families of both the hosts and women workers. Female employers also help poor women from agricultural communities who are seeking higher education for their children in Chiuchin. Employers sometimes offer their godchildren from the agricultural communities subsidized room and board, and women's wage labor helps pay school expenses. In many cases, women employers and laborers are good friends who help each other in the event of serious illness or death in the family.

Nevertheless, the limits to women employers' sense of responsibility for laboring women indicate that economic interest plays some part in shaping these social and economic relationships. For example, one impoverished single mother in Chiuchin does not evoke the same amount of concern on the part of female merchants as do other poor women. In part, women's negative reaction to this single mother stems from her difficult personality. She is a terribly unhappy women who makes all-consuming demands on anyone who offers help and soundly criticizes those who limit their assistance. She has voluntarily isolated herself from available economic and friendship networks. This woman has not adapted herself to her unfortunate position as a single mother with a large number of illegitimate children. One aspect of the townswomen's unusually negative and judgmental reactions to this single mother is doubtlessly due to her refusal to become a laborer for merchants in town. Unlike other impoverished women, this single mother has steadfastly held on to a very marginal, "independent" business based on the sale of fruit to tourists from the coast. She has paid dearly for her independence and receives minimal sympathy from other women.

In contrast, another impoverished single mother with an equivalently large family is a very vital part of women's society in the town. She is steadily employed as a laborer and appears to be very satisfied with her work in the businesses of others. Although she lacks immediate kin in the town, this woman has created a close and caring network of affinal relatives, fictive kin who are the godmothers of her children, and female friends. Aside from the different personalities involved, the contrasting reactions to these women appear to be related to their differential willingness to perform tasks useful to women employers.

Networks: A Strategy for Dealing with Economic Marginality

Neither business owners nor laborers have much economic security in Chiuchin. All townspeople operate within the constraints of the national economy which establishes the monetary value of *sierra* products and the coastal goods offered in local stores and restaurants. In Chiuchin, both merchants and laborers adapt to the resulting economic uncertainty by maximizing their alternatives in commerce and agriculture. Individuals maintain and cultivate ties with agricultural

Andean women frequently spin wool while they herd
sheep, walk to and from the fields, or sit to converse with
each other. The yarn is later knitted into sweaters and socks
by women or woven into blankets and ponchos by men.

Chiuchin is a commercial center linking two districts of agricultural towns with urban, coastal commerce. The regional
secondary school and the rural extensions of national
government bureaucracies are located in Chiuchin.

Mayobamba is perched in the mountains above Chiuchin.
This agricultural town contains large expanses of communal fields as well as irrigated private property. The road
link from Mayobamba to Chiuchin was completed in 1968.

Three generations of Mayobamba women are represented in this household. Women's family ties remain very important despite the enormous changes brought about by the expansion of the cash economy and migration.

Two Mayobamba women enjoy the midday sun in the central plaza. The woman on the right holds an earthenware jar in which *chicha*, a corn beer, has been prepared.

A daughter who has migrated to Lima on the coast visits her mother, a businesswoman, in Chiuchin. Both women and men develop *sierra*-to-coast networks to broaden their access to crucial resources.

Except in extraordinary circumstances, only one bus a day serves the region. Buses and trucks transport agricultural surpluses, commercial goods, visiting relatives, school teachers, agricultural extensionists, national police, traveling merchants, and wholesalers between the coast and the *sierra*.

A widow from an agricultural town visits Chiuchin on business. Women throughout the region participate in trading networks that link agricultural and commercial towns in the *sierra*.

Rural women play major roles in the household as the managers of agricultural stores and domestic consumption. For this middle-aged generation of women, literacy rates in Spanish are very low, limiting their possibilities for local political participation and coastal migration.

A widow from an agricultural town harvests corn. Widows have a particularly difficult time gaining access to cash with which to pay laborers for assistance in the fields.

A Chiuchin merchant prepares potato soup for a special family feast called a *pachamanca*. For the feast, lamb, potatoes, cheese, beans, and herbs are layered and roasted in an underground oven of heated stones.

The presence of restaurants and boardinghouses in
Chiuchin gives rise to greater opportunities for women in
the cash economy. These women are day laborers preparing
food and laundering sheets. The absence of electricity and
running water in homes makes these labor-intensive tasks.

Successful Chiuchin merchants have built additions to their shops to accommodate tourists visiting the local mineral baths. The husband and wife shown here have combined the management of a boardinghouse, a restaurant, and a dry goods shop.

Women in Mayobamba do not, according to the sexual division of labor, load burros to transport harvest. This Chiuchin woman merchant, with help from a male employee, loads pack animals during a highland trading expedition.

Men and women sort potatoes at the harvest of a private plot. Men tend to underestimate women's participation in agricultural production; women tend to emphasize the interconnectedness of men's and women's tasks.

A Mayobamba woman emerges from her kitchen to bring supplies to her husband in the field. Women see meal preparation and delivery as integral aspects of agricultural work.

Plowing is a male specialization in this region of the Andes. Actually, all women and most men must contract and pay those few men who specialize in plowing as well as the wealthy agriculturalists who own oxen.

Irrigation is a male specialty in both the agrarian and the commercial towns. This field belongs to a wealthy merchant; its large size and flatness are atypical.

Mayobambinos celebrate an annual festival to bless the communal dairy herd and transfer the responsibility of herdsman to a new *comunero*. The men's hats are decorated with special cheeses produced from the herd. The cow is adorned with a new ear ribbon braided by young women.

ayobambinos decorate the statue of
e community's patron saint and
uardian of the herd, San Juan.
nce a year, a priest is invited to say
ass for the fertility of the herd.
ownspeople wait until he has left to
gin their own ritual, which
cludes dancing the saint on the
cks of the cows.

During a festival, *comunera* — widows and single mothers who officially head households — form a semicircle in front of a table where community officials are seated. The rest of the community occupies benches ringing the main plaza.

A Mayobambina serves *chicha* at a festival. Corn beer is prepared by female heads of households as part of their service to the community.

Mayobamba *comuneros* gather for the annual transfer of the responsibility for the church treasures. Formal politics remains a male activity in the agrarian town.

A funeral procession emerges from the church in Chiuchin. Wakes lasting all night precede funerals.

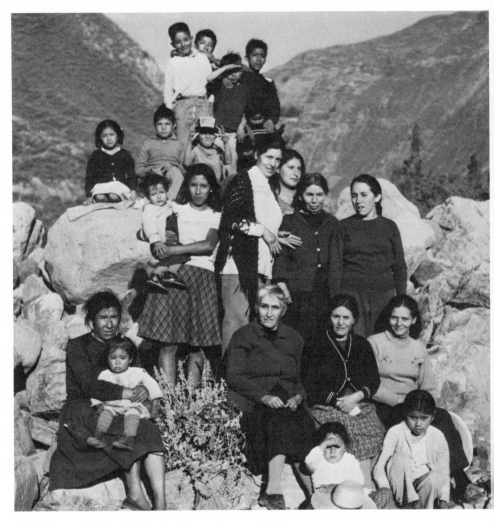

Chiuchin women, including both merchants and laborers,
have considered organizing a committee to pursue their
own development priorities.

communities where cows and sheep can be pastured, staples grown, and exchanges of commercial and agricultural products transacted.

Women in Chiuchin are especially adept at maintaining kinship and trading networks which cross-cut communities and economic strata.[4] Some impoverished widows and single mothers from the agricultural communities have become incorporated into these networks as trading partners. Burro trains ascend steep mountain trails bringing small groups of three or four women from the commercial town. Sometimes visits are made to relatives to whom the women make gifts of commercial goods, knowing that at a later date these gifts will be reciprocated with agricultural staples. On other trips women buy or barter for agricultural surpluses. Widows from the agricultural communities help organize trading expeditions, feed their Chiuchin guests, and take care of the burros. In turn they are offered gifts, assisted in agricultural tasks, and sought as laborers by their Chiuchin connections. Some women from the agricultural communities have used these networks to compensate for the difficulty of soliciting local agricultural laborers and the scarcity of cash income in agricultural towns. In effect, these women have used networks in an attempt to reduce their vulnerability as members of the agricultural underclass.

Networks are sociologically and economically flexible. Members include distant kin and affines; some women cement partnerships by becoming godmothers to each other's children. The scope of exchanges in goods and work is particularly wide ranging; transactions involve barter, gifts, cash purchases, mutual aid, labor exchanges of different kinds of work, and wage labor. Any given trading expedition from Chiuchin is composed of women from different economic strata who share access to burros and each other's company on the way to a highland community. Once there, individual women go off to make separate transactions often utilizing different forms of exchange for highland products. Individuals join forces once again for the descent. On other occasions, highland women bring agricultural surpluses and uncarded wool to Chiuchin or come to work for women merchants. Some women stay for short periods of work, others establish secondary homes in Chiuchin so that they can take care of their children who are attending high school.

Significantly, the active participants in these female networks are described by their migrant sisters in Lima as being unusually dynamic and independent for *sierra* women. Elite women in Chiuchin who run businesses are noted for being organizers and doers who have more of a say in household decisions than women of petty merchant and independent agricultural families. They are said to have benefited from business dealings with the public, including people from outside the region. They are considered to be more highly educated and more knowledgeable. Their Mayobamba counterparts, in terms of strata position, are said to be much less outgoing, more isolated from other women, and less assertive in the home. In Mayobamba most elite women are thought to be restricted by fathers and husbands unless they manage to gain education on the coast. In contrast, the women noted for independence in Mayobamba come from the poorer strata where widows and single mothers must work in the lower commercial settlements by necessity. The women who successfully find wage labor with other women in Chiuchin are thought to be much more active and assertive than the married women of the wealthier strata who are felt to lead more restricted lives because of their dependence on husbands. Mayobamba men do not like their wives to work in commercial towns where they will have their own cash earnings.

In sum, when we look at the impact of economic stratification in Mayobamba and Chiuchin there is a sharp contrast in the meaning of such status for men and women. Whereas the categories are generally the same for men in both communities, they do differ for women. Women in the upper strata in Mayobamba are there because of derived status and their tenure in that strata is dependent upon their relationship to husband, father, or brother. In Chiuchin women's status is more likely to be a result of independent or shared control of economic resources. Moreover, women's location at the upper end of the economic scale implies different behaviors in the two communities. In Chiuchin women in the wealthier strata often have been the instigators of mutually beneficial assistance networks which cross-cut strata and towns, increasing other women's access to cash. Women in the wealthy strata of Mayobamba are less likely than poor women to be involved in cooperative networks either within the community or as part of highland-Chiuchin exchange networks. Instead, upper strata women in Mayobamba appear to be experiencing greater restrictions as a result of their families' increased involvement with cash crops and coastal, market-oriented production.

As we have noted before, in neither town does economic participation free women from sexual hierarchy or the limitations of sex-role stereotyping, nor does it translate into parity with men. But in order to understand the full complexity of this process we must first examine the relationship of women to the political institutions which govern their lives.

Notes

1. In Mayobamba and Chiuchin ethnic differences are largely overshadowed by economic class and regionality. Peasants do not identify themselves as Indians, and "caste-like" ethnic stratification—as reported for Hualcán, a settlement heavily influenced by a neighboring *hacienda* (Stein 1961)—is not a distinct dimension of inequality in these settlements. Ethnicity has been noted as a highly flexible identification in a number of community studies analyzing change (see Fuenzalida et al. 1970). Adams (1959) analyzes the shift from a caste system to a class system in Muquiyauyo, and Doughty (1968) discusses the deemphasis of Indian ethnicity in Huaylas, an agrarian district which lacks fully developed official peasant communities (*comunidades campesinas*) but organizes communal public works. In a major, recent work on Cuzco, van den Berghe and Primov (1977, p. 123) conclude that

> peripheral areas, then, approximate more closely the classic plural society model. . . . Conversely, on the main axis of acculturation, entire towns assume an in-between character, and the majority of their populations are not clearly classifiable as either Indian or mestizo.

2. See Deere (1977*b*) for a comprehensive discussion of class formation in the Cajamarca region. For comparative analyses of stratification in Andean communities, see Deere and León de Leal (n.d.); Stein (1961); Doughty (1968); and van den Berghe and Primov (1977). See also Isbell's (1978) analysis of "social classes" in a nonmarket economy.
3. For similar findings of the effect of increased class stratification on the activities of wealthy peasant women, see Deere (1978).
4. See Sacks (1979) and Leghorn and Parker (n.d.) for different theoretical approaches to the analysis of women's networks in cross-cultural perspective. For insightful case studies of women's networks, see N. Nelson (1979); S. Brown (1975); and Stack (1974).

VII

Consciousness and Participation in a Patriarchal Power Structure

Two images characterize popular understandings of the political relationship between Andean women and men. The first pictures a man astride his burro followed at a distance by a woman on foot, weighted down by either a child or firewood or by some other substantial burden. This image graphically conveys the total and unquestioned subordination of woman to man. The second characterization pictures a woman seated by her hearth preparing the evening meal, yet all the while haranguing her husband about local political issues and carefully instructing him about her views on how he should vote at an upcoming public assembly. This woman allows her husband public recognition as the authority within the family while privately influencing decisions. Both images portray Andean women's apparently limited political participation: the first to argue that women by virtue of their total subordination are apolitical, devoid of political concerns and uninterested in having a political voice. The second characterization is used to argue that despite appearances women actually exercise political control through behind-the-scenes manipulation.[1] These images are stereotypes found in both mestizo notions about Andean women and, from time to time, in academic studies.[2] Our data suggest, in fact, that *neither* image accurately reflects the complexity of Andean women's political interests and involvements.[3]

Disparate views of Andean women's political participation result largely from definitional disagreements over what constitutes an active interest in political issues. For example, if one defines interest in politics as participation in national political parties or concern with national elections, then it follows that Andean women evidence much lower rates of political involvement than Andean men.[4] Our experi-

150

ence, however, leads us to suggest that this would be a mistaken interpretation, assigning to women apolitical attitudes which fail to take into account those structural impediments to national-level participation that women encounter in greater degrees than men. Such structural impediments would include the higher rates of Quechua monolingualism among women which disqualify them from national-level participation, reduced rates of contact with national society as a result of different male-female migratory and employment opportunities, and lower levels of interest on the part of national political parties in the recruitment of peasant women into their organizations. These impediments are important in assessing the differential rates of male and female participation in national political life.

To avoid narrowly defining political participation as voting behavior or participation in national party politics, we are concerned with the local communities' definitions of what constitutes a political issue, who controls the definition of issues, and how control is perpetuated.[5] We approach politics in terms of the exercise of power and influence in highly structured decision making arenas as well as in situations where control is disputed or negotiated. On the one hand, we will look at politics as the control of formal decision making by community groups. On the other hand, we want to examine politics as (1) the exercise of power outside the formal channels of government through the control and manipulation of issues before they reach the political agenda and (2) the impact of unquestioned cultural and ideological biases operating on the definition of political issues and participation.[6] In analyzing Andean politics we are interested in power structures as regulators of access to crucial resources as defined by the community. We are also concerned with power structures as organizations through which some citizens define social reality and enforce those definitions on others. The differential involvements of men and women in agenda setting, in formal decision making, and in exerting power and influence to shape community affairs are our central concerns.[7]

By using this broader definition of political interest and participation, a more complex view of Andean women's situation emerges. In examining women's political behavior within local community politics, we have found restricted and highly circumscribed levels of participation combined with high levels of political awareness and consciousness. In this chapter we describe the gaps between women's participation and consciousness, between women's representation in local politics and their perceptions of political issues. We ask if women are adequately represented under the present political systems. To deal with the issue of representation we must answer a number of antecedent questions about the local organization of politics and political world views. For instance, does the present level of women's participation reflect their political interests and consciousness? Do women view their level of participation as adequate? Do women and men view women's participation in community political life in the same ways? We also want to ask about the extent to which the economic issues raised in our analysis of sexual divisions of labor and economic stratification affect women's political participation.

From the outset we should note that we are examining two distinct forms of political organization. Mayobamba has an indigenous community government as part of its community structure. In contrast, Chiuchin, as a town without firmly entrenched political institutions, is governed sporadically by district officials, national government extension agents, and ad hoc citizen organizations. Thus we must also ask if differences in political organization account for variations in women's perceptions and patterns of participation in the two communities. Let us begin by examining the nature of local level participation in Mayobamba and Chiuchin and then analyzing the implications of these patterns for the two prevailing images of Andean women's political behavior.

Defining Political Issues in the Agrarian Context

The people of Mayobamba are well informed about national politics and aware that the state defines their social reality—institutionally through the courts, the police, the military, and the schools; developmentally through regional projects and agrarian reforms; and economically through governmental pricing of staples and gasoline. Yet rural populations also realize that there is enough play in the articulation of national and local politics so that they can ignore or sometimes even effectively protest the national governmental initiatives they disagree with (cf. Bourque and Warren 1979b). The geographical isolation, small size, and status of Mayobamba as a peasant community have allowed the settlement to maintain a measure of autonomy in local administration.

In Mayobamba, local politics reflect the directions of economic change. Just as Mayobamba's communal land tenure has been forced to accommodate the growing importance of private land and cash crops in the twentieth century, so too the community has been torn by collectivist and individualist definitions of government and development. In the 1970s, the key political issues from the local perspective have involved controversies over the organization of a sheep cooperative, the extension of potable water to private homes, and the restriction of *comunero* status to full-time, resident agriculturalists. While these issues may appear to be rather mundane and pragmatic to an outsider, in fact each has involved an implicit political debate over the definition of the local community. Through these controversies, agriculturalists debate such questions as future forms of community leadership and possible goals for locally motivated participation in national politics.

Like many peasant communities, Mayobamba is characterized by great tension between its collectivist political organization and growing differences in individual wealth and economic positions. Traditionally the community defined membership as the duty to collaborate in the cultivation of communal fields, the undertaking of public works, the care of communal dairy herds, and the communal administration of the settlement. Proceeds from the collective potato harvest of community lands finance local development projects such as school buildings, public water faucets, and the repair of irrigation works. In addition, part of the community harvest is stored and drawn on by any *comunero* in serious financial need due to crop failure. The collectivist model of community also calls on all heads of households to participate in the civil administration of the settlement. In theory each *comunero* rotates through all local political offices during his lifetime and at some point heads the community as its president.[8]

Increasing economic stratification has fostered a more individualistic model of community. Those who hold this contrasting set of values argue that the collectivist model and the obligations of communal membership are a brake upon the improvement of individuals within the community. Local male elites would prefer a more individualistic model of community, one which would allow for greater participation and leadership from the economic progressives. For these individuals, participation would include forging effective ties with provincial and national political officials who might provide access to opportunities and resources for the community or local individuals. Local elites realize that not all members of the community are committed to their image of development and that not all *comuneros* are sufficiently literate, articulate in Spanish, and socially confident to deal with coastal authorities. Consequently they believe that only those *comuneros* with the appropriate skills should be elected to the presidency of the community. They strongly oppose the collectivist model of a rotating presidency.

In addition to the question of how leadership positions are to be filled, recent political debates in Mayobamba have dealt with the implementation of local development projects. For instance, in founding a community sheep cooperative Mayobamba argued over whether all members should have equivalent shares in the cooperative or whether wealthier individuals might increase their investments and thus receive higher returns. In this particular case the more egalitarian alternative won, although in another local development project involving the extension of potable water to homesites, the more individualistic, elite-oriented segment of the population carried the day. In this instance, the community treasury paid for the installation of tubing to the settlement and individuals paid for connections to their homes. Only those with sufficient money to pay for the homesite connections received direct benefits from the community's investment in tubing. In 1978 debates over the extension of irrigation canals to a new zone of private land were taking on similar twists and divisions.

The not-so-hidden agenda behind arguments over who should be president, how a second sheep cooperative should be organized, and whether to extend irrigation works to a new area of private fields is a definitional debate over Mayobamba's future as a collectivist versus a more individualistically organized economically stratified community. At this point in Mayobamba, the basic issue of which form of community to stress is still negotiable and hotly contested among the town's *comuneros*. No one has the power to enforce his definition unilaterally on others, and the presidency remains a rotating position. Yet these debates are important indicators of the growing importance of economic stratification in community life. Younger male economic elites in their 30s and 40s favor developing closer ties to the coast and creating a nonrotating presidency.[9] The rest of the community has responded with more situational stances, at times protesting national policy that would restrict peasant access to the center, at other times, standing firm on more collectivist and egalitarian notions of community development.

What is not disputed by either element are several fundamental functions of the settlement's *comunero* organization. The *comunero* form of household representation serves as the vehicle for undertaking all local public works including road maintenance, irrigation canal repairs, and public building construction. Both wealthy and poorer Mayobambinos share a concern with providing community services that would be left undone if not effectively organized on a local level.

Women's position within Mayobamba's political debates, development projects, and *comunero* system is remarkably uniform. On the whole, women have not played an active part in the debate over the major issue on the community's political agenda; that is, which principle will govern the organization of the community. Women do not stand to gain politically from this debate because neither the collectivist nor the individualistic, elite-based model of leadership and development would widen women's general patterns of political involvement. Regardless of the compromises or more decisive outcomes of negotiations over specific issues, an individual woman's access to participation would remain unchanged. Moreover, these debates do not address Mayobamba's system of household representation through *comuneros,* which is the critical issue for women's political participation.

Growing economic stratification has not brought women into politics either in a public decision-making capacity or in behind-the-scenes manipulations of the definitions of leadership and development. For example, even in families where men desire more individualistic political control as a result of their newly acquired economic position, the women to whom they are related have not been brought into the political arena. As we argued in chapter 6, women married to men in the wealthy strata of the agricultural community are economically active, but isolated at home where they spend their workday cooking for laborers in addition to their domestic duties. These women are largely dependent on husbands for their economic position. Women's involvements in labor exchanges or women's networks are greatly restricted in this economic strata. Paradoxically those forces which gave rise to a greater desire for individualized political leadership among men have distanced women from the public arena and limited their community participation. It is important to note that women have also been severely constrained in political participation in the collectivist community. This becomes apparent in more detailed examinations of the *comunero* system and local government.

Political Implications of the Comunero System

Formal government in Mayobamba is organized on the basis of family representation through officially designated heads of household, called *comuneros*. The complexity of *comunero* status derives from two important elements. First, the status is a set of political privileges, entitling the holder to voice, vote, and cyclical leadership within the community. Second, *comunero* status requires the payment of a labor tax through participation in community public works projects called *faenas*. Few men would be particularly anxious to have *comunero* status if it only implied the obligation to contribute time and labor. *Comunero* status also implies political rights, in essence the right to participate in public decisions. Given the nature of the issues that local government controls, this is viewed as an important forum for protecting individual and family interests.[10]

In Mayobamba local government consists of the assembly of all *comuneros* and the board of officers including an elected president, vice president, secretary, treasurer, and five other councilmen charged with distinct administrative responsibilities. Community officers are elected each January to serve for a year. As mentioned above the pattern has been to rotate offices among all *comuneros,* so that all adult men eventually take on each responsibility for local governance. Community government has control over the allocation of water and communal land; it also regulates community herds of cows and sheep. The officers are responsible for selecting a communal herder to care for the animals and oversee the sale of surplus animals when the assembly so determines. The assembly also decides how the proceeds from the sales will be used. Community officers administer community pastures, determine who can use those pastures, and organize the system of vigilance which keep stray animals out of productive fields.

In short the community's governmental apparatus has a great deal of control over local resources. Mayobambinos hold and measure wealth in terms of private irrigated property, but the water which makes private property valuable is distributed by the community. The potato, upon which Mayobambinos base their subsistence, is grown on land which belongs to the community and distributed among its members by local officials. Serving as an officer of the community involves time, effort, and the expenditure of personal resources. It can be an onerous obligation. However, to be excluded from such an obligation would be to be removed from the most important decisions before the group.

Mayobamba men say that each family is represented by a single *comunero* and as long as there is a male to take on this role, it should be done by a man. In any given family, brothers become *comuneros* as they marry, while sisters must gain access to representation and resources through their fathers and husbands who are *comuneros*. Only when a woman has been widowed or when she is a long-term single mother and no longer attached to her father's family does she receive *comunera* status. Nevertheless, few women are free from the impact of the labor tax dimension of the *comunero* system. Directly or indirectly women bear some of the burden of the tax. Women who are not heads of household must replace their fathers or husbands in the fields when the men are occupied in community projects. Older single mothers and widows with *comunera* status must meet the labor tax directly by contributing to communal projects. Yet, these women are not given a full set of political rights as a result of their participation in communal projects.[11]

The labor tax requirement of the *comunero* system functions as a regressive tax in that it is disproportionately disadvantageous for poor women and men. Those with limited wealth, either in land or cash, are disadvantaged by the demand for equal work from all. Because the labor tax is assessed equally in a situation where wealth is unevenly distributed, the effect of the law is to help the rich get richer and the poor poorer.

The obligations of *comunero* status can be extremely heavy, demanding the contribution of time which might otherwise be spent in private concerns. Many *comuneros* attempt to avoid some of the more onerous responsibilities within the community. If a *comunero* fails to meet his community obligations he is fined. It is possible to pay a substitute to perform one's work obligation, if someone can be found to do it. Failure to meet one's work obligation, or barring that, to pay assessed fines, can result in removal from the official roster of the community and the loss of rights to communal land. Significantly those cases in which an adult male has avoided the full set of obligations incumbent on *comunero* status have been among the sons of men with extensive holdings of private land. These individuals produce enough on private land so that the loss of community land would not spell disaster for them.

Wealthy *comuneros* also enjoy special advantages within the labor tax system for public works. These *comuneros* are able to take advantage of the option to pay a fine (in the form of a cash penalty or the purchase of cash products for work groups) in lieu of contributing a day's labor. This option allows the wealthy individual to devote himself to private fields while poorer *comuneros* must provide their own labor and lose time from their private holdings.

Like poor men, single mothers and widows who are *comuneras* are disadvantaged by the regressive labor tax. They have less access to cash and thus may be forced to convert produce or livestock into cash in order to meet communal obligations. Poor men solve this problem by showing up personally to work on *faenas*. Women are not as fortunate. In instances such as road construction and irrigation canal repairs, key tasks are deemed too demanding physically for women. As a substitute for heavy physical labor, women are required to supply cash or such commercial products as alcohol and cigarettes for work parties. This is not always an attractive alternative for women whose opportunities to generate cash are minimal. Ironically, traditional community participation in the *comunero* system, in effect, forces women's additional involvement in the wage labor economy where they are by far the lowest paid segment of the labor force.

The older female *comuneras* are especially disadvantaged by this system. Generally women are granted *comunera* status only after the deaths of fathers and husbands. Women may enter the system at an age where their male counterparts are actually retiring from *comunero* status and asking sons to take over family representation. In other words, women become *comuneras* when they are least capable of completing their responsibilities and successfully influencing local politics to reflect their interests. Widows complain vociferously about the hardship of serving out *comunera* obligations, pointing out that they have limited access to cash at this point in their lives and the demands upon it are heavy. These women must supply cash products both for communal work projects and to pay for the male labor they need in agriculture. They also feel that the male *comuneros* have increased the obligations which widows must fulfill. Some complain they were not given a full year free of communal service to mark their period of mourning for a dead husband. Others say they have been asked to take on tasks which they are unable to complete and, as a result, are forced to pay other *comuneros* to complete the responsibilities for them. Finally there are instances in which the male *comuneros* have changed the nature of women's contribution from a work obligation, which women have the skills to accomplish, to a cash contribution.

A redefinition of female responsibilities for communal projects occurred recently in the case of a dispute over who should cook for work groups constructing a high altitude irrigation dam. In the past women had met their work obligation on this *faena* by cooking for workers at the construction site. In 1978, the male *comuneros* argued for a change, saying that there was considerable dissatisfaction among the men about the perceived favoritism of the women in serving the food at communal projects. According to the men, the female *comuneras* failed to give the men equal portions and kept the best pieces of meat for themselves. This alleged inequity caused considerable bad feelings among the men. Male *comuneros* now praise the ability of their two new male cooks to distribute meat evenly among them. Female *comuneras,* who can no longer participate as cooks, must now meet their obligations in this *faena* by supplying cash products such as rum, tobacco, and coca.

One of the reasons that the men could make this new arrangement, despite the fact it disadvantages cash-poor female *comuneras,* who would prefer to cook, is that men make such decisions on their own. In addition to the differential economic implications of *comunero* obligations, the political privileges of *comunero* status are awarded only to men. Whereas women share in those aspects of *comunero* status which imply a work obligation, they receive none of the benefits of political participation and decision making that men enjoy.[12] Women, whether or not they are *comuneras,* are generally barred from voting, leadership, and participation in public decisions. As a result they have limited influence on which activities constitute their labor contribution and what projects the community should undertake.[13]

Women's participation in community service is not exhausted by studying those women who formally become *comuneras.* In fact, married women are informally but thoroughly involved in community positions that are felt to require the efforts of both husband and wife to complete successfully. In these instances, however, it is the man who is given the official position and title; the wife's participation in the task does not entitle her to participation in the official affairs of the community.[14] For instance, a male *comunero* is assigned the task of caring for the community cows (about sixty head of dairy cattle) for a year, in return for which he is freed from other communal *faenas* and can use the milk from the community cows for his own cheese production. In both the daily milking of the cows and the manufacturing of cheese his wife's labor is indispensable. The task of caring for the community cows is recognized as being especially time consuming and people try to avoid it. Moreover, it would be impossible to complete this community service without the assistance of a wife, an older daughter, or other female relatives (and easier if one has all three).

The festival which marks the end of the *comunero*'s year of service as the community herder includes the active participation of the *comunero*'s wife and her friends. During a day-long celebration, to ensure the herd's fertility, dozens of small rounds of cheese, made from the milk of the community herd, are used as decorations for town officials, guests, and *comuneros*. When the community's cows are brought to the central plaza to be counted and paraded before the image of the town's patron saint, the *comunero* who has served his year as herdsman and his wife lead the procession twirling banners, dancing, and singing songs about the successful completion of the heavy responsibility.

Even though the *comunero*'s wife participates actively in this aspect of the ceremony, it is the *comunero* alone who speaks to the community president, presenting him with the cows and explaining the number of births, deaths, and sales that have occurred during the year. His wife may stand behind him and remind him of details, but it is he who is the responsible authoritative voice of the family.

Similarly the *comunero* charged with the care of the church's treasures takes on a year of community service which is completed with his wife's collaboration. As with the care of the community animals, the responsibility of caring for the church requires activities that make it especially appropriate for men and women to share the task. The cleaning and guardianship aspects of this position are traditionally associated with women. In the case of the church, the *comunero* and his wife are responsible for cleaning, opening and preparing the church building for fiestas, in addition to the care of the community's religious treasures.

The ceremony for transferring this guardianship occurs in early May when the church is opened for the day and all *comuneros* gather in front of it on benches or around a large table. A younger literate *comunero* records the transfer of church property from one guardian to the next. The *comunero* reads a description of an item, and the retiring guardian enters the church where his wife sits on one side of the vestry with several large chests of church treasures. The retiring guardian asks his wife for the item, and she either tells him where it is or gets it for him. He then takes the item outside and turns it over to the *comunero* with the record book. After it has been checked off, the treasure is given to the new guardian, who brings the item back in to the opposite side of the church where *his* wife sits ready to receive the treasure. This continues for about four hours. The two women chat with one another as they search for items or put them away. Meanwhile the *comuneros* stand outside, noting which *comuneros* have failed to attend the ceremony (so that they can be fined half a day's wages), or busy themselves repainting the four crosses which guard the entrances to the community. As the transfer progresses, the men enjoy each other's company drinking together and chatting so that by midway in the afternoon a good proportion of the men are inebriated. With the exception of the wives of the retiring and incumbent guardians, none of the women of Mayobamba attend the ceremony.

An interesting exception to the pattern of exclusively male leadership and official participation in community organizations occurred in 1975 with the appointment of a Mayobamba woman to a minor position in the community's Parents' Association of the elementary school, an organization roughly equivalent to the PTA. The young woman appointed was not at all sure what the position would entail. Her mother was rather distressed at the selection, saying that this responsibility should not have been imposed on her daughter, that her daughter's eldest child had not been in school long enough for this to seem fair. Several Mayobamba men explained the woman's selection as an attempt to punish men who had sent their wives to the meeting personally to avoid the chance of being selected. In short, there was a range of local interpretations of the significance of this woman's selection, yet no one suggested that her appointment reflected a trend to broaden women's participation.

Mayobamba's *comunero* system as a form of political representation
and taxation has far reaching consequences for maintaining economic
stratification based on wealth and sex. Male control of local government and decisions concerning *comuneros* of both sexes is one structural outcome of this system of household representation. Through
the *comunero* system, men define important aspects of women's social
reality. For example, they decide when sexual divisions of labor can be
violated (as in the case of male cooks for work parties), and when
conventional divisions of labor can be used to justify necessary but
unrewarded female participation in community service (as in wives'
assistance of herdsmen and church guardians). For women, however,
participation in service to the community does not translate into political power or formal office. Even though recent local administrations
have complained about a lack of available men for posts and some
men have been asked to serve twice, women have not been brought
into local government as decision makers.

Perceptions of Political Participation in Mayobamba

Our discussion thus far has concentrated on how power is exercised in
Mayobamba politics through agenda setting and community decision
making. We find that women's participation is restricted in both their
ability to determine what comes up for decision as well as the ultimate
resolution of contested issues.

How men and women explain and justify differential participation
helps us understand the role of social ideologies—which structure
values and explanations of how the world operates—in shaping and
reproducing inegalitarian relations. Thus it is not only men's control
of crucial resources, but also the cultural justifications of why that
should be the case, which become important for understanding
women and men's relationship to one another. Of particular importance in this case is the fact that Mayobamba men and women have
differing explanations for women's limited political participation.
Men say that women do not need to participate as *comuneros*, attend
assemblies, or vote because men adequately represent the family.
They do not, however, say that they take their wives' opinions into
account when deciding a communal issue, nor do they feel it necessary to ask the women about opinions before making communal decisions. Mayobamba men are aware of the contrast between community

and national politics in the sense that women have both voted and held office at the national level. The men indicate that it is simply not the custom for women to hold public office in Mayobamba. One man went on to emphasize, "You simply can't change that; it is one of the things that people won't change."

Other men explain that female political participation is limited because women are not as fluent in Spanish and are often illiterate. These same factors do not, however, restrict men from participating in community government: illiterate men have been president of the community, attended assemblies, and voted in community elections. Higher literacy among women may help to eliminate this particular explanation for limiting women's political participation. Yet, more fundamental cultural justifications for the exclusion of women may prove more resistant to change. The opinions of the president of Mayobamba about proper male-female roles exemplifies these values.

> The man always has to be on top, has to order, to command. The man has to give ideas to women. He has to take care of the children, to sustain them and his wife. Men know more; women don't know anything.
>
> Men may cook for a day or two, and women may go to the fields for a while, but each has his separate place. If both cooked, who would work in the fields?

Men tend to view their dominance as both natural and extensive: it is not limited to the public realm nor to areas of particular male expertise. Although men may at times emphasize the functional aspects of the sexual division of labor, one cannot conclude that the men feel each sex's tasks are equally important.

Women's explanations of their nonparticipation in institutionalized politics are somewhat distinct. While they are aware of their higher rates of illiteracy, they do not focus on this explanation. Rather, women cite community values, customary patterns of decision making, and attitudes about women's capabilities. Here are two explanations women offer for their limited participation.

> It is still the case that here a woman is calculated to be an inferior being, a less competent thing that cannot participate. She is only fit to help at home, not publicly.

> Some women get accustomed to the fact that their husbands are the heads of everything; others want to participate. But the majority give up leadership to their husbands.

Note that women are aware that they are viewed as less capable, "an inferior being." Significantly, however, women do not see this status as given in nature, but rather as male evaluation. As the second statement suggests, women may resist men's attempts to monopolize control, however, in the end they give in to male demands for leadership.

One woman, when asked if widows or *comuneras* could hold communal office, summarized her understanding of the mechanisms involved as follows:

> Up until the present time they haven't . . . because the men don't give them the opportunity to participate. They figure that a woman is incapable of carrying out responsibilities. They don't give her leadership or opportunity, and by custom this continues. Never is she given a role in the governing board.

These quotes exemplify the range and complexity of women's self-perception with regard to public participation. In addition they indicate that some women identify subordination with restricted participation and male attitudes toward women.

Women and men perceive their participation in community service in distinct ways. Women in the company of other women during festivals speak of having passed through a particular community office and share reminiscences of the demanding nature of the work. This is especially true for offices requiring great expenditures of time, as in the case of community herders. Men on the other hand tend to portray themselves as the sole occupants of these official positions, while acknowledging their wives' assistance in those tasks closely associated with women's work.

This pattern of women's wider definition of participation, in contrast to men's narrow conception of official participation as formal office holding, parallels the patterning we found in male and female definitions of work in chapter 5. Married women's broader notion of participation makes their service to the community meaningful to the women themselves.

Differences in the perception of community service may well block married women's consciousness of the sex-based inequities of the *comunero* system. Older widows and single mothers are much more aware of the special demands the system makes on women. As in the case of the definitions of economics and work, it is men's, not women's, conception of participation that is given value by the local power structure.

Neither Mayobamba men nor women claim that there is mutual consultation between husbands and wives over community decisions. A man's notion that he represents his family as a *comunero* means, in Mayobambino terms, that he fulfills the community work obligations. It does not mean that he feels he must faithfully represent the concensus of his household in community discussions and decisions.

The notion of the *comunero* as a Lockean representative, instructed by his constituents, the family, as to how to vote, and what opinions to express, appears in other descriptions of male-female relations in the Andean Quechua family. To quote Núñez del Prado Béjar:

> The man is the spokesman, that is to say he collects the opinions of the various members of his household and puts forth these decisions. In no way is it he who makes the decisions for his family, nor does he impose his point of view or his criteria in an authoritarian fashion. [1975*b*, p. 627]

We have not found this form of representation to hold for Mayobamba. Moreover neither men nor women convey this image of male representation as either their expectation or their ideal. Thus the view of Andean women as powerful behind the scenes manipulators of men does not ring true to Mayobamban perceptions of their political behavior.

Returning to the questions which we posed at the outset of this chapter it appears from our reading of political life in Mayobamba that there is a discrepancy between the present level of women's participation in the community and the level of their political interests. Women are as deeply concerned by the distribution of resources as are men. They discuss local production, water problems, and they have definite ideas about which public works should be undertaken. When speaking about local Mayobamba politics women are neither apolitical nor politically uninterested. They have definite views about how particular officials perform their specific tasks and about the overall administration of the town. Women are also aware that their opinions are frequently not taken into consideration by the male assembly.

Whereas men may explain that there is no need for more than one *comunero* per family, neither they nor their wives claim that the *comun-*

ero represents the collective interests of the family unit. Men and women offer different explanations for restricted female participation; when offering the same explanation, such as illiteracy, they tend to assign it different saliency. Finally it seems to us a mistake to assume a commonality of opinion between men and women, as husbands and wives or as *comuneros* and *comuneras,* on the decisions before the community. In fact, it appears that in the case of the *comuneras,* some of the decisions taken by the men alone (for instance, the question of how to handle cooking obligations on community work projects) are very much at odds with the desires of the women.

Political Issues and Women's Political Participation in Chiuchin

The people of Chiuchin have a heightened awareness of the impact of national politics on rural populations as a result of their role as the critical link for communication, transportation and commerce between the coast and the highland communities. It is not unusual to hear a Chiuchin merchant grumbling about the scarcity of small gasoline-powered motors and offering a critique of Peru's import substitution policies as an explanation. Other merchants worry that their coastal suppliers are hoarding commodities which fall under the national government's pricing policy in hopes that they will make windfall profits with new hikes in price ceilings. Still other townspeople wonder if someone's contacts with coastal authorities might prove useful in speeding the construction and staffing of a new public health center.

Chiuchinistas do not seek isolation and autonomy for their town. Rather they value strategic links with the coast that will benefit commerce and promote the town as a regional commercial capital for the ten highland communities it serves. In many ways Chiuchin has successfully captured regional stature, although the formal political capital of the district remains a remote and very conservative highland agricultural community. Chiuchinistas know that there is little chance of having the title of political capital transferred to their settlement. Instead, they have promoted the centralization of as many economic, administrative, and educational functions as possible in Chiuchin so that the town will become the de facto capital. This strategy for development is the primary theme behind the agenda of issues that have been locally debated during the last decade.

In Chiuchin, the educated, merchant elites control local politics. On the whole these merchants agree that close ties to the coast and the location of outposts of coastal institutions in Chiuchin will bring prosperity and progress to the town. They also believe that for Chiuchin to attain economic dominance, the town needs the participation of highland communities in development projects. Unlike the highland communities, however, Chiuchin lacks an officially recognized *comunero* structure through which to make local policy, to mobilize individuals for community projects, and to represent the town's interests to the center. Instead, Chiuchin is ultimately subject to district officials, most of whom come from and reside in the higher agricultural communities. In the absence of locally elected officials or a history of communal cooperation through *comuneros,* local activity in Chiuchin is organized on an ad hoc basis. Usually this means that when there is a project a local merchant will take the initiative to organize a committee, invite the district authorities, and attempt to generate support for the given project.[15]

Chiuchinistas are well aware of the difficulties of working with an unofficial political structure and the limits that its lack of full legitimacy places on their development strategies. Townspeople recognize that their lack of an institutionalized mechanism for organizing and carrying out projects also restricts what the community accomplishes and in some instances seems to determine what the community decides to undertake. Townspeople openly discuss their desire for more widespread cooperation for accomplishing public works, which they believe would be ideally organized through a *comunero*-like system of labor contributions. In fact, Chiuchinistas have been unsuccessful in replicating this model of political organization in their settlement for several reasons: the national government has not recognized the town as an official community, the town has no communal resources to distribute among potential *comuneros,* and merchants prefer to play off individualistic competitive interests against more collective goals on an ad hoc basis.

The consequences of a nontraditional political structure have been uneven for women. On the one hand, as we shall explain below, the ad hoc nature of organization has facilitated elite women's political participation. On the other hand, it has influenced the kind of activities which the town is likely to pursue, giving highest priority to those projects for which outside coastal aid can be secured, and postponing many local improvement projects to which women give higher priority than do men.

For the town, political issues in the seventies can be placed on a continuum reflecting local perceptions and reactions to them. Those issues which link and broaden access to coastal and regional resources and are based on considerable outside aid would represent one end of the continuum. Those concerns which are more specifically geared toward improving local life and which depend primarily on local labor and resources would stand at the other end. We would include the construction and staffing of a health center and comprehensive school (*nucleo*),[16] and the distribution of scarce coastal commodities to local merchants for sale in the first set of issues. The second set would include issues such as the construction of a local soccer field, the extension of potable water to individual homes, the construction of a new bridge to the local thermal baths, and improvement of the town plaza.

It is, of course, true that the health center and the nuclear school are intended to improve local life, but their ultimate success and primary purpose is more clearly directed toward enhancing the ties between the rural population and the national government and garnering for the local area the resources of the national political system. Moreover, in an important sense, the success of these projects is more clearly dependent on the responses of national decision makers.

The major unquestioned assumption underlying all political issues in Chiuchin is the belief that, like it or not, the most *realistic* development goals for the town involve increased ties with coastal society and national organizations. Through such connections, it is anticipated that the rural standard of living will rise and the economy grow. Also coastal ties will help to channel young people to urban areas where employment opportunities are wider. Given the small land base, steadily growing population, and the aspirations of the youth for coastal lifestyles, *sierra* communities have little choice but to export population to cities. Both men and women agree on this strategy and share this set of values. There is also considerable agreement on this issue across economic strata in Chiuchin.

Despite their strong commitments to coastal-oriented development, Chiuchinistas have complex and sometimes ambivalent attitudes toward the emissaries of coastal organizations. Townspeople are very critical about poorly conceived development efforts and inept personnel assigned to the *sierra*.[17] Development projects heavily dependent on the coast have substantial elements of uncertainty due to the difficulty of finding personnel for these projects, the inconsistent policy decisions of frequently changing central government administrators, and the consequent local risk of constructing buildings that may never be utilized. Posting personnel to the *sierra* is a significant problem that illustrates the difficulties and limitations of the development strategy adopted by Chiuchin. For the comprehensive school and health center to be effective the central government ministries must send personnel to the facility. Yet, acquiring trained personnel willing to serve in the rural areas is a serious problem because of the resistance of coastal dwellers to being transferred to rural areas. Strong racial, class, and regional prejudices exist in coastal society toward the *sierra* and even when urbanites agree to serve in a rural area their prejudice toward the local population leads to a frustrating work experience for everyone, as well as frequent resignations and turnovers.

Since Chiuchin has very limited resources, political negotiations must sort out priorities for local development projects. The tendency has been for Chiuchin to abandon such projects as a bridge to the thermal baths and the extension of potable water to homes in favor of the establishment of a health center and a comprehensive school. To fully understand the differing implications of these choices for men and women we must examine both women's patterns of participation and men's and women's perceptions of local politics.

In Chiuchin, women have been actively involved in local politics and development efforts. The ad hoc nature of local organization and the absence of traditional governmental structure have meant, in at least some instances, that women's economic power has been more readily translated into political participation. The conjunction between economic power and political participation is especially apparent in Chiuchin because individuals in the town must generate the money needed to undertake an activity. There are no community cows, sheep, or potatoes which can be sold to raise the necessary cash. Moreover, since Chiuchin is not an official peasant community, there is no *faena* system among the citizens. This means that all labor necessary for a given activity must be contracted and paid for with cash. Given the expanded opportunities for women to earn money in Chiuchin, they are not as disadvantaged as Mayobamba women by increased reliance on cash. Access to cash of course varies by economic level (as it does in Mayobamba), but because some Chiuchin women have substantial economic resources by local standards, their contribution to any activity is a central consideration for the success of any project.

Women's broader patterns of participation are evidenced in the case of an ad hoc committee organized to support the creation of a comprehensive school. A great many Chiuchin women have been involved in the school committee, and one woman was elected to serve as treasurer of the group, an important position and one which reflects her ability as an administrator of the largest local hotel and thermal baths. Active women have tended to be those with high levels of economic responsibility in their work: four are in charge of their own businesses, along with three female school teachers who are presently stationed in Chiuchin. This case of increased participation appears to be directly related to economic position and the fact that expanded participation has occurred in a structure not subject to the patriarchal tradition of a *comunero* system.

The ad hoc school committee is a particularly significant political organization in Chiuchin. The committee was organized to pressure the national government to create a comprehensive school with an expanded curriculum that would include both vocational and adult education programs and to locate the facility in Chiuchin. The school is among the most important extensions of the national government in the rural areas. As such it represents an obvious link between the national system and the local community. Members of the ad hoc committee actively discuss the nature of local-to-national ties and strategies for lobbying for benefits from the national system at the same time as they receive considerable exposure to political manipulation and calculation beyond the confines of the local community. Consequently membership on this type of committee is a significant indicator of political participation. It is also important to note the difference between the parents' association of Mayobamba and the ad hoc school committee in Chiuchin. The Mayobamba group has not engaged in activities other than advising the local school teacher and planning local activities. Thus not only are more women involved in

Chiuchin, but they participate in substantially more political activities.

One can see how participation on the Chiuchin school committee is both a result of expanded political opportunities for Chiuchin women and the means by which greater political consciousness and wider political skills can be acquired.

While there is far greater female participation in the ad hoc school committee than in Mayobamba, this has not translated into district level leadership positions. There are no Chiuchin women serving as members of the district council, nor are women members of the police force. Nevertheless, while women in Chiuchin have not yet achieved district level offices, they demonstrate a level of political consciousness and a recognition of both opportunities for and constraints upon their political participation.

Perceptions of Political Participation in Chiuchin

As with the *comuneras* in Mayobamba, the women of Chiuchin have a set of political concerns and articulately discuss the issues which are central to them. In many instances Chiuchin women share a common set of values with men, particularly with regard to supporting projects such as the comprehensive school and health center which have direct benefits for their children. On the other hand, they give much higher priority to those projects which figure at the other end of the continuum, involving local level improvements and depending on local resources for their completion. Women, while supporting the extension of ties to the coast, are reluctant to see these goals pursued exclusively and at the cost of much needed local improvements. They are aware that the importance men assign to regional development projects differs from their own ranking, yet they let the town maintain these priorities because they anticipate important benefits for their families.

Furthermore, men and women in Chiuchin have distinct rankings for *local* improvement projects. The result of those different rankings have been that projects favored by the men are completed first and projects favored by women listed last on the town's agenda. Women are conscious of these differences and are interested in changing them.

Small groups of Chiuchin women regularly gather in the afternoons to share sewing skills and from time to time their conversation turns to local politics. Frequently they consider the inability of the community to accomplish some longed for improvement. In one such conversation a middle-aged mother of four commented:

> It seems to me that we women would do a better job of unifying the community. Men don't do anything; they get drunk, go out to make themselves happy by discussing things, and there it ends. But women, I believe, would do it better. We need a central plaza, drainage, and electricity. I think it would be best if we would create a committee of women with someone to advise us. It hurts me that my town is backward, that there isn't any progress. Soon we will need progress so that there is some advancement for the children, so there isn't so much unemployment. Everyone goes to Lima. We can't leave behind our beautiful homeland without doing something.

Women in this discussion went on to point out to each other which Chiuchin women they could count on for a pressure group and what issues they might organize around. They discussed concrete changes to make women's lives easier such as insuring a regular supply of water in the town and extending it to private homes so that women would not have to go to the river or the central spigots to haul water, and funding a community generator so that women would have better light when they work at night.

In conversation these women direct their political concerns toward local issues that would improve the conditions of specifically female tasks. In town politics such projects are given second place to efforts enhancing ties to coastal resources. Because both men and women agree to some extent about the value of the first end of the continuum, the most intense negotiation takes place where local projects must be decided upon. The ability of the men to direct the town's limited resources to accomplish the projects they identify as top priority—such as the construction of a soccer field—gives rise to resentment among the women who decry the loss of interest in the bridge to the baths, town electrification, and extension of the potable water system to homes.

A factor that has stopped these women from organizing their own committee is the response they anticipate from men in the community. One woman imagined the town's response to a woman activist on such a committee: "They would say, 'She's crazy; she has a lot of time on her hands.'" (Who would say this?) "The men. . . . Many times to avoid all the quarrelling we decide not to do anything, to avoid an argument." Chiuchin women say that men do not consider them polit-ically competent or their political equals. One businesswoman charac-terized her frustration with negative male attitudes as follows:

> When the men come to a meeting that is attended principally by mar-ried women, they say, "Well, we can't get anything done. There are only women here and with only women we can't decide anything." The men wouldn't dream of making a woman president of a committee; they reject the names of the women immediately. Worse still, some of the women accept this idea of themselves, the views of men. They agree with the men and say, "What can we do here? We're only women."

When Chiuchin women evaluate their own participation they con-vey a sense of dissatisfaction with the little they have been able to accomplish in the town and their hopes of doing a great deal more. Women's frustrated desire to organize politically is clear evidence that their political participation is not successfully accomplished through manipulation of husbands. Were this the case women would not be contemplating new forms of political organization through which to articulate demands relating directly to their concerns as women.

Chiuchin men also recognize that there is no necessary conjunction between the political concerns of men and women. In fact, the men argue that differing priorities is one of the reasons they resist wom-en's participation in community meetings.

Chiuchin women know their priorities for necessary local im-provements are different from those of the men. Chiuchin men also believe and fear women may have different preferences, but they choose to attribute these differences to outside manipulation and to use susceptibility to manipulation as a justification for continuing to exclude women. A former district mayor explained that men objected to women attending their meetings for fear that the women would want to undertake projects the men were against and force the men into obligations they did not want. He recalled one instance in which a local strong man had wanted the communities of Checras district to collaborate in the construction of a school. The *comuneros* had been reluctant to agree to the project, which would have required an in-creased labor contribution. As the mayor recalls events, the strong man convinced women that it was a good idea and insisted that they be allowed into the meeting. When the idea for the project came up for discussion he called on the women he had coached to speak in favor of the project. As the mayor explains it, the men were ashamed to voice their objections in front of the women, particularly when the women had offered to collaborate whether or not their men went along with the school.

The mayor's story suggests that some Chiuchin men view women as too open to outside manipulation. Thus men worry that women's political participation might lessen men's control over the political agenda. Some Chiuchin men indicate that they feel that qualified women would make good administrators and would probably do the job as well as men. Verbally they favor the participation of active women in such positions as the treasurer of local groups. However, most men feel that women in general are less prepared than men to participate in community affairs because of lack of education. Some point out that the lower level of education for women is not their fault but rather the mistake of earlier generations who had undervalued their daughters.

Actively involved Chiuchin women have a desire to participate in local political decisions and an emerging sense of themselves as women with a particular contribution to make. Clearly they would like to get more of their concerns acted upon. As a partial explanation of this high level of social concern and political consciousness, one might point out that Chiuchin women have had extensive experience in dealing with the outside world. They are public people engaged in businesses which require them to deal with strangers. Hence the geographical location of Chiuchin may have served to enhance these women's personal skills and self-confidence. This appears to carry over into evaluations of their abilities as compared to men. Individual women who are proprietors of their own businesses often consider themselves at least as capable as their brothers and husbands in areas such as business decisions, the ability to deal with outside businessmen, and the skills to negotiate and bargain skillfully. Moreover, the absence of traditional community political institutions has opened new participatory opportunities on ad hoc committees for those individual women who have higher economic status.

Our data from Chiuchin and Mayobamba suggest that women demonstrate high rates of political awareness and consciousness, particularly in those areas directly related to their own and their families' well-being. Women's lack of power to manipulate issues before they are to be decided is tremendously important because it restricts women's effective influence to only those questions addressed in community agendas. In both communities there are fundamental orientations to politics and decision making that disadvantage women. Women find these aspects of local politics—such as the *comunero* system of Mayobamba or the coastal direction of development in Chiuchin—particularly difficult to influence because they are not subject to direct negotiation in community politics.

Women's participation is circumscribed both by the persistence of traditional political structures from which they have been excluded and by a prevailing set of attitudes held by men which mark the women as less capable for political and public activity. Women are aware of these negative evaluations and in some instances report that these attitudes limit their willingness to participate. Fear of ridicule, of public criticism, and of not being taken seriously restrict women's desire to influence the distribution of the community's resources and cause women to avoid the public realm. Thus, while women's subordinate status does not mean that they are apolitical, men's dominance of political life and male definitions of women's capacities and their appropriate roles have affected women's participation.

Our analysis of these Andean women parallels some of the current reevaluation of women's political participation in the United States. McCormack (1976) observes that it may be a mistake to assume that "men and women share the same political reality." A more comprehensive understanding of women's political behavior, she argues, begins with the recognition that women and men often do not share the same political environment. Different opportunities, opinions, and societal expectations shape contrasting political environments and perceptions of the political system.

Finally, we have shown that both prevailing images of Andean women are inadequate. Rural women in Mayobamba and Chiuchin are neither apolitical nor powerful behind-the-scenes manipulators of their men. They are more accurately portrayed as a group with a set of political priorities that lacks adequate representation, a group with a desire to expand their political participation and influence but frustrated by prevailing attitudes, structures, and the active opposition of some men. Women's acceptance of the community's ranking of development goals, despite their own preferences, has not always worked to women's advantage. The next chapter pursues this issue by examining this region in the context of national economic and political change in the 1960s and 1970s.

Notes

1. This image seems to be derived in part from an upper-middle-class myth similar to thinking found in the United States that the most successful strategy for a woman to pursue is to convince her husband that her desires are actually his. In other words, she must get him to carry out her wishes without his realizing that he is being manipulated. Variations on this include a division of labor between a "private" woman and a "public" man. This model assumes a commonality of interests between both parties and a consensus on what is, finally, publicly expressed.

2. Flores-Ochoa in his study of the pastoralists of Paratia describes the sources of male authority and suggests that both the male role and male lines of descent predominate. He goes on to add: "However, the role of the woman is still important; her opinion counts heavily in family decisions and her option for divorce is evidence enough that she is in no way submissive to her husband. In the absence of the husband, it is she who runs the household, although theoretically the male children assume these responsibilities. *Women are in fact the power behind the throne*" (1979, p. 68; emphasis ours). See also the discussion in Cornejo (1978, p. 11). For both images see Bourricaud (1967, p. 184).

3. The perpetuation of both stereotypes is located in their partial accuracy. As we have argued, these Andean women experience subordination in a variety of fashions, as in the first stereotype. With respect to the second stereotype, women of course attempt to influence men in their homes and in the family, and they have some impact on them. The question is whether or not they are able to achieve effective political participation and accomplish their goals through such behind-the-scenes strategies of influence. For comparative data see Andradi and Portugal (1978); Bourricaud (1967); Carpio (1974,1976); and Crespi (1976).

4. Electoral statistics on male-female participation and registration from last census clearly indicate this pattern. Illiterates voted nationally for the first time in 1980.

5. We are not arguing that local power relations are unaffected by national politics. Of course in most instances they are clearly tied to one another, though not always in a unilinear or predictable fashion. However, if we hope to fully appreciate an individual's interest in politics, our focus should not rely solely upon national politics where the structural constraints previously assessed abound.

6. This recalls the debate set out in chapter 2, drawn from the discussions of power of Robert Dahl vs. Bachrach and Baratz.

7. Our concentration is on the institutionalized and nonformal processes of community decision making and the distribution of local authority rather than women's participation in sporadic resistance activities such as land invasions and food strikes. Andean women, like women throughout the world, have found their place at the head of invading peasant communities or strike lines. Such participation, however, does not necessarily transfer into institutionalized local politics. Mayer notes this distinction in his discussion of women in Tangor. He reports that community assemblies are all male gatherings and that "Women tend not to participate, but the time they were invited to do so by the *inspector de comunidades* [a visiting Lima official] they turned out to be much more vocal in expressing opposition to the demands of the *inspector*" (1974, p. 249). For a summary of the material on Latin American women's involvement in rural and urban guerrilla movements see Jaquette (1973*b*). Kaplan explores the processes of mobilization among working-class and peasant women in Europe, West Africa, and China in her synthetic work-in-progress entitled *Feudalism to Feminism: Women's Social Movements and Political Consciousness* (n.d.). See Whyte (1976) for the general pattern of Peruvian peasant activism.

8. For comparative analysis of the role of the community see Mayer (1974); Isbell (1978); and Brush (1977). Brush notes a recent trend in Urchubamba to limit membership in the community. In Tangor, Mayer remarks on the tendency to complain about participation in the community. Similar patterns of resistance to community projects were noted in the Checras district by Bourque et al. (1967).

9. Mayer describes a similar pattern of migration in Tangor: "The benefits of working outside are translating themselves into an internal differentiation by which the more successful members become a leading elite which uses the community for its own private benefit" (1974, p. 555). In speaking about the tendency to adopt the *presidency* organization of the community as opposed to the traditional system, Mayer notes that in Tangor this is accompanied by the rejection of Indian ethnic identification (1974, p. 240). Indian identity is denied in both Chiuchin and Mayobamba (Bourque and Warren 1978*a*).

10. For a discussion of the benefit of community membership in other Andean communities, see Mayer (1974).

11. In certain circumstances women who are not *comuneras* are asked to perform services for the community. As one woman explained it, if a single woman has children who use the community school, then there will be some expectation that she contribute to the community. Service will not be as onerous as that of the *comuneros* and *comuneras*. For instance, it may mean providing lunch or lodging for a visitor. Women as wives perform additional services for the community by making *chicha* (corn beer) for fiestas or serving a meal for fiesta guests.

12. In Mayobamba a woman's economic position has not yet allowed her to overcome her disenfranchisement as a female. However, in the neighboring community of Jucul there is one instance of a woman achieving political

and social power as a result of wealth. This woman is the widow of the wealthiest man in the district, a local strong man. The widow has inherited most of his wealth and plays a role in the community affairs.

13. This pattern of female participation varies somewhat throughout the Andes. Andean women's participation in defense and recuperation of community lands has been described by a number of observers including Mayer (1974) and Neira (1964). At the level of community politics Mayer found limited female participation in community meetings and affairs. Isbell concludes that, contrary to the local ideal of maintaining equilibrated relationships between the sexes in the community of Chuschi, "women have very little direct influence in the political life of the community except to have an equal voice in elections" (1978, pp. 217–18).

14. While there is evidence of men and women sharing responsibilities and joining forces to complete the man's obligations, this does not constitute a separate civil-religious hierarchy for women such as Isbell reports for Chuschi in Ayacucho (1976). There is no evidence that such a female hierarchy existed historically in Mayobamba.

15. *Campesino* (peasant) communities, like Mayobamba, achieve their status as a community through official government recognition and registration. The history of Peruvian *campesino* communities is rich and politically fascinating and has received considerable attention in the scholarly literature. (See, for example, Castro Pozo 1924; Dobyns 1964; Ritter 1965; Davies 1974.) Chiuchin has no communal lands nor was it ever organized as a community. Rather, Chiuchin's lands were originally part of the lower extensions of the highland communities of Mayobamba and Canin, providing these communities with access to a milder ecological zone. These lands were appropriated by the Catholic church after the conquest and in the twentieth century, with the decline of church influence and the loss of a local priest, the church's holdings were sold off to private buyers. As a result Chiuchin lacks the basic requisite for community status, a history of inalienable communal land.

16. The plan to establish comprehensive schools (*nucleos*) throughout rural Peru was part of the *Ley General de Educación: Decreto Ley 19362* promulgated by the Revolutionary Government in March, 1972. Drysdale and Myers summarize this new organizational form as an attempt to make the educational facilities in each district "resources potentially available to children and adults of the district" (1975, p. 266). These authors see the comprehensive school policy as the national government's attempt to better integrate the rural areas of Peru into national life. They report that "by the end of 1973, over two hundred and fifty *nucleos* were in operation!" (p. 268).

17. See, for example, the discussion in Bourque and Warren (1979b).

VIII

Women, Social Change, and National Development

It is impossible to talk about Andean women without referring to the changing social context of their lives. Rural populations have not neatly replicated the family, economic strata, or community power structures from generation to generation. Rather, social, economic, and political institutions as well as rural perceptions and values have responded to the increasingly pervasive influence of urban, national Peruvian society. This final chapter focuses on Chiuchin's and Mayobamba's involvements in national patterns of change. We analyze the dimensions of change—such as national economic development, increasing integration into the national economy, expanding educational opportunities, and rural-urban migration—that have had great influence on rural life. Our goal is to understand the differential impact of rapid social change on women and men and to explore the role of the Peruvian state in recent transformations of rural society.

The Multiple Meanings of Social Change and Development

Students of social change have been forced to rethink their evaluations of the costs and benefits of change. In general, scholars have shifted away from the use of concepts like modernization and Westernization, which assume that changes paralleling the routes taken by Western Europe and the United States will ultimately lead to similar, largely positive results. Initially modernization theories argued that industrialization, urbanization, the commercialization of agriculture, and the destruction of the peasantry would lead to economic development. In these models development was associated with increas-

179

ing national integration, democratic participatory institutions, and a higher standard of living for an increasing proportion of the population.[1]

Industrialization and urbanization, however, have failed to produce anticipated levels of economic growth, political integration, and stability. The limited success of the Latin American countries that adopted early modernization strategies led to reassessments and alternative explanations of change. It is not surprising that important critiques of modernization and Westernization were proposed by scholars living and working in societies where the expectation that major social transformations would accompany these development strategies had been widely and optimistically embraced.

Current reanalyses argue that since the colonial period Latin American countries have been directed toward economic and technological dependence on Western Europe and the United States, and that social change along the lines previously traveled by the industrialized nations increases, rather than lessens, that dependence. Present patterns of dependence promote an international division of labor in which underdeveloped countries focus their economies on raw material production, labor intensive commercial agriculture, and labor intensive light industry. National economies in the Third World now require international capital, new technologies, and advanced training for economic expansion. In filling such needs these countries face weakened political autonomy, the concentration rather than distribution of wealth, the creation of consumer needs requiring wider imports from industrialized countries, and renewed cycles of dependence on advanced capitalist economies. This reassessment of modernization has also been applied to patterns of social change within Latin American countries. Dependency analysts argue that the economic relation of developed nations to the less developed parallels, in key respects, the economic relation of urban centers to rural communities within Latin American countries. The closer the ties between urban and rural sectors, the greater the dependence and underdevelopment of the rural areas.[2]

The contrasting evaluations of development are very much a part of the present controversy over alternative strategies that Third World individuals and societies might use in seeking a higher standard of living, or merely in responding to the impact of Western economic structures and values on their own societies. Should change in the guise of development be embraced as a solution to the problems of poverty, powerlessness, and subordination? Or should it be avoided and identified as a false prophet leading only to new forms of domination and dependence?

**The Differential Impact of Change
and Development on Women and Men**

During the past ten years there has been a comparable reassessment of modernization and dependency by scholars interested in the relation between social change and sexual subordination. The assumption of many development experts is that social change first benefits those groups previously most advantaged, but that in time benefits filter down to all levels of society. For modernization to occur, these experts feel that it is essential to "bet on the stronger" to lead the process. In effect, this means that the greatest benefits initially accrue to the more privileged members of society, usually the upper-middle or middle classes.[3]

Only recently have students of social change paid explicit attention to the fact that these development policies also "bet on men," not only in preference to women, but often at the cost of women. As in the modernization-dependency debate, most development policies and programs assume that men will pass along the benefits they derive from modernization to the women with whom they live. That is, through their familial associations with fathers, husbands, or brothers women will benefit in due course; just as peasants will, in good time, receive the trickle down benefits of urbanization and industrialization.

Assumptions concerning the benefits of social change for women have been questioned from two perspectives. Social scientists have found that women in developed, industrialized countries have not, in fact, experienced the full range of improvements in status and opportunities presupposed by the modernization model. Along these lines, McCormack, a political sociologist, criticizes modernization theorists for failing to consider that

> in the sequence of changes from traditional to modern society, women become better educated, enjoying more leisure and discretionary income than at any other time in human history, only to encounter options in education, consumption and life styles that were so gender-

typed that the effect was new and more subtle types of discrimination. [1976, p. 3]

In a similar critique, Nash points out that women in industrialized nations still cluster at the bottom of the economic scale and women's rates of labor force participation depend less on distinctions between "developed and developing" and more on a government's commitment to full employment (1977, p. 166).

Current critical studies also seriously question the improvement of women's status in Third World societies presently undergoing rapid social change. These analyses direct attention toward such aspects of development as the expansion of capitalist economies, the consolidation of the state's political control over the countryside, and the influence of international development projects on men and women. Analyses of development that consider the distinct experiences of women and men are still relatively rare, but pioneering studies that have been carried out in the last decade show the importance of reassessing development from this fuller perspective. These analyses reinterpret women's responses to social change, modernization, and development in light of the specifically female experience with change. Women's behavior—which has been termed conservative, traditional, or even irrational when measured against male responses—takes on a different meaning when seen from the reality of women's structural position. Men's and women's differing responses to social change need no longer be explained by reference to women's reputedly innate dispositions or inadequacies. Rather, such variation is explained by studying the specific impact of changes on women and women's consciousness, and their responses to the differential consequences of change for the sexes.

For example, one of the major changes that contemporary economic development has introduced to rural areas is the expansion of peasant involvement in the cash economy. A number of studies now demonstrate that dependence on cash-based economies affects men and women differently. The consequences for women of shifts to cash crop production, petty commerce, and wage labor employment depend on the following factors: (1) the social values and perceptions orienting and constraining women's participation in the market economy; (2) women's access to cash producing activities; (3) women's access to new technology and technological assistance; and (4) the attitudes associated with increased economic stratification.[4] Third

World women have not been passive when they have sensed that change would bring a loss in their influence, status, or control over resources. Rather, they have resisted such changes. Women's resistance, however, has often been labeled conservatism or been neutralized by the intervention of outside groups, supporting the "trickle-down" view of modernization.[5]

In rural Peru the growing importance of the cash economy has undermined women's role as the administrator of family harvests. Unless women successfully transfer their administrative influence from domestic economics to key tasks in the cash economy, they lose an important source of control over family resources. Yet the transfer of women's economic roles is difficult because the urban mestizo economy (which has been the source of cash-oriented transformations of rural economies) severely restricts the roles and skills open to women. As we discussed in chapters 5 and 6, the shift from subsistence to cash production has far-reaching consequences for women's roles in agriculture and for increased stratification.

To fully comprehend the significance of economic change for the distribution of power between men and women and among the different strata of rural society, one must consider three additional aspects of social change: the national government's formulation of policy affecting rural settlements, the impact of expanded educational opportunities on rural populations, and the employment options offered by migration to urban coastal labor markets. All three aspects of change exemplify the increased institutional contact between the highlands and the coast and the complex interplay between rural and urban value systems. National governments, through rural development policies, as well as longer-term macroeconomic forces, shape rural realities. Yet peasant power structures often filter and redirect specific policies or map out alternative ways of dealing with economic change. The issue then is to analyze the interplay between the state, peasant power structures, and competing value systems in order to come to a more comprehensive understanding of the divergent outcomes of social change for the sexes.

The Revolutionary Military Government: Women's Place in National Reforms

The study of social change should take into account the national forces responsible for directing social policy. Our consideration of national policy begins by examining the efforts of the Peruvian military to define women's problems and to organize programs to meet some of their needs. The military government, which came to power in Peru in 1968, proclaimed itself a revolutionary government committed to the restructuring of Peruvian society. Government statements emphasized citizen participation within organizations specifically chartered to channel the involvement of various sectors.[6] Given the reformist bent of the government, one must ask how a military government committed to major changes in Peruvian society addressed the question of women and their participation. Specifically, how did political leaders conceptualize the problems of women's inequality, subordination, and lack of participation? To what extent did the government commit resources to broadening women's access to participation in national society? Were women conceived of as a specific sector which required representation through a participatory organization?

One provision of government policy which addressed the question of women was *Plan Inca*.[7] This policy statement, read for the first time in public by the President in July 1974, was the national government's official assessment of Peru's ills and its plan for restructuring Peruvian society. Like many official policy statements, *Plan Inca* was an ambitious and articulate statement of rhetorical ideals, not an accurate guide to government behavior. In fact, the government identified many more ills than it was able to deal with effectively through reforms and development policies.

Article 23 of *Plan Inca* outlines the situation of Peruvian women, government objectives, and remedial actions as follows:

  a. *The Situation*
    1. The Peruvian woman does not effectively exercise her citizenship rights.
    2. Women's access to high political and administrative posts and other activities is very limited.
    3. A man disposes of the goods of a marriage without the consent of his conjugal partner.
    4. There is discrimination against women in obtaining employment and in their remuneration.
    5. There is unjust and inhuman treatment of the single mother.
    6. The low cultural level of the majority sharpens the abusive treatment of men toward women.
  b. *The Objectives*
    1. Effective equality with men in rights and obligations.

c. *Actions*
1. Propitiate women's participation in all high level activities and offices.
2. Eliminate all discriminatory treatment that limits the opportunities or affects the rights and dignity of women.
3. Promote co-education.
4. Guarantee that the common property of a marriage will not be disposed of by the unilateral decision of the husband.

Article 23 of *Plan Inca* was never adequately implemented. There were, however, certain initiatives in government agencies which affected rural women's lives: the establishment of training programs with specific responsibilities for rural women, the Agrarian Reform Law D.L. 17716, and the recruitment of women into the military. In some instances, these initiatives proved to be counterproductive for women. In other instances, the positive intentions of government policies were subverted because of the resistance of local citizens.[8]

The government initiative with least impact in this area of Peru was the creation of ACOMUC, the Association for Cooperation with the *Campesino* Woman. Founded in 1972 to "promote fundamental values of the *campesino* family through the education of family members" (Deere 1977*b*, p. 27), ACOMUC activities reached Chiuchin and Mayobamba only once, when the organization attempted to establish a sewing cooperative in the neighboring district capital. Few women participated, the effort languished and eventually disappeared. While ACOMUC had few activities in this area, its cars and personnel were very evident in the Cajamarca region to the north. In this region, however, Deere (1977*b*) reports that the programs of the agency were directed at the upper levels of the peasantry and ignored women's central role in agriculture. The ACOMUC programs emphasized cottage craft industries directed at the tourist trade, despite the fact that women's responsibilities in agriculture gave them very limited time for other activities.

Similarly, the Agrarian Reform Law ignored the central role of women in agriculture. Promulgated in June 1969, the law provided for sweeping changes in the countryside: the expropriation of large landholdings, the redistribution of land among those who worked the land, and the reorganization of agricultural production on a cooperative basis. The law proved disadvantageous for women; it granted rights to land and participation in the new cooperative structure to the male head of household. Thus, the agrarian reform reinforced males' access to critical resources and restricted women's participation in the groups which make decisions about those resources. In accordance with the provisions of the Agrarian Reform Law, the male head of household, rather than the family, received title to land or membership in the cooperative. Thus married women would have no rights to the land or cooperative membership if left widowed and with a son over eighteen.[9] In short, the Agrarian Reform Law undervalued women's contributions to agricultural production, left their inheritance rights vulnerable in some cases, and severely restricted their participation within the new production cooperative structure.

The Agrarian Reform Law is an especially instructive case because, despite its many defects, the law was recognized as fostering major changes in the rural areas. Thus, it is a good example of how government policy affects men and women differently, as well as how the institutions of the state can foster a dependence that did not previously exist. This reform created mechanisms beyond the control of rural women which helped to perpetuate female subordination. The establishment of ACOMUC and the Agrarian Reform Law are examples of the application of coastal models which fail to comprehend the reality of Andean women's labor force participation. In these nationally directed reforms, government policy failed to distinguish between the interests of men, women, and families.

On the other hand, local citizens sometimes subvert national government initiatives which have the potential of providing women with wider access to skills and a broader basis for participation. The government's decision to recruit women into the military is one such example of rural manipulations of national policy. The military organized several female reserve units and some rural women expressed interest in inscription.[10] Unfortunately, this was an instance in which local attitudes and values prevented a national government initiative from being effectively utilized by women.

The basis for recruitment into the military was registration, required of all males over sixteen and single females over sixteen without children. In the district of Santa Leonor this process is handled by the district secretary, a local *comunero* with high school level training. District secretaries keep track of all birth, death, and marriage records. This authority lends itself to high levels of personalistic service and manipulation. District secretaries facilitate procedures for friends for a small fee, adjusting dates and ages when necessary. The personalistic nature of the job also allows these officials to frustrate individuals' access to the various certificates and records they need, either in hopes of a monetary reward for the document or, at times, simply as a demonstration of power.

In the case of women's military registration, the district secretary found the idea of women's military participation ludicrous and attempted to stall their efforts to register. In the first year of registration four women and sixteen men from Santa Leonor registered. Although there were very few single, childless women to begin with, those who attempted to register were dissuaded by the official. In one case a young woman was quite anxious to inscribe herself for military duty. She had been to the coast, secured the necessary photographs, and returned to the district secretary to complete her registration. The secretary delighted in telling the tale of how the woman, in an attempt to look her best for the photograph, had worn a barrette. He rejected her application arguing that the military would not accept a photograph that included such adornments. She would need to get new pictures. He further counseled her to save the cost of another trip to the coast for the photographs, pointing out that the cost of travel would exceed the fine for registering a year late.

Thus a rural woman who was interested in pursuing the opportunities that might be available through military training found herself blocked by a local official. This man's position of authority gave him control over the channels of access to the larger national system. In effect, he had the capacity to determine women's access to sources of change emanating from the national government.

Education as a Source of Expanded Options

The expansion of the educational system is a second example of the complexity of local-national interaction. Education is a central process for national integration since it provides literacy, math skills, and specialized knowledge for participation in an increasingly industrial and technological world. Education also implies the transfer of values through the structure of the curriculum, the messages conveyed by school materials, and the teachers who staff the schools. Ultimately, the impact of expanded educational opportunities for women in the rural communities will be related to the values imparted by the school system, the local population's responses to those values, and the opportunities for women to use knowledge and skills in the wider community. As in the case of recruiting women into the military, there are disjunctures between the aims of national policy and the desires of the local population.

Under the military government there were some initiatives to use the school system to improve women's status. The military government's Educational Reform Law of 1972 addressed the question of women's education in article 2.

> Education will be oriented toward the revaluing of women, offering them the maximum opportunities for full and free personal development, which is the only authentic basis of their decisive function in the family and their creative participation in the process of transformation and improvement of Peruvian society. [quoted in Heyman 1974, p. 150]

Attention was also directed at the content of primary school texts by Peruvian social scientists acutely aware of the capacity of texts to convey implicit and explicit values about appropriate male, female, and children's behavior. One such study, *¿Cuesta arriba o cuesta abajo?* was published by a private Peruvian social research organization, DESCO, in 1973. In this book, the authors note that the image of women portrayed in school texts was strongly associated with the concept of *marianismo,* the long-suffering, spiritually superior woman. The social scientists summarized the treatment of mothers in the texts as follows:

> The mother could not be a mother without being self-sacrificing. . . . The mother is the synthesis of love, sacrifice and sanctity. . . . This being [the mother] is considered in the texts as a religious symbol, as something celestial. [Boggio et al. 1973, pp. 33,34]

The authors of this study call for a reevaluation and rewriting of such texts, pointing out that the values they express are inconsistent with participatory citizenship in a reform setting.

Similarly, groups of women within SINAMOS, the agency created by the military government to promote and oversee popular participation, wanted to attack the question of women's status. They tried to create materials to confront sexism in the government bureaucracy and in the wider society. Through the development of cartoons patterned after the Argentine comic strip "Mafalda," they attempted to question women's limited participation and restrictive roles. They wanted to make this issue an ongoing part of SINAMOS programs.

The agency as a whole, however, suffered from grave internal difficulties and an ambiguous relationship to the military government. The women's program was an infinitely small part of its activities and disappeared along with the dismantling of the agency in 1975.

The educational reform was never fully implemented in the rural areas. Similarly, neither the efforts of the SINAMOS women, nor the DESCO study had an impact on the curricula of the Mayobamba and Chiuchin schools. As the Mother's Day skits indicate, ideal women were still portrayed as long-suffering, frequently abused objects whose passive acceptance of personal sacrifice made them appropriate for veneration. The skits and the Mother's Day celebration in Chiuchin were the projects of the mestizo school teachers. The dual-edged nature of the message conveyed—that women, especially mothers, should be honored, combined with the particular submissive behaviors for which they are to be venerated—demonstrates the paradoxical nature of the social values which are communicated through the school system. Teachers in Chiuchin and Mayobamba make efforts to impart their own norms to rural students. The three female Chiuchin teachers' most specific concerns were to instill in the female students the importance of coastal notions of virginity and modesty. Mestizo norms, as noted by a variety of observers, often provide an extremely restrictive role for women. While we have argued that women are subordinated in Andean society, we are not suggesting that they will be any less subordinated in coastal mestizo society. This is the ultimate paradox represented by social change directed at the acceptance of coastal mestizo norms.[11]

This is not to deny that the new skills, self-confidence, and mastery imparted through greater educational opportunity might give rise to unanticipated consequences, including an expanded version of women's competence and proper roles.[12] Given the relatively recent extension of education to Andean women, the consequences of these opportunities are not entirely clear.

Andean women have traditionally received less formal education than men. Boys attend school with more regularity and for longer periods of time, leading to substantial differences in educational achievement by sex.[13] Moreover, before the military government's conversion to coeducation, the staff available to rural females had fewer accredited school teachers than that available to the boys. In most rural communities, a boy's school was established first, followed several years later by a decision to give the boy's facility over to the girls and build new classrooms for the boys.

The patterns of educational participation are a reflection of cultural values about the appropriateness of education for girls, as well as a calculation on the part of families with limited resources about the wisest way to employ those resources. This is a circular and self-fulfilling argument that works against women. Once women are excluded from the educational system, they become far less effective participants in any other aspect of society which requires educational attainment.

Education in Mayobamba and Chiuchin:
Widened Options and Persistent Attitudes

Public education is a relatively recent addition to Santa Leonor and Checras. Up until the 1940s most primary education was handled privately and available to only a few children of the local elite. Indeed the end of local strong man (*gamonal*) dominance is dated by townspeople to the expansion of public education in the region and the possibility for nonelites to acquire education.[14] In the late 1940s and early 1950s the communities established primary schools, beginning with the first three years of training and eventually extending themselves to five grades.

By the 1960s when district residents petitioned the government for a secondary school, the extension of the road from the coast to Chiuchin made the commercial center the logical place for the new facility. Other highland communities showed some resistance, arguing that Chiuchin was not a formal community, did not have enough students of its own, and that the vast majority of the students would have to travel to Chiuchin from the high altitude agrarian communities. Despite the merit of these arguments, none of the highland communities was willing to let any other be the site for the school. The arguments in favor of Chiuchin's centrality, the access of regular transportation to the coast, and the presence of the necessary services for the teaching staff (such as restaurants, the hot baths, and rooming houses for teachers) finally prevailed and the school began to function in 1965.

The founding of the secondary school, however, coincided with the dramatic increase in local migration to Lima. Land invasions around the capital made an urban relocation a viable option. The ease of migration coupled with some well-founded reservations about the quality of *sierra* education led to a gradual decline in the high-school-age population and the reduction of the high school's category to that of a two-year annex by the early 1970s. The educational reforms of the military government began to have some effect in Chiuchin by 1974 when local leaders petitioned to have a comprehensive high school established in Chiuchin.[15]

The period from 1974 through 1978 included the establishment of the comprehensive high school and the expansion of the regional school system, followed in quick succession by the nuclear school's collapse due to the contraction of government reforms and a bitter teachers' strike. Instead of the far-flung activities ideally encompassed by the comprehensive school (such as the expansion of technical and adult education), the Chiuchin school is now a traditional five-year high school with a curriculum similar to that found throughout the nation. The teaching staff has been reduced from a high of fifteen during the brief period of the comprehensive school to a present full-time staff of seven. The seven teachers have a total of eighty-eight students distributed as shown in table 1.

In the end, parents have not been totally displeased by the loss of the nuclear school. They watched the growing teacher bureaucracy with concern. On the other hand, they pointed out that while the nuclear school existed there was greater control of teachers by the administrators and less teacher absenteeism. With the present arrangements, parents are faced with some difficult calculations with respect to the rural schools since sending a child on to secondary school means substantial cash expenditures. Unless one has relatives

Table 1. Chiuchin High School Students,
by Year and Sex

Year	Males	Females
Fifth	8	2
Fourth	8	1
Third	8	8
Second	14	6
First	20	13
Total	58	30

in Chiuchin, room and board must be secured at a cost of about S/600 a month in 1974 or S/1,000 in 1978. In addition, there are the costs of books and uniforms. Families must weigh the cost of education in Chiuchin versus education on the coast. The comparative cost depends upon where the family has relatives and the perceived difference in the quality of education offered.

As the cost of living soared after 1976, the attractiveness of the local Chiuchin high school increased, counteracting to some extent the long-term reservations about the ability of teachers sent to the rural areas, and strong resistance to parts of the educational reform. One aspect of the reform concerned teaching boys skills, such as weaving and embroidery, generally associated with women in this area. Most boys, especially the younger ones, found the activity great fun. But the reactions of rural fathers to their sons embroidering was strongly negative.

In this educational environment, with the expansion and contraction of rural facilities, the situation of rural women has rapidly waxed and waned. The small gains they have achieved may be threatened by the deterioration of the secondary school system.

The women of Mayobamba and Chiuchin often discuss the importance of education, their efforts to attain it and the obstacles that they encounter. Women of thirty-five years of age, such as Hilaria and Concepción, as discussed in chapter 1, fought with their fathers to secure higher education. In Hilaria's case she was unsuccessful: "My mother wanted my older sister to go on to study but my father wouldn't allow it. So she never got to study. She married very young at sixteen. I wanted to study as well but he would only allow me to take a sewing course." Concepción, on the other hand, was successful. With her mother's help she convinced her father to allow her to accompany a brother to the coast. She attended high school there, achieving a diploma with distinction. Despite her own tremendous efforts to achieve education, this opportunity will not be extended to her own daughter. Given her very limited resources, Concepción has made a choice to support the educational prospects of her sons.

Today, fathers in Chiuchin are beginning to see the need to educate daughters. The following are typical statements from men, linking changes they perceive in their own society to the need for education:

Now it is just as important to give a profession to the girls as well as the boys; times are harder, more unfavorable now.

Before parents didn't feel it was necessary to educate their children. They thought their children would always live as they had, from the income of the fields. But that is no longer possible. We plant but we don't harvest [an adequate] production. It seems as if the earth has tired; there are always crop diseases and plagues. For these reasons, it is important that children look for another way to gain their livelihood.

Despite these changing attitudes, the 1972 census data from this region (the districts of Santa Leonor and Checras) suggest that women are still disadvantaged educationally. Although rural education is broadly available and parents now enroll girls as well as boys, there is still a disparity between men's and women's literacy rates as demonstrated in table 2.

The first column of the top half of table 2 demonstrates the sexual imbalance in the total population: women represent 53 percent and 52 percent of the population over five years old in each district. As the illiteracy rates in the second column show, men represent 27 percent of the illiterate population above five, while women in 1972 comprised 73 percent of the illiterate population in each district. In 1972, 37 percent of the population of Checras and 31 percent of the district of Santa Leonor was illiterate.

The bottom half of table 2 demonstrates the direction and speed of change by focusing on the population from five to twenty-five years of age, that group presently in the school system or most recently involved in it. Illiterates still comprise 33 percent of the Checras population and 31 percent of the population of Santa Leonor. The first column shows that the sexual imbalance is slightly less for this age group in Checras and disappears in Santa Leonor where each sex composes 50 percent of the population.

While women still comprise 54 percent and 57 percent of the illiterates in the two districts, their overrepresentation in this category has been markedly reduced. The greatest discrepancy between males and females in the ages five through twenty-five occurs in the youngest age groups five to nine years of age in Santa Leonor where many more boys are reported as literate. This suggests a variety of explanations: a tendency to start girls in school somewhat later, slower rates of acquiring literacy skills for girls related to their greater dependence on Quechua, or misreporting in the census.[16] No such contrast occurs in the Checras data for this age group.

Despite the improvements reflected in the census statistics, education experts suggest that greater educational opportunity and achievement, in and of itself, cannot guarantee equity between the sexes.[17] The ideological content of education, the assumptions and stereotypes that become part of the curriculum, and the societal values that give education meaning will have a dominant impact on the overall influence of education.

To note the limitations of education for the reevaluation of women is not to deny its fundamental importance as a necessary if not suffi-

Table 2. Literacy Rates by Sex and District

	Total		Illiterates		Literates	
	n	%	n	%	n	%
For the Total Population above Five Years of Age						
Checras district						
Males	(920)	47	(197)	27	(723)	58
Females	(1,047)	53	(533)	73	(514)	42
Total	(1,967)	100	(730)	100	(1,237)	100
Santa Leonor district						
Males	(821)	48	(141)	27	(680)	58
Females	(873)	52	(386)	73	(487)	42
Total	(1,694)	100	(527)	100	(1,167)	100
For the Population between Ages Five and Twenty-five						
Checras district						
Males	(458)	48	(147)	46	(311)	49
Females	(492)	52	(170)	54	(322)	51
Total	(950)	100	(317)	100	(633)	100
Santa Leonor district						
Males	(418)	50	(111)	43	(307)	52
Females	(424)	50	(146)	57	(278)	48
Total	(842)	100	(257)	100	(585)	100

Source: Censo Nacional de la Población, 1972. Lima: Instituto Nacional de Estadística.

Note: Adapted from *Cuadro 20, Población censada de la República, por alfabetización y sexo.*

cient factor influencing change in women's status. Moreover, some rural men seem to recognize education's far-reaching, perhaps threatening potential. For instance, in Mayobamba when the local school teacher attempted to organize a women's club in the hopes of increasing women's participation he was met with considerable resistance from the men. The men objected to the club; they felt women should stay home and were reluctant to see women with their own organization. Some men objected to women being out at night for club meetings. The club eventually failed.

In another instance a Mayobamba woman explained the reluctance of some *sierra* men to educate their daughters, by recounting this story from a neighboring town in the central *sierra*.

> They say the men there prefer to marry women who can't read, because if a man receives a letter or a document from someone and the woman can read it, the woman might want to get involved in the matter. She might cause a fight, and that would be very objectionable.

Any assessment of education as a source of social change must recognize its dual nature. Given the direction of change in Peruvian society, both literacy and the skills taught in the educational system will be important ingredients for individual mobility. Without doubt, such skills increase women's independence and their personal options. This seems to be recognized by Andean men as well; at times helping them see the importance of educating their daughters and at other times leading them to restrict the educational opportunities of their wives. It seems equally clear that the social values found in the Peruvian curriculum do not expand women's opportunities.[18] The wider community's values, in both rural settlements and urban mestizo society, further restrict the political options offered by education.

In short, our analysis suggests that Nash's assessment of the role of education in women's subordination is accurate for Andean populations as well: education is neither the culprit nor the solution.

> The plea for greater educational opportunities is a quasi solution for a structural situation that maintains women in subordination to the male sector of the work force at every level. To give lack of education as the reason for discriminatory status is to confuse agency with agent. [Nash 1976, p. 14]

This is not to argue, however, that Andean women can do without

education. The direction of change in Peruvian society is clear, and
education will be a requirement for participation. Nevertheless, education will not guarantee Andean women equality with men any more
than it has guaranteed it to any other group of women.

Migration as a Source of Urban Opportunities

Of all the aspects of social change we have discussed rural-urban
migration is the most concrete demonstration of greater national integration. While not directed by the national government, migration
poses critical problems for political leaders. Moreover, government
policies toward the rural areas have a substantial impact on the migration choices and strategies of rural citizens.

Migration and urban growth are intimately tied in Peru. The expansion of squatter settlements in the outskirts of Lima has been
dramatic. In the 1940s squatter settlements represented less than 1
percent of Lima's population; by 1972, D. Collier (1976, p. 144) reports, this figure had become 25 percent, or approximately 850,000
people. Such population shifts have far-reaching political consequences; they increase demands for urban services, initiate new patterns in voting power, and pose new problems of national political
integration.

While both men and women migrate, the experiences for each in
the city are different. Like men, women find their first jobs through
kin networks, but women have a narrower range of employment
available to them. Men migrate more frequently than women and are
more likely than women to move without children and families.
Women, in contrast, usually come to the city with family members or
with their future employer.

Chaney (1977) reports that in Peru both male and female migrants
aspire to factory jobs. Despite long hours and difficult working conditions, factory jobs offer social security benefits, sick pay, and paid
vacations. However, migrant women are less likely than migrant men
to find such jobs. The manufacturing sector of the Peruvian economy
is unable to absorb all the workers seeking employment. As a consequence, most women end up in the service sector. In fact, the number
of women with employment in manufacturing has declined over time.
This has occurred simultaneously with increased migration of women
into the cities (see table 3).

Table 3. Percentage of Peruvian Population Economically Active in Manufacturing, by Sex, 1940, 1961, and 1972

	1940	Percentage	1961	Percentage	1972	Percentage
Men	165,516	43.6	294,983	71.8	340,422	75.4
Women	214,765	56.4	115,997	28.2	123,185	24.6
Total	380,281	100.0	410,980	100.0	463,607	100.0

Source: Peruvian national census of 1940, 1961, 1972, adapted from Villalobos, n.d., p. 1.

The figures show that the change, from roughly equal participation to male dominance in manufacturing, occurred during the period of large-scale migration to Lima, between 1940 and 1961. Chaney points out that as male migrants come to dominate this part of the labor force the consequences for women are two-fold: women are forced out of the industrial labor force and pushed into the least attractive jobs in the service sector. In countries like Peru, where the absorptive capacity of industrial manufacturing is limited, not only will this labor force be male, but, in addition, men who cannot find work in this sector will tend to secure the better paying jobs in the service sector. This forces women "into the lower echelons of the tertiary sector, and specifically into domestic service" (Chaney 1977, p. 41).

Women seldom move out of the service sector: women who start as domestic servants, which is the most frequent occupation, will remain domestic servants. If they become pregnant and lose their domestic position they will probably move laterally into the ranks of street vendors. Upward mobility out of the class of domestic servants is rare.[19]

Thus migration does not offer women the same employment opportunities it does for men, nor does it offer them comparable opportunities for mobility. To understand the role of migration in the lives of rural women, let us turn to the data from Mayobamba and Chiuchin to examine how migration is viewed.

Migration: Contrasting Models of Success

Rural-urban migration has dramatically increased with the growth of the national school system and the extension of roads into this area of the *sierra.* In the past twenty years a substantial segment of the rural population moved to larger urban settings, primarily to Lima. Mayobamba and Chiuchin are a part of a national pattern of population shifts. The motives for migration are many; who moves and why are fundamental questions, as well as how the migrants fare in the city and how the rural community fares without the migrants.

In both Mayobamba and Chiuchin men migrate first and most frequently.[20] A great many younger and middle-aged women in Mayobamba and Chiuchin have had some migratory experience and returned to the *sierra*. For the generation from 16 to 25 years both men and women have migrated in large numbers and their absence in the *sierra* community is especially noticeable. For men this absence extends into the generation from 25 to 35.

The process of migration is best understood as one aspect of the process of family network construction. The attempts of families to establish a network of mutually beneficial linkages between the coast and the *sierra*, between cash and subsistence economies, are attempts to maximize individual and family options. In short, these networks represent a development strategy created and elaborated by rural citizens. In the present context of high economic uncertainty in Peru their critical functions become apparent.[21]

When seen as one aspect of a network strategy, it is possible to understand migration not so much as a permanent rejection of the *sierra* (though in many cases there is a permanent transfer of residence) but rather, as a temporary situation from which specific advantages are sought. Migration is thus related to an overall view of family relationships which includes both *sierra* and coastal connections.

A family's choices about migration are intimately tied to their options in the rural areas. For instance, education is one of the main reasons cited for coastal migration. Families with trusted relatives on the coast can send a child to live with their kin while studying. Where no such connection exists, entire families may be forced to move themselves to the city to insure the kind of educational opportunity they want for their children. Educated individuals then have the chance to try their skills to find a place in coastal society.

Wealthier families are most likely to establish family coastal connections. They require that one of the children, educated on the coast, return to the *sierra* to manage the family's interests. Extremely poor families may never have the opportunity to migrate to find better work. The group most likely to become permanent migrants are the excess children of families whose rural holdings are insufficient to support the entire group, as well as those children of wealthier families who form part of the family's coastal connections.

For the family with some property in the rural area the member with least success on the coast will be relegated to the *sierra* to watch over their interests. If all members of the family find coastal success and no one is willing to remain in the *sierra*, the family may attempt to rent their land to a more distant relative in the rural community. Very seldom does a family totally relinquish its rural rights and ties, even when there is no longer a resident member. In the past ten years, while substantial migration has taken place, only two families have completely divested themselves in Mayobamba and one in Chiuchin. The cases in Mayobamba were the direct result of the families' success on the coast and their fear that the military government's reforms would divest them of their property without compensation if they did not act to sell it first.

The reciprocal importance of network ties between the coast and the *sierra* manifests itself in the attempts of migrants to maintain their connections with their original communities.[22] One mechanism by which such ties are maintained is the establishment of regional clubs in Lima for the ex-residents of a town, district, or province. The clubs are vehicles to help new migrants adjust to the urban environment.[23] In Mayobamba and Chiuchin the clubs have been effective resources for funding local improvements in the rural communities. This continuing commitment to their natal community allows migrants to maintain mutually beneficial linkages to their rural relatives and holdings. The clubs also demonstrate the success of male migrants to those back home and to those from the old community who have moved to the city.

The clubs have assisted in broadly based public improvement projects such as the construction of a medical post in Chiuchin and the purchase of equipment for the schools. On the whole, however, for this region of Peru the clubs tend to be men's organizations which emphasize male interests and priorities. For instance, in both Chiuchin and Mayobamba the construction of soccer fields received the club's assistance. Soccer, a sport in which women do not participate, serves as an important vehicle for maintaining male friendships.

While the coastal clubs may be of some assistance in speeding the adjustment of migrants to the city, the process of urbanization can be difficult, particularly for women. One Mayobamba woman explained why some women have been reluctant to migrate or found it an unsatisfactory alternative:

> Frequently the women [who migrate to Lima] are sad. They want to go to the fields. They don't like being in one single, small house. Here in the *sierra* they have several large houses. I've seen two cases of women who couldn't adjust to the coast. Elena went to the coast to live and took all her children. But she just couldn't do it; she said it was driving her crazy. She wanted to come back to Mayobamba because she couldn't get adjusted. She didn't like the atmosphere in Lima, she didn't like the way of life. In the first place it bothered her to go to the market, to spend money and buy just a little bit of all the things. Here [in Mayobamba] she didn't have to go to the market, and she had everything in great quantity: *ocas* [a tuber], milk, potatoes, cheese. It bothered her to spend money. For example, for her to spend 100 *soles* was to spend a lot of money, and it worried her to have to spend so much.
>
> The other case was my cousin. She went to Huaral [a coastal provincial city north of Lima, just off the Pan American highway]. The money bothered her too; everything had to be bought and there wasn't enough money. She could only buy a little bit. She had the children with her and they always wanted bread. She got very worried. After six months she came back. It's very difficult for a woman with children or an older woman to get adjusted. In Mayobamba they have their storerooms, there's cheese and milk and potatoes. [If] it's only rarely that one buys coffee or noodles or things like that, then you don't mind it. But on the coast one has to go to the market every day, and that worries many women.

The mother's frustration at her children's requests for bread reflects the fact that products only occasionally consumed in the rural communities become necessities on the coast. Thus one's inability to purchase them becomes more pressing. The need for bread in Mayobamba can be met by potatoes; in Huaral, with its bakeries, the children insist on bread.

Underlying this discussion are two factors. Women on the coast have less opportunity than men to earn cash, yet they find themselves economically more dependent upon cash than in rural, agricultural Mayobamba. Moreover, the issue continually mentioned by these women is the loss of control over food supply. As we have noted, the administration of the family's food supply is an important area of independent judgment and decision making for an Andean woman. She is responsible for assuring that the proper amount of food is kept for family consumption, and she oversees consumption on a day-to-day basis. Thus when women decry their increased dependence on cash and the need to purchase food in Lima they are identifying and bemoaning the loss of an important source of authority and independence.

Women's loss of control also occurs when they lose their livestock through migration. A very successful Mayobamba migrant eventually convinced his mother to join him on the coast. In order to leave for Lima the mother had to sell her cows. The son thought this would be a simple matter but found instead that every time he succeeded in selling a cow, his mother cried all night. She had five cows, each with a name. The son came to understand that for his mother the cows represented her "fortune, interests, worries, security and independence." The mother had a difficult time adjusting to life in Lima, and so on weekends the son tried to cheer her up by taking her to a rural area where she could see cows. Unfortunately this only made her depressed once again.

As with stores of food, care of animals is a woman's responsibility and source of independence. Animals are a form of ownership which women have been able to retain and, as opposed to land, the kind of property a woman is likely to inherit. Migration to Lima means the loss of this source of income and security.

Thus the process of migration can leave a woman doubly disadvantaged. They have limited earning power in the coastal economy and, in addition, they have been removed from those sources of independence and control they previously exercised.

Mayobamba and Chiuchin women who do migrate usually secure employment in the urban setting through family connections with successful migrants. Domestic service is the most frequent employment for women from this region. Some report high levels of satisfaction with their experience as domestic servants, citing work in foreign or wealthy families. Women who work as domestics and then return to the *sierra* often cite their need to care for parents or a need to take over the family business as factors which motivated their decisions to return. The unpleasant aspects of domestic service and the birth of children are other important factors which encourage women to return home. Many employers will not allow their servants to keep children with them. Unless the new mother can send the baby home to her own mother or sister in the *sierra,* the migrant woman will be forced to leave her post and seek employment elsewhere. Again, opportunities for women are extremely limited in the city and some women may choose to return to the *sierra* if they have any options there.

Our understanding of Mayobamba and Chiuchin migratory patterns suggests that there are two distinct patterns of migratory success, one male, the other female. Two cases of successful migrants demonstrate that some factors which are neutral or insignificant in the case of men carry great weight in the lives of women and vice versa. Carlos and Concepción, as we will call them, are similar people in terms of their intelligence, industry, and desire to improve themselves. The structural elements of their experiences demonstrate the distinct opportunities which migration presents to men and women, and the different barriers encountered by each.

First a male success story about Carlos and his poultry business. Carlos came from a relatively poor family without extensive holdings in Mayobamba, although he was favored by kinship ties to some of the wealthier Mayobamba families. Carlos's father died when he was a boy (thus making him, in local terms, an orphan despite the fact his mother is living). Given his limited local options he decided to move to Lima. He studied in a night school and eventually found a good job on an urban poultry farm. The poultry business was expanding rapidly in Lima and as a bright, hard-working young man he found a place in it. He married, but his first wife died quite suddenly. He remarried, had one daughter, and, in conjunction with his brother, expanded their poultry distribution system. Later, he created a series of positions for other migrant kin from Mayobamba. Some of the young men worked in wholesale distribution with him; other female relatives were set up in market stalls to retail the poultry. By 1975 he had a network of over a dozen Mayobambinos, primarily relatives, employed in various aspects of his business. Besides providing for his relatives he assisted the town in a number of public works projects. He provided the community with doors and windows for the new school, with gates for the stadium, and he contributed materials to the town hall. Finally, he served as the primary sponsor of the town's patron saint fiesta. He marked the occasion by bringing two truck loads of Lima residents and a ten-piece band to Mayobamba for the celebration. In effect, he has reversed his earlier social position; members of the town's wealthier families now depend on him, and he is much sought after as a godfather for local children. His role in the fiesta was a public opportunity to mark dramatically his mobility.

In contrast to the male success stories, women who succeed as migrants invariably marry a man who proves to be a good provider and a responsible husband. One local account of a woman's experience emphasized her marriage to a member of the national police force. Significantly, in a counterpart male story, becoming a police officer is the signal of success.

Concepción, whose life we presented in chapter 1, is a successful female migrant. Yet her experience demonstrates the different consequences of marriage and childbearing for men and women, the different options available to each in the urban setting and, in contrast to Carlos, indicates the different strategies for success adopted by male and female migrants.

Concepción studied on the coast, received a high school diploma, and pursued entrance to the University. She married while still a student and dropped out of school after the birth of her first child. The untimely death of her young husband left her stranded. Determined to remain on the coast, she continued to work as a market vendor as part of Carlos' poultry business and counted on her rural family for assistance. Concepción, in turn, has become the central figure in the family's network of rural-urban ties. The costs of raising her family pushed her into another marriage. Her new husband, however, resented her children and her strong ties to her family. This latter issue was especially significant in that Concepción's ties to her family were her one sure source of assistance. Even if the new husband resented her family she could not risk their certain support for his uncertain loyalty. She found herself, in 1978, torn over the deterioration of both her relationship to her second husband and her uncertain economic position in the highly inflationary urban economy, but committed to remaining there as the center of her extended family's link to the coast.

Carlos and Concepción are good examples of the patterns in Mayobambinos' migratory experience. Carlos's move to the city allowed him to overcome the disadvantages of his orphan status. The lack of a father was not a serious drawback for him once he left the community. His marriage and his children in no way limited the options open to him. He played a direct part in the town's development efforts and celebrated his success by sponsoring the community fiesta. He has no intention of permanently returning to Mayobamba and is an outspoken critic of the community's inability to achieve more far-reaching change. Indeed, he has become a symbol of modernization.

For Concepción, on the other hand, marriage and childbirth blocked her educational plans and limited her employment options. The job opportunities open to her as a mother with young children in the city are limited. Skills such as truck driving, which Carlos acquired and used to great advantage, are sex-typed as male activities. Whereas Carlos's ties to his family in Mayobamba became less important to his success and more a means of demonstrating it, in Concepción's case the maintenance of her rural family ties were critical for her survival. This became especially clear in the case of her second marriage where she was being forced to choose between these ties and the new marital union.

In sum, migration has a differential impact on men and women. Men are likely to migrate originally for education, to acquire a new skill, or to find employment in the mines or in some branch of industry in the city. They are also more likely to be successful migrants and remain in the city. If they permanently settle in the city, they are more likely to participate in the migrants' club, and to seek prestige by their gifts and service to their hometown.

For women, migration occurs less frequently and offers few options. For older women and women with children, migration separates them from sources of security and subsistence without offering new and comparable options. Significantly, women are more likely than men to return to the *sierra*. Women migrants succeed through advantageous marriages and the maintenance of strong family rural-urban networks.

The difference in male-female migration patterns, as well as the different opportunities open to men and women in the urban areas fosters sexual imbalance in the *sierra*. Women outnumber men in Mayobamba and Chiuchin and in both the districts of Santa Leonor and Checras. In some communities this has affected community government. Evidence from several highland communities suggests that the higher percentage of women in the rural areas has extended their control of land and participation in local government. Communities with a dearth of *comuneros* may be willing to accept community service and even leadership from women.[24] However, this does not imply that such a shift is imminent or the *sierra* will become a bastion of female power.

The network relations of families between coast and *sierra* ensure that coastal patterns of success will continue to influence the local communities. One consequence of this influence would be the pattern already noted in our discussion of Lima migrant clubs: to the degree that coastal groups and values influence rural *sierra* decisions through their financial contributions, men will continue to have the determining voice. This will be further reinforced by the distinct opportunities of males and females on the coast.

Patterns for the Eighties: Rural Responses to Economic Crises

By any measure the years from 1974 on have been a critical period in Peruvian national life. The revolutionary military government showed deepening divisions by 1974. In early 1975 the government suffered its most dramatic setback when a police strike was followed by riots, looting, and burning in downtown Lima. President Juan Velasco Alvarado was replaced by Francisco Morales Bermudez, and the revolution, already severely compromised, began to grind to a halt. The nation's economy deteriorated rapidly, the public debt rose, and production fell. The country experienced 300 percent inflation from 1975 to 1978. Sources of hope, such as the successful exploitation of oil discoveries in the Amazon, faded. The military, which was initially viewed in 1968 as Peru's salvation from a corrupt civilian government, became the focus of public disenchantment. The change in public attitudes was due in large part to the military's privileges, lack of austerity, and apparent corruption. Struggling civilians were quick to comment on officers' fancy homes, eight-cylinder American cars, and high salaries. Antimilitaristic attitudes were accompanied by such major public protests as the general strikes of July, 1977, and May, 1978, which involved widespread public disturbances and resulted in a number of deaths and increased repression.

Chiuchin and Mayobamba have been deeply affected by these major currents of change. The relative prosperity and hopeful attitude toward the economy in 1974, evidenced locally by the expansion of tourist rooms and the mechanization of some aspects of local production, had given rise in 1977–78 to despair over the land's poor productivity and the low prices for agricultural products. The gap caused by inflation resulted in cutbacks in stock in Chiuchin shops and in the disappearance of several small stores in Mayobamba.

As the economic situation deteriorated families changed their educational plans for their children. They faced the impossibility of sending a son on to school or realized that a choice would have to be made between a son or a daughter. There was a great deal of talk about reversion to earlier subsistence patterns: substituting lard for cooking oil and a barley/grain brew for coffee, and cutting back on coastal products such as sugar and rice. Merchants in Chiuchin sought more agricultural land and spent more of their time in agricultural production on what small plots they had, as opposed to their shops where trade and merchandise had been severely limited. Some merchants sought *comunero* status in order to gain access to community land. The communities rejected their overtures, recognizing the importance of the changes in economic conditions and the increased value this gave to their land.

Even the long-term trend of rural-urban migration was undergoing some reversals as the cost of living on the coast soared, employment opportunities dwindled, and strikes closed schools. There has not been enough reverse migration to identify this as a major trend. Families who had established a foothold in the city with the construction of a home in a squatter settlement appear to be reluctant to leave their urban outposts. Rather, one sees a pattern of strengthening the rural links in a family's network by the return of parents or a sibling to the rural community. Some of the families originally from the highland communities returned to Chiuchin rather than their natal community. They prefer Chiuchin's transportation links and the amenities that the commercial center offers.

Chiuchin affords both limited cash employment and the possibility of reestablishing network ties with the highland agricultural communities. People from highland Mayobamba say that Chiuchin is all cash, all business, and there is no community there. In comparison to the agricultural communities that is, of course, an accurate description. But in contrast to Lima, life in Chiuchin is far closer to an agricultural community, while still providing some ties to a cash economy and to the coast. Freedom from some of the restrictions and obligations of *comunero* status in a highland community is, for most returning migrants, an advantage, although all would like greater access to land, communal or private.

For women, Chiuchin represents employment opportunities and options not found in the rural community. It is unclear if these opportunities will remain, given the deteriorating economy and the return of migrant families. Will competition with returning male migrants for Chiuchin's employment opportunities eliminate some of the access to cash women now enjoy? A similar question might be directed at the local attempts to lessen dependence on the cash economy by a return to more autonomous patterns of subsistence farming. How is this trend likely to influence male and female patterns of power and authority?

While we note these trends as intriguing reversals of development and modernizing patterns, it seems unlikely that there will ever be large scale return migration to the *sierra,* and even more unlikely that reverse migration would be accompanied by a permanent return to traditional practices or ways of life. Instead, rural-urban linkages will remain an important strategy for Andean Peruvians and the rural base of those linkages will most likely not be lost but rather further elaborated.[25] A woman like Concepción, while committed to living in the urban environment, asserts that if it were necessary for her to return to Mayobamba to retain her family's land she would do it. However, despite the sexual imbalance in the *sierra* and the commitment of women like Concepción to their *sierra* lands and their networks, men's domination in the *sierra* is unlikely to change. Those aspects of men's control, reinforced by coastal experience, are unlikely to be challenged given the lack of any commitment in coastal society to equalizing the relationship between men and women. Even minor returns of males to the *sierra* may ultimately prove detrimental to those opportunities which temporarily opened up for women in Chiuchin.

While one should not underestimate the skills of Chiuchin women it is not at all certain to us that the particular circumstances which gave them increased opportunities, compared to those available in the highland community, will survive an influx of men with greater coastal training, skills (such as the ability to drive), cash reserves, or a more developed coastal network. In other words, the advantages which Chiuchin offered women were economic and political opportunities related to the structural differences between the two communities. As we have noted the social values which define attitudes toward men and women have not been substantially altered in Chiuchin, nor do coastal values offer a more positive model of male-female interaction. On the other hand, Chiuchin women also demonstrate greater awareness of their subordinate status. We suspect that they will resist those aspects of social change which they identify as likely to decrease their options.

Notes

1. This model of political and economic development has undergone several critiques. For the historical development of the critique see Huntington (1971); for the most thorough treatment of the issues see Black (1976); for a comparison of development and dependency, with an emphasis on Latin America, see Chilcote and Edelstein (1974).

2. The dependency school is large and varied. For a discussion of this variation see Bath and James (1976) and Chilcote and Edelstein (1974). For the historical development of the concept see Frank (1969) and Kahl (1976). For a recent statement see Cardoso and Faletto (1979).

3. The obvious exception would be revolutionary change in which the ideology of the revolution explicitly addresses the redistribution of society's goods and then implements redistribution, usually by eliminating the privileges of the most favored groups. Radical transformations are rare and, despite the self-chosen title of Peru's "revolutionary military government," significant redistribution of resources has not occurred in Peru (Webb 1975; Stepan 1978).

4. Specific cases are found in Boserup (1970); Bossen (1978); Bourque and Warren (1976a, 1979a); Chaney and Schmink (1976); Deere (1976, 1977a, 1977b); Deere and León de Leal (n.d.); Dixon (1978); Huston (1979); Morin (1970); Nash (1976, 1977); Newland (1979); and Staudt (1976).

5. See for instance Babb (1976); Nash (1976, 1977); Rubbo (1975).

6. There is an extensive literature on modern Peru. For those interested in a fuller discussion of the policy initiatives of the present government, see Chaplin (1976); Cotler (1975, 1978); Lowenthal (1975); Palmer (1973, 1980); and Stepan (1978).

7. *Plan Inca*'s official title is *Plan del Gobierno Revolucionario de la Fuerza Armada*. Published in 1974, it contained an analysis and plan of action for thirty issues in Peruvian national life. The military claimed the *Plan* had been drawn up before it took power in 1968. See Schipske (1975) for a discussion of national level initiatives directed at women.

8. Massell (1970) reports a similar pattern of subversion of national government efforts to promote women's equality in the Soviet Union.

9. For a fuller discussion see Deere (1977*b*) and the initial critiques of the law by Sara LaFosse (1969).

10. There is a similar American pattern. Many poor rural women have found the United States Army an important source of opportunity and a vehicle for mobility. Women are not on active duty in any of the three branches of the Peruvian military, although some reservists in the air force and army have received special training. Women are likely to play a somewhat larger role in the *Guardia Civil,* the national police force. In 1979 two hundred women graduated from a year long, specially designed course training them to help tourists, to direct traffic especially around schools, and to assist with cases of child disappearance.

11. See for example Gissi Bustos (1976) and Stevens (1973). Heyman (1974) in a study of Peruvian high school students found that "as one moves from the less urban and more indigenous areas of Peru to the larger more mestizo coastal cities greater rigidity exists as to what job is appropriate for each sex and fewer options are open to the individual" (p. 132). For an extended discussion of the impact of mestizo values on the rural educational system see Paulston (1971), especially chapters 3 and 4.

12. One can never fully predict the consequences of education. No matter what the values obstensibly conveyed, and these are often conservative, the effect of rising expectations may be radically different. To draw a parallel from the United States, Cott (1977) points out that the content of the nineteenth-century ideology which argued for women's higher education justified the need on the basis of women's distinct characters and the necessity of providing special training and skills for their "separate sphere." Despite this justification, the experiment had unanticipated consequences. As Conway has demonstrated, the first generation of women college graduates came away with a missionary zeal to use their new skills to improve society and the lot of women. Higher education was instrumental in equipping them with the opportunity and sense of personal efficacy to challenge the status quo and carve out a new and more active role in society, albeit while explaining their behavior in terms of the dominant ideology (Conway 1964, 1971–72). For the important impact of education on women during the early republican period in the United States see Norton (1980).

Women's higher education did not retain the drive to create new and expanded roles for women. Rather, as women's educational opportunities expanded in the mid-twentieth century to include most of the middle class, the impact of college education lessened to the point where its major function was to ingrain a revitalized version of women's secondary status, defining their principal responsibilities in the home as the educated wives and mothers of men (Chafe 1977; Conable 1977; Conway 1974).

13. See for example Doughty and Negrón (1964); Bourque et al. (1967); Vazquez (1965); and Paulston (1971).

14. See the discussion in Bourque and Warren (1978*a*) for the specifics in this region and Paulston (1971) for the national pattern.

15. Nuclear schools, reminiscent of the nuclear schools first established in

1945 in rural Peru, were intended to provide a range of instruction for both children and the community.

16. The disadvantage of starting school later is that by the time girls complete primary school they will be too old to attend a regular secondary school. Regular secondary schools restrict entrants to those under seventeen. Older students must attend a night school. Parents are reluctant to send their daughters to a night school in an urban area for fear of abuse and harassment.

17. See the studies by Boggio et al. (1973); Heyman (1974); and Standing (1976).

18. See Paulston's (1971) critique of Peruvian education and (1973) the study of the curriculum by Boggio et al.

19. The pattern identified by Chaney (1977) for Peru matches the findings of Arizpe (1977) for Mexico and Jelin (1976) for Brazil. Chaney notes that the pattern for Latin America contrasts with the experience of domestic servants in the first industrializing countries, such as Britain and the United States, where domestic service was a route of upward social and economic mobility for some groups. See M. Smith (1971) for further information on domestic servants and Safa (1977) for women's role in the labor force.

20. This finding by Morris et al. (1968) matches the male-female migration rates for Peru reported in the UNESCO study by Orlansky and Dubrovsky (1978, p. 6). For further data on women and migration see Jelin (1977).

21. Chaney (1977) notes that the maintenance of rural-urban networks are the poor's means of outwitting those who predict they cannot survive in the city. Our data suggests that these networks may be especially important to women. Tilley and Scott (1978, p. 143) find a similar pattern in the urbanization processes of France and England.

22. Isbell (1974, 1978), Roberts (1975) discuss the importance of migratory networks.

23. See Mangin (1970) and Doughty (1970).

24. For examples see Castillo (1964) and Bourque and Warren (1976a, 1976b).

25. The importance of such ties to both highland and coastal families was demonstrated in the resistance of communities to the provisions of the Agrarian Reform Law restricting the rights of migrants to hold land in the community. Despite the fact this provision would have opened up new land for those who remained in the community, only rarely did a community move against a migrant's land, and then only when the migrant no longer had relatives to watch over his interests (Bourque and Warren 1978b).

IX

The Dynamics of Sexual Subordination

As we have affirmed in the last eight chapters, the analysis of sexual subordination presents special challenges. We have approached the riddle of women's continued subordination, despite changes in their public roles and economic options, by (1) developing the conceptual tools to identify and analyze the structural and ideological mechanisms of subordination, (2) examining alternative theoretical formulations of sexual hierarchy, and (3) analyzing women's and men's lives as they respond to the forces of social change in a particular cultural setting. Our goal has been to further the *interpretive* understanding of contemporary sexual hierarchies, rather than to create predictive, statistical explanations of discrete behaviors or to enter into debates concerning the first causes of sexual subordination. The decision to stress interpretive explanations arises from our interest in the meanings of sexual differentiation for the participants within a cultural tradition. Predictive and causal explanations frequently dismiss cultural meanings as being secondary to large-scale social processes. In contrast, we attempt to show how the cultural meanings assigned to sex differences are manipulated by individuals and tied to social institutions so as to perpetuate sexual hierarchies.

Our approach to sexual subordination benefited greatly from recent developments in the social sciences. Model building in the 1970s produced a spectrum of theoretical approaches to sexual subordination, including what we term the separate spheres, the sexual division of labor, the class analysis, and the social ideology approaches. Our evaluation of these frameworks reflects a commitment to pursue the interconnections between economics, politics, and other social systems; to investigate power structures as they constrain thought and behavior, yet are subject to individual manipulation; and to generate approaches fruitful for detailed ethnographic analysis as well as for comparative studies and generalizations about the cross-cultural experience of social change.

Our review of the literature on women's status in cross-cultural perspective convinced us that a combination of the social ideology and class analysis approaches would be most useful for conceptualizing sexual hierarchy in society. We have not, however, attempted a seamless theoretical synthesis of the two perspectives. Instead, we have decided to work from a social ideology perspective, while also incorporating analyses of agrarian class structures and economic dependency relations between rural and urban spheres. The social ideology approach, with its focus on the interconnections of sex role stereotyping, sexual divisions of labor, and institutionally structured access to crucial resources, is particularly well suited for documenting the ways sexual hierarchy is perpetuated. Our hope has been to overcome the weaknesses of approaches which focus on disembodied sex role stereotypes by studying the grounding of social ideologies in the material conditions and power structures of a society. With this amplified social ideology approach we have been able to address such questions as: What are the cultural mechanisms that perpetuate sexual subordination? How do these mechanisms change with increasing economic development and national integration? How do women act to limit the economic impact of sexual subordination? To what extent does class position override sexual subordination in shaping women's and men's political interests and patterns of mobilization?

We have analyzed the profound changes in men's and women's lives that accompany the increasing class stratification of rural settlements, the reorientation of agrarian production to national markets, and the closer political connections between the highlands and the urbanized coast. Economic development and state expansion into rural affairs have undermined rural autonomy in local political, economic, and cultural affairs. The loss of autonomy has accelerated since the 1960s with road construction, new schools, and increasing rates of coastal migration.

The impact of these broad changes has been different for the agricultural and the commercial settlements. For example, in Mayobamba, official representatives of the state, not traditional community elders, now regulate marriage, marital conflicts, legitimacy, and inheritance. In the process women have recognized certain protections provided by legal marriage; yet, they have also lost many roles that earlier gave them specialized authority in the domestic economy and community medicine. Women's limited local participation and community influence reflect the growing importance of national police who enforce coastal laws, the reorientation of local farming to meet the needs of coastal markets, and the increasing local reliance on coastal medicines and medical facilities when they are accessible.

These patterns of change have allowed Mayobamba men to consolidate their control over the local arenas of political and economic decision making, reinforcing female dependence on fathers, brothers, and husbands. That young women seek alternatives in migration and education and that female migrants harshly judge the traditionalism of *sierra* men in these circumstances is not surprising. What women fail to see is that part of the male authoritarianism they criticize is the product of coastal contact and the consequent erosion of women's earlier sources of influence.

Women in the commercial settlement of Chiuchin have been exposed to the same forces of social change. For the moment, some of these women are the beneficiaries of shifting patterns of local authority and the increasing integration of the coastal economy and rural subsistence patterns. Chiuchin's success as a commercial center for the distribution of coastal products is tied directly to the penetration of the cash economy into the highlands. In Chiuchin the advantageous aspects of economic development accrue most directly to those women who occupy positions directing local commerce. Due to their independent access to capital, merchant women are able to stress class position in a way that overrides some of the invidious consequences of sexual subordination. Female elites operate successful businesses by joining forces with entrepreneurial husbands, by coordinating a range of enterprises operated by their extended families and by establishing networks of female trading partners in the highland communities.

Women merchants in Chiuchin are concerned with effectively translating their economic positions into political influence for local development projects. These women have encountered stiff male resistance to the political parity of the sexes. However, the lack of a formal town government in this settlement has made women's political participation more negotiable, especially since women must number among the contributors for local projects to be economically feasible. Businesswomen maintain both sex-based and class-based economic commitments and alliances. On the one hand, they are major employers of female wage laborers and activists in highland trading networks; on the other hand, women merchants are involved with the local economic elites of both sexes in negotiations with national authorities for development projects and strategic ties to the coast.

Our study shows that women are not silent or inactive victims in the face of the serious economic consequences of sexual subordination. Women of all economic strata actively locate assistance for masculine tasks in the sexual division of labor, broaden their access to critical resources, influence decision making, and formulate new options based on migration and education for themselves and their children. With the goal of limiting the economic impact of subordination and gaining a measure of independence, women have developed strategies for converting small amounts of capital into businesses, for organizing labor exchanges to harvest each other's fields, and for participating in highland and coastal trading networks. They also enlarge their access to male labor by creating household units through formal marriages or, alternatively, through matrifocal extended families.

Our framework has allowed us to follow the interplay of sexual subordination and class stratification, without analytically reducing either dimension of social inequality to the other. As a result, we have been able to investigate aspects of rural life that might remain unexplored in more conventional studies of either sex roles or agrarian class systems.

For example, we have found that one mechanism for the perpetuation of sexual hierarchy in both agrarian and commercial towns is the cross-class economic cooperation of men which restricts women's access to crucial resources. In Mayobamba, elite merchant-farmers, who own irrigated pastures and teams of oxen, join with skilled laborers, who are specialists in handling difficult animals and heavy equipment, to monopolize the plowing of agricultural fields. Plowing and other agricultural tasks that are male-specialized increase women's dependence on men as husbands or *convivientes* or on wage labor, which is particularly difficult for women to contract. In Chiuchin, regional businessmen cultivate specialized connections to national government authorities who provide school programs, development funds, information, extension agents, and government subsidized coastal products. Patriarchy on the national level reinforces male dominance on the local level, even though women in the town are able to run economically independent households. To gain access to coastal products, Chiuchin women forego their own development priorities in favor of jointly negotiated projects that reinforce men's strategic ties to urban bureaucracies and, consequently, further women's subordination in the process of change.

At the same time as our analysis finds that economic stratification plays an important role in the creation of new mechanisms for the maintenance of sexual hierarchy, we have also discovered that rural women attempt to ameliorate the consequences of their subordinate status by fostering cross-strata, pan-community economic cooperation. Female merchants identify some of their own economic interests with those of other women, especially impoverished highland widows and single mothers, who seek steady work, cash, moral support, and education for their children. We see the resulting female networks as one of the few instances in which access to local and coastal resources is improved for poor rural women. Yet, there are limitations to the remedial capacity of these networks, given the grave problems of impoverished women who bear the full brunt of class exploitation and sexual hierarchy.

One is tempted to ask if women directly link their strategies for limiting the effects of sexual subordination to their understandings of male control in their towns. In other words, do women see certain strategies for solving economic problems as also dealing with issues rooted in sexual politics? This question is a particularly difficult one for the social sciences which have yet to agree on how one might most effectively pursue the issue of "consciousness."

In the course of this study of the women of Chiuchin and Mayobamba, we have examined women's social ideologies, values, perceptions, and understandings of the politics of male-female relationships. By studying women's discussions of power structures, sexual divisions of labor, and their images of sex roles and sexual stereotypes, we have begun to isolate the categories through which women express their ideological analyses. Using this method, with the appropriate ethnographic data, we should be able to ask if and when women's political analyses of their situation give them special insights into sexual subordination. Or, do women's perceptions and social values tend systematically to reinforce their subordination by misportraying the realities of sexual hierarchy?

To effectively characterize women's political analysis (or men's, for that matter), we must also ask how social ideologies are shaped and structured. The cultural creation of social ideologies is a particularly complicated and controversial issue. For example, Marxist scholars tend to think of ideologies as determined by the material conditions of society and the requirements for the reproduction of the dominant mode of production. Social ideology in this framework would be a dependent variable. In contrast, "consciousness," in the context of the contemporary American women's movement has often been viewed as an awareness individuals either have or lack. In this usage consciousness is rooted in individual (as opposed to collective) insights into the politics of interpersonal relations with or without reference to the structural constraints of the social order, or the impact of the situational context on its expression.

Our Peruvian data show the complexity of social ideologies and perceptions. Women's analysis of the mechanisms that perpetuate sexual subordination varies between Mayobamba and Chiuchin. In both communities women maintain definitions and perceptions of social reality that are distinct from ideologies forged by local power structures and are not predictable solely on the basis of class. In Mayobamba, women's distinct definitions of work (e.g., irrigation) and community service (as the community herder or church guardian) give meaning to subordinate roles that are otherwise unrecognized. However, these views of participation appear to block women's full understanding of the structural contribution that the *comunero* system makes to the sexual subordination of married women (over and above its acknowledged impact on impoverished female heads of household).

In Chiuchin, women are explicit about the different priorities they would give local development projects and the demands they would make if they were to organize to exert political influence. Women outline men's negative attitudes and efforts to discourage women's participation. While their understanding of local politics has been enhanced by participation on the ad hoc committees that negotiate with coastal organizations, women have not explicitly and systematically linked men's ability to control access to the coast with their continued dominance in rural life.

Women in both communities are keen observers of change: they are adept at evaluating the impact of change on their own sources of control and influence. In many instances, however, they are forced to balance one positive aspect of change against elements which undermine some aspect of their status. The transfer of childbearing to coastal hospitals is a case in point. Women desire some of the benefits of health technology available in coastal hospitals, but this alternative has undermined the position of the skilled midwives in the rural communities. Coastal childbirth also increases women's dependence for vital services on the cash economy in which they are competitively disadvantaged.

Education also demonstrates the importance of understanding women's social analyses that seemingly stand behind paradoxical responses to change. Women recognize the benefits to be garnered from their children's education and many, who struggled to educate themselves, know its particular importance to women. However, when women are faced with limited resources for their children, they may opt to favor the male children. They feel their sons have the greatest chance of success and consequently will be most likely to provide support for the mother's old age. One can hardly dismiss the cultural logic of the choice or fail to appreciate its difficulty. Nor can one assume that these are static priorities.

A comprehensive analysis of women's social ideologies as they relate to the consciousness of inequality and change will require additional analytical tools and ethnographic data. Our findings suggest that a good take-off point for such analysis would be the *interplay* of sex and class, as these dimensions of inequality shape social environments, pose problems that evoke evaluations and responses, and play central parts in the cultural construction of social identities.

Our data demonstrate that despite women's analysis of subordination and their efforts to devise strategies to respond to it, there are structural forces arrayed against them. The mechanics of subordination are found in the local economy and political structure; they are integral to the dynamics of family life and embedded in community value systems. Moreover, those forces of outside change—the national government, the educational system, and the possibility of migration—show no clear counter-trend. The cultural values of these outside groups, and the processes that link the *sierra* and the coast, either reinforce existing patterns of male dominance or offer a still

more restricted view of women's roles. In addition, those policy initiatives of national institutions that might challenge patterns of domination have been met by local resistance and subversion. Nonetheless, as
the lives of Andean women demonstrate, inequality is not mechani-
cally perpetuated. Instead, it is negotiated, disputed, and ultimately
changed through the conscious actions of individuals.

Bibliography

Adams, Richard N.
1959   *A community in the Andes: Problems and progress in Muquiyauyo.*
        Seattle: University of Washington Press.
Alberti, Giorgio, and Mayer, Enrique, eds.
1974   *Reciprocidad e intercambio en los Andes peruanos.* Lima: Instituto de
        Estudios Peruanos.
Andradi, Esther, and Portugal, Ana María
1978   *Ser mujer en el perú.* Lima: Ediciones Mujer y Autonomia.
Ardener, Shirley
1975   Introduction to *Perceiving women,* ed. Shirley Ardener, pp. vii–
        xxiii. London: Malaby Press.
Ardener, Shirley, ed.
1978   *Defining females: The nature of women in society.* New York: John
        Wiley.
Ariès, Philippe
1962   *Centuries of childhood: A social history of family life.* New York: Alfred
        A. Knopf.
Arizpe, Lourdes
1977   Women in the informal labor sector in Mexico City: A case of
        unemployment or voluntary choice? *Signs* 3:25–37.
Aronoff, Joel, and Crano, William D.
1975   A re-examination of the cross-cultural principles of task segrega-
        tion and sex role differentiation in the family. *American Sociologi-
        cal Review* 40:12–20.
Babb, Florence
1976   The development of sexual inequality in Vicos, Peru. Special
        Studies Series no. 83, Council on International Studies, State
        University of New York at Buffalo.
Bachrach, Peter, and Baratz, Morton
1962   The two faces of power. *American Political Science Review* 56:947–
        52.
1970   *Power and poverty.* London: Oxford University Press.
Bamberger, Joan
1974   The myth of matriarchy: Why men rule in primitive society. In

Women, culture, and society, ed. Michelle Zimbalist Rosaldo and Louise Lamphere, pp. 263–80. Stanford: Stanford University Press.

Bath, C. R., and James, D. D.
1976   Dependency analysis of Latin America. *Latin American Research Review* 11, no. 3, pp. 3–54.

Black, Cyril E.
1976   *Comparative modernization: A reader.* New York: Free Press.

Boals, Kay
1975   The politics of male-female relations: The functions of feminist scholarship. *Signs* 1:161–74.

Bodley, John H.
1976   *Anthropology and contemporary human problems.* Menlo Park, Ca.: Cummings Publishing Co.

Boggio, Ana; Lora, Carmen; Riofrío, Gustavo; and Roncagliolo, Rafael.
1973   *¿ Cuesta arriba o cuesta abajo?* Lima: DESCO.

Bolton, Ralph
1977   The Qolla marriage process. In *Andean kinship and marriage,* ed. Ralph Bolton and Enrique Mayer, pp. 217–39. Washington, D.C.: American Anthropological Association.

Bolton, Ralph, and Mayer, Enrique, eds.
1977   *Andean kinship and marriage.* Washington, D.C.: American Anthropological Association.

Boserup, Ester
1970   *Woman's role in economic development.* London: Allen and Unwin.

Bossen, Laurel Herbenar
1978   Women and development: A comparison of women's economic and social roles in Guatemala. Ph.D. dissertation, State University of New York at Albany.

Bourque, Susan C.
1971*a*   *Cholification and the campesino: A study of three Peruvian peasant organizations in the process of societal change.* Ph.D. dissertation. Latin American Studies Program. Dissertation Series, no. 21. Ithaca: Cornell University.

1971*b*   El sistema político peruano y las organizaciones campesinas: Un modelo de integración." *Estudios Andinos* 2:37–60.

1975   The clash of empires: Peru's enduring paradox. *Smith College Studies in History* 47:65–81.

Bourque, Susan C.; Brownrigg, Leslie; Maynard, Eileen; and Dobyns, Henry.
1967   *Factions and faenas: A report on the development potential of Checras district, Peru.* Ithaca: Cornell University Anthropology Department.

Bourque, Susan C., and Grossholtz, Jean
1974   Politics as an unnatural practice: Political science looks at female participation. *Politics and Society* 4:225–266.

Bourque, Susan C., and Palmer, David Scott
 1975   Transforming the rural sector: Government policy and peasant response. In *The Peruvian experiment,* ed. Abraham Lowenthal, pp. 179–219. Princeton: Princeton University Press.
Bourque, Susan C., and Warren, Kay B.
 1976*a*   Campesinas and comuneras: Subordination in the sierra. *Journal of Marriage and the Family* 38:781–88.
 1976*b*   Campesinas y comuneras: subordinación en la sierra peruana. *Estudios Andinos* 5, no. 1:77–98.
 1978*a*   Denial and reaffirmation of ethnic identities: A comparative examination of Guatemalan and Peruvian communities. International Area Studies Programs, University of Massachusetts, Amherst, Program in Latin American Studies, Occasional Papers Series, no. 8.
 1978*b*   Political participation and the revolution: Lessons from rural Peru. Latin American Program, The Wilson Center, Smithsonian Institution, Washington, D.C. Working Paper no. 25.
 1979*a*   Female participation, perception, and power: An examination of two Andean communities. In *Political participation and the poor,* ed. John Booth and Michell Seligson, pp. 116–33. New York: Holmes and Meier.
 1979*b*   Individual and collective responses to economic and political change: Lessons from the Peruvian experiment. Paper presented at the Latin American Studies Association Annual Meetings, April 4, 1979, Pittsburgh, Pennsylvania.
 1980   Multiple arenas for state expansion: Class, ethnicity and sex in rural Peru. *Ethnic and Racial Studies* 3, no. 3:264–80.
Bourricaud, François
 1967   *Cambios en puno.* Mexico: Instituto Indigenista Interamericano.
Brown, Judith K.
 1970   A note on the division of labor by sex. *American Anthropologist* 72:1073–78.
 1975   Iroquois women: An ethnohistoric note. In *Toward an anthropology of women,* ed. Rayna R. Reiter, pp. 235–51. New York: Monthly Review Press.
Brown, Susan E.
 1975   Love unites them and hunger separates them: Poor women in the Dominican Republic. In *Toward an anthropology of women,* ed. Rayna R. Reiter, pp. 322–32. New York: Monthly Review Press.
Brush, Stephen B.
 1977   *Mountain, field and family: The economy and human ecology of an Andean valley.* Philadelphia: University of Pennsylvania Press.
Buchbinder, Georgeda, and Rappaport, Roy A.
 1976   Fertility and death among the Maring. In *Man and woman in the New Guinea highlands,* ed. Paula Brown and Georgeda Buch-

binder, pp. 13–35. Washington, D.C.: American Anthropological Association.

Buechler, Hans C., and Buechler, Judith–Maria
1971   *The Bolivian Aymara.* New York: Holt, Rinehart, and Winston.

Bujra, Janet
1979   Introductory: Female solidarity and the sexual division of labor. In *Women united, women divided: Contemporary studies of ten cultures,* ed. Patricia Caplan and Janet M. Bujra, pp. 13–45. Bloomington: Indiana University Press.

Burkett, Elinor C.
1977   In dubious sisterhood: Race and class in Spanish colonial South America. *Latin American Perspectives* 4:18–26.

Burton, Michael L.; Brudner, Lilyan A; and White, Douglas R.
1977   A model of the sexual division of labor. *American Ethnologist* 4:227–51.

Callan, Hilary
1978   Harems and overlords: Biosocial models and the female. In *Defining females,* ed. Shirley Ardener, pp. 200–219. New York: John Wiley.

Callaway, Helen
1978   "The most essentially female function of all": Giving birth. In *Defining females,* ed. Shirley Ardener, pp. 163–85. New York: John Wiley.

Caplan, Patricia, and Bujra, Janet M., eds.
1979   *Women united, women divided: Contemporary studies of ten cultures.* Bloomington: Indiana University Press.

Cardoso, Fernando, and Faletto, Enzo
1979   *Dependency and development in Latin America.* Berkeley: University of California Press.

Carpio, Lourdes
1974   Las mujeres campesinas en el Perú. *Boletín documental sobre las mujeres* 4, no. 2:31–42.
1976   "La mujer campesina: Una alarmante postergación." *Educación* 1, no. 3:9–17.

Carroll, Berenice
1979   Political science, part I: American politics and political behavior. *Signs* 5, no. 2:289–306.

Castillo, Hernan
1964   *Mito: The orphan of its illustrious children.* Ithaca: Cornell University Anthropology Department.

Castro Pozo, Hildebrando
1924   *Nuestra comunidad indígena.* Lima: Editorial El Lucero.

Chafe, William H.
1977   *Women and equality: Changing patterns in American culture.* New York: Oxford University Press.

Chaney, Elsa M.
1974   The mobilization of women in Allende's Chile. In *Women in politics*, ed. Jane S. Jaquette, pp. 267–80. New York: John Wiley.
1977   Agripina: Domestic service and its implications for development. Paper presented at the First Mexican-Central American Symposium on Research on Women, November 7–10, 1977, Mexico, D.F.
Chaney, Elsa M., and Schmink, Marianne
1976   Women and modernization: Access to tools. In *Sex and class in Latin America*, ed. June Nash and Helen Safa, pp. 160–82. New York: Praeger.
Chaplin, David, ed.
1976   *Peruvian nationalism: A corporatist revolution.* New Brunswick, N.J.: Transaction Books.
Chilcote, Ronald H., and Edelstein, Joel C., eds.
1974   *Latin America: The struggle with dependency and beyond.* New York: John Wiley.
Chiñas, Beverly L.
1973   *The isthmus Zapotecs: Women's roles in cultural context.* New York: Holt, Rinehart, and Winston.
Chodorow, Nancy
1978   *The reproduction of mothering: Psychoanalysis and the sociobiology of gender.* Berkeley: University of California Press.
Cloward, Richard, and Piven, Francis Fox
1979   Hidden protest: The channeling of female innovation and resistance. *Signs* 4, no. 4:651–69.
Cole, John W., and Wolf, Eric R.
1974   *The hidden frontier: Ecology and ethnicity in an alpine valley.* New York: Academic Press.
Collier, David
1976   *Squatters and oligarchs: Authoritarian rule and policy change in Peru.* Baltimore: Johns Hopkins University Press.
Collier, Jane Fishburne
1974   Women in politics. In *Women, culture, and society*, ed. Michelle Zimbalist Rosaldo and Louise Lamphere, pp. 89–96. Stanford: Stanford University Press.
Cominos, Peter T.
1973   Innocent femina sensualis in unconscious conflict. In *Suffer and be still: Women in the Victorian age*, ed. Martha Vicinus, pp. 155–72. Bloomington: Indiana University Press.
Conable, Charlotte Williams
1977   *Women at Cornell: The myth of equal education.* Ithaca: Cornell University Press.
Constantinides, Pamela
1979   Women's spirit possession and urban adaptation in the Muslim

northern Sudan. In *Women united, women divided: Contemporary studies of ten cultures,* ed. Patricia Caplan and Janet M. Bujra, pp. 185–205. Bloomington: Indiana University Press.

Conway, Jill K.
1964   Jane Addams: An American heroine. *Daedalus* 93:761–80.
1971–72 Women reformers and American culture, 1870–1930. *Journal of Social History* 5:164–77.
1973   Stereotypes of femininity in a theory of sexual evolution. In *Suffer and be still: Women in the Victorian age,* ed. Martha Vicinus, pp. 140–54. Bloomington: Indiana University Press.
1974   Perspectives on the history of women's education in the United States. *History of Education Quarterly* 14:1–12.

Cornejo Muñoz, Rina.
1978   La socialización de la mujer campesina del Cuzco. AMIDEP Seminario de Investigaciones Sociales acerca de la Mujer. Cuzco: Universidad Nacional San Antonio Abad.

Cotler, Julio
1975   The new mode of political domination in Peru. In *The Peruvian experiment,* ed. Abraham F. Lowenthal, pp. 44–78. Princeton: Princeton University Press.
1978   *Clases, estado y nación en el Perú,* Perú Problema 17. Lima: Instituto de Estudios Peruanos.

Cott, Nancy F.
1977   *The bonds of womanhood: "Woman's sphere" in New England, 1780–1835.* New Haven: Yale University Press.

Crespi, Muriel
1976   Mujeres campesinas como líderes sindicales: la falta de propiedad como calificación para puesto político. *Estudios Andinos,* 5:151–70.

Dahl, Robert A.
1961   *Who governs? Democracy and power in an American city.* New Haven: Yale University Press.

Davies, Thomas M.
1974   *Indian integration in Peru: A half century of experience, 1900–1948.* Lincoln: University of Nebraska Press.

Davis, Natalie Z.
1975   *Society and culture in early modern France.* Stanford: Stanford University Press.

de Beauvoir, Simone
1952   *The second sex.* Translated by H. M. Parshley. New York: Alfred A. Knopf.

Deere, Carmen Diana
1976   Rural women's subsistence production in capitalist periphery. *Review of Radical Political Economics* 8:9–18.
1977*a*   Changing social relations of production in Peruvian peasant women's work. *Latin American Perspectives* 4:48–69.

1977*b*   The agricultural division of labor by sex: Myths, facts and contradictions in the northern Peruvian sierra. Paper presented at the Joint Meeting of the Latin American Studies Association and the African Studies Association, November 2–5, 1977, Houston, Texas.

1978   The differentiation of the peasantry and family structure: A Peruvian case study. *Journal of Family History* 3:422–38.

Deere, Carmen Diana, and León de Leal, Magdalena

n.d.   *Women in agriculture: Peasant production and proletarianization in three Andean regions.* Unpublished Manuscript, International Labor Organization.

Dinnerstein, Dorothy

1976   *The mermaid and the minotaur: Sexual arrangements and human malaise.* New York: Harper Colophon Books.

Divale, William Tulio, and Harris, Marvin

1976   Population, warfare, and the male supremacist complex. *American Anthropologist* 78:521–38.

Dixon, Ruth B.

1978   *Rural women at work: Strategies for development in South Asia.* Baltimore: Johns Hopkins University Press.

Dobyns, Henry F.

1964   *The social matrix of Peruvian indigenous communities.* Cornell Peru Project Monograph. Ithaca: Cornell University Anthropology Department.

Doughty, Paul L.

1968   *Huaylas: An Andean district in search of progress.* Ithaca: Cornell University Press.

1970   Behind the back of the city: Provincial life in Lima. In *Peasants in cities: Readings in the anthropology of urbanization,* ed. William Mangin, pp. 30–46. Boston: Houghton Mifflin.

Doughty, Paul, and Negrón, Luis

1964   *Pararín: A break with the past.* Ithaca: Cornell University Anthropology Department.

Douglas, Ann

1977   *The feminization of American culture.* New York: Alfred A. Knopf.

Draper, Patricia

1975   !Kung women: Contrasts in sexual egalitarianism in foraging and sedentary contexts. In *Toward an anthropology of women,* ed. Rayna R. Reiter, pp. 77–109. New York: Monthly Review Press.

Drysdale, Robert S., and Myers, Robert G.

1975   Continuity and change: Peruvian education. In *The Peruvian experiment: Continuity and change under military rule,* ed. Abraham F. Lowenthal, pp. 254–301. Princeton: Princeton University Press.

DuBois, Ellen Carol

1980   Politics and culture in women's history. *Feminist Studies* 6, no. 1: 26–36.

Dumont, Louis
   1970   *Homo hierarchicus: An essay on the caste system.* Chicago: University
            of Chicago Press.
Dwyer, Daisy Hilse
   1978*a*   Ideologies of sexual inequality and strategies for change in male-
            female relations. *American Ethnologist* 5:227–40.
   1978*b*   *Images and self-images: Male and female in Morocco.* New York: Co-
            lumbia University Press.
Eisenstein, Zillah R., ed.
   1979   *Capitalist patriarchy and the case of socialist feminism.* New York:
            Monthly Review Press.
Elmendorf, Mary
   1976   *Nine Mayan women: A village faces change.* Cambridge, Mass.:
            Schenkman.
Elshtain, Jean B.
   1974   Moral woman and immoral man: A consideration of the public-
            private split and its political ramifications. *Politics and Society*
            4:453–73.
   1979   Methodological sophistication and conceptual confusion: A
            critique of mainstream political science. In *Prism of Sex,* ed. Julia
            Sherman and Evelyn Torton Beck, pp. 229–52. Madison: Univer-
            sity of Wisconsin.
Engels, Frederick
   1942   *The origin of the family, private property and the state.* New York:
            International Publishers.
Etienne, Mona, and Leacock, Eleanor, eds.
   1980   *Women and colonization: Anthropological perspectives.* New York:
            Praeger.
Faithhorn, Elizabeth
   1976   Women as persons: Aspects of female life and male-female rela-
            tions among the Kafe. In *Man and woman in the New Guinea high-
            lands,* ed. Paula Brown and Georgeda Buchbinder, pp. 86–95.
            Washington, D.C: American Anthropological Association.
Fee, Elizabeth
   1974   The sexual politics of Victorian social anthropology. In *Clio's con-
            sciousness raised: New perspectives on the history of women,* ed. Mary S.
            Hartman and Lois Banner, pp. 86–102. New York: Harper &
            Row.
Fee, Terry, and Gonzalez, Rosalinda, eds.
   1977   Women in changing modes of production. *Latin American Per-
            spectives* 4:38–47.
Fernea, Elizabeth W.
   1969   *Guests of the sheik: An ethnology of an Iraqi village.* New York:
            Doubleday.
   1976   *A street in Marrakech.* New York: Doubleday.

Flores-Ochoa, Jorge A.
1979   *Pastoralists of the Andes.* Translated by Robert Bolton. Philadelphia: Institute for the Study of Human Issues.
Frank, André Gunder
1969   *Capitalism and underdevelopment in Latin America.* New York: Monthly Review Press.
Friedl, Ernestine
1975   *Women and men: An anthropologist's view.* New York: Holt, Reinhart, and Winston.
Frieze, Irene H.; Parsons, Jacquelynne; Johnson, Paula; Ruble, Diane; and Zellman, Gail
1978   *Women and sex roles: Social psychological perspective.* New York: Norton.
Fuenzalida, Fernando; Mayer, Enrique; Escobar, Gabriel; Bourricaud, François; and Matos Mar, José
1970   *El Indio y el poder en el Perú.* Lima: Moncloa.
Gilder, George F.
1973   *Sexual suicide.* New York: Quadrangle.
Gissi Bustos, Jorge
1976   Mythology about women, with special reference to Chile. In *Sex and class in Latin America,* ed. June Nash and Helen Safa, pp. 30–45. New York: Praeger.
Goldberg, Steven
1973   *The inevitability of patriarchy.* New York: Morrow.
Goldschmidt, W., and Kunkel, E. J.
1971   The structure of the peasant family. *American Anthropologist* 73:1058–76.
Gomm, Roger
1979   Bargaining from weakness: Spirit possession on the south Kenya coast. In *Women and society,* ed. Sharon W. Tiffany, pp. 120–43. Montreal: Eden Press Women's Publications.
Gough, Kathleen
1975   The origin of the family. In *Toward an anthropology of women,* ed. Rayna R. Reiter, pp. 51–76. New York: Monthly Review Press.
Green, Philip
Forthcoming *The pursuit of inequality.* New York: Pantheon.
Harding, Susan
1975   Women and wards in a Spanish village. In *Toward an anthropology of women,* ed. Rayna R. Reiter, pp. 283–308. New York: Monthly Review Press.
Hardman, Martha James
1976   Andean women. *Faces of change,* Bolivian Series Films and Essays. American Universities Field Staff.
Harris, Olivia
1978   Complementarity and conflict: An Andean view of women and

men. In *Sex and age as principles of social differentiation,* ed. J. S.
LaFontaine, pp. 21–40. New York: Academic Press.

Harrison, Brian
1978   *Separate spheres: The opposition to women's suffrage in Britain.* New
        York: Holmes and Meier.

Hartmann, Heidi
1976   Capitalism, patriarchy and job segregation by sex. In *Women and
        the workplace: The implications of occupational segregation,* ed. Martha
        Blaxall and Barbara Reagan, pp. 137–69. Chicago: University of
        Chicago Press.

Hastrup, Kirsten
1978   The semantics of biology: Virginity. In *Defining females,* ed. Shir-
        ley Ardener, pp. 49–65. New York: John Wiley.

Heyman, Barry Neal
1974   Urbanization and the status of women in Peru. Ph.D. disserta-
        tion, University of Wisconsin.

Hubbard, Ruth, ed.
1979   *Women look at biology looking at women.* Cambridge, Mass.:
        Schenkman.

Huntington, Samuel P.
1971   The change to change: Modernization, development and politics.
        Comparative Politics 3:283–322.

Huston, Perdita
1979   *Third world women speak out.* New York: Praeger.

Ifeka-Moller, Caroline
1975   Female militancy and colonial revolt. In *Perceiving women,* ed.
        Shirley Ardener, pp. 127–57. London: Malaby Press.

Isbell, Billie Jean
1974   The influence of migrants upon traditional social and political
        concepts: A Peruvian case study. In *Anthropological perspectives on
        Latin American urbanization,* vol. 4, ed. W. A. Cornelius and Felicity
        Trueblood, pp. 237–59. Beverly Hills: Sage Publications.
1976   "La otra mitad esencial: Un estudio de complementaridad sexual
        en los Andes." *Estudios Andinos* 5:37–56.
1978   *To defend ourselves.* Austin: University of Texas Press.

Jaquette, Jane S.
1973a   Literary archetypes and family role alternatives: The woman and
        the novel in Latin America. In *Female and male in Latin America,*
        ed. Ann Pescatello, pp. 3–28. Pittsburgh: University of Pittsburgh
        Press.
1973b   Women in revolutionary movements in Latin America. *Journal of
        Marriage and the Family* 35, no. 2:344–54.
1976   Female political participation in Latin America. In *Women in the
        world,* ed. Lynne B. Iglitzin and Ruth Ross, pp. 55–76. Santa
        Barbara: Clio Press.

Jaquette, Jane S., ed.
1974   *Women in politics.* New York: John Wiley.
Jelin, Elizabeth
1976   The Bahiana in the labor force in Salvador, Brazil. In *Sex and class in Latin America,* ed. June Nash and Helen Safa, pp. 129–46. New York: Praeger.
1977   Migration and labor force participation of Latin American women: The domestic servants in the cities. In *Women and national development: The complexities of change,* ed. Ximena Bunster et al., pp. 129–41. Chicago: University of Chicago Press.
Jopling, Carol
1974   Women's work: A Mexican case study of low status as a tactical advantage. *Ethnology* 13:187–95.
Kahl, Joseph
1976   *Modernization, exploitation and dependency in Latin America: Germani, Gonzalez Casanova and Cardoso.* New Brunswick, N.J.: Transaction Books.
Kanter, Rosabeth Moss
1977   *Men and women of the corporation.* New York: Basic Books.
Kelly, Joan
1979   The doubled vision of feminist theory: A postscript to the "Women and Power" Conference. *Feminist Studies* 5, no. 1:216–27.
Knaster, Meri
1976   Women in Latin America: The state of research, 1975. *Latin American Research Review* 11:3–74.
Koonz, Claudia
1977   Mothers in the fatherland: Women in Nazi Germany. In *Becoming visible: Women in European history,* ed. Renate Bridenthal and Claudia Koonz, pp. 445–73. Boston: Houghton Mifflin Co.
Kuhn, Annette, and Wolpe, Ann Marie, eds.
1978   *Feminism and materialism.* London: Routledge and Kegan Paul.
La Fontaine, J. S., ed.
1978   *Sex and age as principles of social differentiation.* New York: Academic Press.
Lambert, Bernd
1977   Bilaterality in the Andes. In *Andean kinship and marriage,* ed. Ralph Bolton and Enrique Mayer, pp. 1–27. Washington, D.C.: American Anthropological Association.
Lamphere, Louise
1974   Strategies, cooperation, and conflict among women in domestic groups. In *Women, culture, and society,* ed. Michelle Zimbalist Rosaldo and Louise Lamphere, pp. 97–112. Stanford: Stanford University Press.
1977   Anthropology. *Signs,* 2:612–27.

Langness, L. L.
   1979   Sexual antagonism in the New Guinea highlands: A Bena Bena
          example. In *Women and society*, ed. Sharon W. Tiffany, pp. 256–
          78. Montreal: Eden Press Women's Publications.
Leacock, Eleanor Burke
   1972   Introduction to *The origin of the family, private property and the state*
          by Frederick Engels, pp. 7–68. New York: International Pub-
          lishers.
   1975   Class, commodity and the status of women. In *Women cross-
          culturally, change and challenge*, ed. Ruby Rohrlich-Leavitt, pp.
          601–16. The Hague: Mouton Press.
   1977   Women, development, and anthropological facts and fictions.
          Latin American Perspectives 4:8–17.
Leacock, Eleanor, and Nash, June
   1977   Ideology of sex: Archetypes and stereotypes. *Annals of the New
          York Academy of Science* 285:618–45.
Lefebvre, Henri
   1971   *Everyday life in the modern world.* Translated by Sacha Rabinovich.
          New York: Harper Torchbooks.
Leghorn, Lisa, and Parker, Kathy
   n.d.   *Womensworth: Toward a matriarchal economy.* New York: Routledge
          and Kegan Paul.
Levy, Marsha
   1973   Playing the field: Anthropologists at work. Unpublished senior
          honors thesis, Princeton University.
Liebowitz, Lila
   1975   Perspectives on the evolution of sex differences. In *Toward an
          anthropology of women*, ed. Rayna R. Reiter, pp. 20–35. New York:
          Monthly Review Press.
Lowenthal, Abraham, ed.
   1975   *The Peruvian experiment: Continuity and change under military rule.*
          Princeton: Princeton University Press.
McCormack, Thelma
   1976   Towards a nonsexist perspective on social and political change. In
          Another voice: Feminist perspectives on social life and social science, ed.
          Marcia Millman and Rosabeth Moss Kanter, pp. 1–33. New York:
          Octagon Books.
Magdoff, JoAnn
   1977   The tillage of his husbandry: A symbolic analysis of change in
          male and female identity in an industrializing town in central
          Italy. Ph.D. dissertation, Princeton University.
Mangin, William, ed.
   1970   *Peasants in cities: Readings in the anthropology of urbanization.* Bos-
          ton: Houghton Mifflin.
Massell, Gregory
   1970   Traditional structures as obstacles to revolutionary change: The

case of Soviet central Asia. In *Politics and society,* ed. Eric Nordlinger, pp. 266–87. Englewood Cliffs: Prentice-Hall.

Mayer, Enrique José
1974   *Reciprocity, self-sufficiency and market relations in a contemporary community in the central Andes of Peru.* Ph.D. dissertation. Latin American Studies Program. Dissertation Series no. 72. Ithaca: Cornell University.

Meggitt, M. J.
1976   A duplicity of demons: Sexual and familial roles expressed in western Enga stories. In *Man and woman in the New Guinea highlands,* ed. Paula Brown and Georgeda Buchbinder, pp. 63–85. Washington, D.C.: American Anthropological Association.

Michaelson, Evalyn Jacobson, and Goldschmidt, Walter
1971   Female roles and male dominance among peasants. *Southwest Journal of Anthropology* 27:330–52.

Millett, Kate
1970   *Sexual politics.* Garden City, New York: Doubleday.

Millman, Marcia, and Kanter, Rosabeth Moss, eds.
1976   *Another voice: Feminist perspectives on social life and social science.* New York: Octagon Books.

Morin, Edgar
1970   *The red and the white: Report from a French village.* New York: Pantheon.

Morris, Earl Walter
1970   Acculturation, migration and fertility in Peru: A study of social and cultural change. Ph.D. dissertation, Cornell University.

Morris, Earl W., ed.
1964   *Etapas para el desarrollo socio-económico de Mayobamba.* Lima: Folletos del Proyecto Perú-Cornell.

Morris, Earl W.; Brownrigg, Leslie; Bourque, Susan C.; and Dobyns, Henry F.
1968   *Coming down the mountain: The social worlds of Mayobamba.* Ithaca: Cornell University Anthropology Department.

Murdock, George P., and Provost, Caterina
1973   Factors in the division of labor by sex: Cross-cultural analysis. *Ethnology* 12:203–25.

Murphy, Yolanda, and Murphy, Robert F.
1974   *Women of the forest.* New York: Columbia University Press.

Nash, June
1976   A critique of social science roles in Latin America. In *Sex and class in Latin America,* ed. June Nash and Helen Icken Safa, pp. 1–21. New York: Praeger.

1977   Women in development: Dependency and exploitation. *Development and change* 8:161–82.

1978   The Aztecs and the ideology of male dominance. *Signs* 4:349–62.

1980   Aztec women: The transition from status to class in empire and colony. In *Women and colonization: Anthropological perspectives*, ed. Mona Etienne and Eleanor Leacock, pp. 134–48. New York: Praeger.

Nash, June; Corradi, Juan; and Spalding, Hobart, eds.
1977   *Ideology and social change in Latin America*. New York: Gordon and Breach.

Neira, Hugo
1964   *Cuzco, tierra y muerte*. Lima: Populibros.

Nelson, Cynthia
1974   Public and private politics: Women in the Middle Eastern world. *American Ethnologist* 1:551–63.

Nelson, Nici
1979   "Women must help each other": The operation of personal networks among Buzaa beer brewers in Mathare Valley, Kenya. In *Women united, women divided: Contemporary studies of ten cultures*, ed. Patricia Caplan and Janet Bujra, pp. 77–98. Bloomington: Indiana University Press.

Nerlove, Sara B.
1974   Women's workload and infant feeding practices: A relationship with demographic implications. *Ethnology* 13:207–14.

Netting, Robert McC.
1969   Women's weapons: The politics of domesticity among the Kofyar. *American Anthropologist* 71:1037–45.

Newland, Kathleen
1979   *The sisterhood of man*. New York: W. W. Norton.

Norton, Mary Beth
1980   *Liberty's daughters: The revolutionary experience of American women 1750–1800*. Boston: Little, Brown, and Company.

Núñez del Prado Béjar, Daisy Irene
1975*a*   El rol de la mujer campesina quechua. *América Indígena* 35:391–401.

1975*b*   El poder de decisión de la mujer quechua andina. *América Indígena*, 35:623–30.

Orlansky, Dora, and Dubrovsky, Silvia
1978   *The effects of rural-urban migration on women's role and status in Latin America*. UNESCO: Reports and Papers in the Social Sciences.

Ortner, Sherry
1974   Is female to male as nature is to culture? In *Women, culture, and society*, ed. Michelle Zimbalist Rosaldo and Louise Lamphere, pp. 67–87. Stanford: Stanford University Press.

Palmer, David Scott
1973   *Revolution from above: Military government and popular participation in Peru, 1968–1972*. Ph.D. dissertation. Latin American Studies Program. Dissertation Series. Ithaca: Cornell University.

1980   *Peru: The authoritarian tradition*. New York: Praeger.

Paul, Lois
1974   The mastery of words and the mystery of sex in a Guatemalan village. In *Women, culture and society,* ed. Michelle Zimbalist Rosaldo and Louise Lamphere, pp. 281–300. Stanford: Stanford University Press.
Paul, Lois, and Paul, Benjamin
1975   The Maya midwife as sacred specialist: A Guatemalan case. *American Ethnologist* 2:707–26.
Paulston, Rolland
1971   *Society, schools and progress in Peru.* Oxford: Pergamon Press.
Pollock, Nancy
1972   Women and the division of labor: A Jamaican example. *American Anthropologist* 74:689–92.
Reiter, Rayna R.
1975*a*   Introduction to *Toward an anthropology of women.* New York: Monthly Review Press.
1975*b*   Men and women in the south of France: Public and private domains. In *Toward an anthropology of women,* ed. Rayna R. Reiter, pp. 252–82. New York: Monthly Review Press.
Ritter, Ulrich Peter
1965   *Comunidades indígenas y cooperativismo en el Perú.* Estudios Sobre la Economía Ibero-Americana, Universität Göttingen: Ibero-Amerika Institut Für Wirschafts forschung.
Roberts, Bryan R.
1975   Center and periphery in the development process: The case of Peru. In *Urbanization and inequality,* vol. 5, ed. W. A. Cornelius and Felicity Trueblood, pp. 77–106. Beverly Hills: Sage Publications.
Rodriguez de Muñoz, Carmen, and Roca de Salonen, Elsa
1978   *Compilación y análisis de leyes sobre la condición jurídica y social de la mujer Peruana.* Lima: Universidad Nacional Mayor de San Marcos.
Rogers, Susan C.
1975   Female forms of power and myths of male dominance: A model of female/male interaction in peasant society. *American Ethnologist* 2:727–56.
Rubbo, Anna
1975   The spread of capitalism in rural Columbia: Effects on poor women. In *Toward an anthropology of women,* ed. Rayna R. Reiter, pp. 333–57. New York: Monthly Review Press.
Rupp, Leila
1978   *Mobilizing women for war.* Princeton: Princeton University Press.
Sacks, Karen
1975   Engels revisited: Women, the organization of production, and private property. In *Toward an anthropology of women,* ed. Rayna R. Reiter, pp. 211–34. New York: Monthly Review Press.

Bibliography

1976 State bias and women's status. *American Anthropologist*, 78:565-69.

1979 *Sisters and wives: The past and future of sexual equality.* Westport, Conn.: Greenwood Press.

Safa, Helen Icken
1974 *The urban poor of Puerto Rico: A study in development and inequality.* New York: Holt, Rinehart, and Winston.
1977 The changing class composition of the female labor force in Latin America. *Latin American Perspectives* 4:126-36.

Saffioti, Heleith I. B.
1977 Women, mode of production, and social formation. *Latin American Perspectives* 4:27-37.

Sangree, Walter H.
1979 Going home to mother: Traditional marriage among the Irigwe of Benue-Plateau State, Nigeria. In *Women and society*, ed. Sharon W. Tiffany, pp. 188-206. Montreal: Eden Press Women's Publications.

Sara Lafosse, Violetta
1969 La ley de reforma agraria (no. 17716) y sus implicaciones en la estructura familiar. *Serie, Documentos de Trabajo*, no. 3. Taller de Socialización, Pontífica Universidad Católica del Perú, Lima.
1978 La mujer y la familia en contextos sociales diferentes. AMIDEP Seminario de Investigaciones Sociales acerca dè la Mujer. Cuzco: Universidad Nacional San Antonio Abad.

Saulniers, Suzanne Smith, and Rakowski, Cathy A.
1977 *Women in the development process: A select bibliography on women in Sub-Saharan Africa and Latin America.* Austin, Tx.: Institute of Latin American Studies, the University of Texas at Austin.

Schipske, Evelyn
1975 An analysis of the consejo nacional de mujers del Perú. *Journal of Interamerican Studies and World Affairs* 17, no. 4:426-38.

Schlegal, Alice
1977 Male and female in Hopi thought and action. In *Sexual stratification: An anthropological view*, ed. Alice Schlegal, pp. 245-69. New York: Columbia University.

Sharma, Ursula
1979 Segregation and its consequences in India: Rural women in Himachal Pradesh. In *Women united, women divided: Contemporary studies of ten cultures*, ed. Patricia Caplan and Janet M. Bujra, pp. 259-81. Bloomington: Indiana University Press.

Sherif, Carolyn Wood
1979 Bias in psychology. In *The prism of sex: Essays in the sociology of knowledge*, ed. Julia Sherman and Evelyn Torton Beck. Madison: University of Wisconsin Press.

Sherman, Julia A., and Beck, Evelyn Torton
1979 *The prism of sex.* Madison: University of Wisconsin.

Silverblatt, Irene
1978   Andean women in the Inca empire. *Feminist studies* 4:37–61.
1980   "The Universe has turned inside out . . . There is no justice for us here": Andean women under Spanish rule. *Women and colonization: Anthropological perspectives,* ed. Mona Etienne and Eleanor Leacock, pp. 149–85. New York: Praeger.

Sklar, Kathryn Kish
1973   *Catherine Beecher: A study in American domesticity.* New Haven: Yale University Press.

Slocum, Sally
1975   Women the gatherer: Male bias in anthropology. In *Toward an anthropology of women,* ed. Rayna R. Reiter, pp. 36–50. New York: Monthly Review Press.

Smith, Daniel Scott
1974   Family limitation, sexual control and domestic feminism in Victorian America. In *Clio's consciousness raised: New perspectives on the history of women,* ed. Mary S. Hartman and Lois Banner, pp. 119–36. New York: Harper & Row.

Smith, Margo Lane
1971   Institutionalized servitude: The female domestic servant in Lima, Peru. Ph.D. dissertation, Indiana University.

Smith-Rosenburg, Carroll
1980   Politics and culture in women's history. *Feminist Studies* 6, no. 1: 26–36.

Stack, Carol
1974   *All our kin.* New York: Harper Colophon.

Standing, Guy
1976   Education and female participation in the labour force. *International Labour Review,* 114:281–98.

Staudt, Kathleen A.
1976   Agricultural policy, political power and women farmers in western Kenya. Ph.D. dissertation, University of Wisconsin.

Stavenhagen, Rodolfo
1975   *Social classes in agrarian societies.* Garden City, New York: Anchor Books.

Stein, William W.
1961   *Hualcán: Life in the highlands of Peru.* Ithaca: Cornell University Press.

Stepan, Alfred
1978   *The state and society: Peru in comparative perspective.* Princeton: Princeton University Press.

Stevens, Evelyn
1973   Marianismo, the other face of machismo. In *Female and male in Latin America,* ed. Ann Pescatello, pp. 89–101. Pittsburg: University of Pittsburg.

Stone, Lawrence
    1975   The rise of the nuclear family in early modern England: The
            patriarchal stage. In *The family in history*, ed. Charles Rosenberg,
            pp. 13–58. Philadelphia: University of Pennsylvania Press.
Tanner, Nancy, and Zihlman, Adrienne
    1976   Women in evolution part I: Innovation and selection in human
            origins. *Signs* 1:585–608.
Tilly, Louise A., and Scott, Joan M.
    1978   *Women, work, and family.* New York: Holt, Reinhart, and Winston.
Turnbull, Colin M.
    1961   *The forest people.* London: Chatto and Wendus.
van den Berghe, Pierre L., and Primov, George P.
    1977   *Inequality in the Peruvian Andes; class and ethnicity in Cuzco.* Col-
            umbia, Mo.: University of Missouri Press.
Vázquez, Mario C.
    1965   *Educación rural en el Callejón de Huaylas: Vicos.* Lima: Editorial
            Estudios Andinos.
Villalobos, Gabriela
    n.d.   La madre trabajadora: el caso de las obreras industriales. Centro
            de Estudios de Población y Desarrollo, C.E.P.D., Lima, Perú, Se-
            ries C, no. 1.
Wallace, Anthony
    1970   *The death and the rebirth of the Seneca.* New York: Alfred A. Knopf.
Warren, Kay B.
    1978   *The symbolism of subordination: Indian identity in a Guatemalan town.*
            Austin: University of Texas Press.
Webb, Richard
    1975   Government policy and the distribution of income in Peru,
            1963–1973. In *The Peruvian experiment*, ed. Abraham F. Lowenthal,
            pp. 79–127. Princeton: Princeton University Press.
Whyte, William F.
    1976   Rural Peru: Peasants as activists. In *Peruvian nationalism: A cor-
            poratist revolution*, ed. David Chaplin, pp. 241–51. New Brunswick,
            N.J.: Transaction Books.
Wilson, Edward O.
    1978   *On human nature.* Cambridge: Harvard University Press.
Young, Kate
    1978   Modes of appropriation and the sexual division of labor: A case
            study from Oaxaca, Mexico. In *Feminism and materialism*, ed. An-
            nette Kuhn and Ann Marie Wolpe, pp. 124–54. London: Rout-
            ledge and Kegan Paul.
Zaretsky, Eli
    1976   *Capitalism, the family, and personal life.* New York: Harper & Row.
Zihlman, Adrienne L.
    1978   Women in evolution, part II: Subsistence and social organization
            among early hominids. *Signs* 4:4–20.

Index